Local government and democracy in Britain

Manchester University Press

Local government and democracy in Britain

Neil Barnett and J. A. Chandler

MANCHESTER UNIVERSITY PRESS

Copyright © Neil Barnett and J. A. Chandler 2023

The right of Neil Barnett and J. A. Chandler to be identified as the authors of this work has been asserted in accordance with the Copyright, Designs and Patents Act 1988.

This book will be made open access within three years of publication thanks to Path to Open, a program developed in partnership between JSTOR, the American Council of Learned Societies (ACLS), University of Michigan Press, and The University of North Carolina Press to bring about equitable access and impact for the entire scholarly community, including authors, researchers, libraries, and university presses around the world. Learn more at https://about.jstor.org/path-to-open/

Published by Manchester University Press
Oxford Road, Manchester M13 9PL

www.manchesteruniversitypress.co.uk

British Library Cataloguing-in-Publication Data
A catalogue record for this book is available from the British Library

ISBN 978 1 5261 5064 6 hardback
ISBN 978 1 5261 9133 5 hardback

First published 2023
Paperback published 2025

The publisher has no responsibility for the persistence or accuracy of URLs for any external or third-party internet websites referred to in this book, and does not guarantee that any content on such websites is, or will remain, accurate or appropriate.

EU authorised representative for GPSR:
Easy Access System Europe – Mustamäe tee 50, 10621 Tallinn, Estonia
gpsr.requests@easproject.com

Typeset
by Cheshire Typesetting Ltd, Cuddington, Cheshire

Contents

Preface   vi
Abbreviations   viii

Introduction   1
1 The evolution of the twentieth-century system   21
2 Theorising local government in Britain   52
3 Changing the boundaries   71
4 Can local governments govern? Powers and resources   97
5 Restructuring democracy within local authorities   123
6 Central control and local autonomy   146
7 How have local authorities coped with change?   171
8 Local government as expedient agencies of central government   199
9 Is there any possibility of change?   218
Conclusions and reflections   243

Appendix 1   253
Appendix 2   254
References   255
Index   287

Preface

This study emerged in part from the realisation that local government in Britain has since the beginning of this century, and especially since 2010, been restructured so rapidly that almost all textbooks and studies of the system – including those written by the authors of this volume – are now monuments to history rather than current practice. Most of the change to the local government system has been to deconstruct the institution to the extent that it could be claimed that local government is largely not local in any popularly used version of the term. Neither does it now govern in its own right, but is obliged to follow the dictates of central government rather than the interests of its electors. The authors, who have been active in local government earlier in their careers and have since been writing and teaching local government as academics, are concerned to show what is happening to local government and local democracy, and also to make clear that local government matters. A central concern of this study is not only to demonstrate how far local government has declined in terms of being a central pillar of liberal democratic governance in Britain, but also to show how this trend undermines the efficacy of liberal democracy in the nation.

Local government is not, we argue, an institution that should be manipulated by central government to be the scapegoat for inequality and social decline in Britain but must be founded in a stronger moral position within political thought and practice. This study is, therefore, not only an introduction to the role and position of local government in the 2020s but also argues from a normative perspective that recent developments are generally antipathetic to the rights and duties of citizens in shaping the neighbourhoods in which they live. As the title suggests, we focus on local government in Britain, but accept that issues we touch on – the constitution and the effects of Brexit, for example – are issues affecting the United Kingdom. Also, several of the texts and sources we draw on refer to the United Kingdom, and it is inevitable that both territorial entities permeate debates around local government. We also refer in places to local government in Northern Ireland where we feel this serves to underline our points about the size and service responsibilities of local government. Overall, we encourage a greater awareness of the enduring qualities of local government even amidst the most hostile of climates, which holds out the hope that, if better constituted, it can be the underpinning of a genuine sense of people's well-being and capacity to shape their environment, and a major contributor to the welfare of society as a whole.

We would, however, like to acknowledge the support that has been given to the study of local government by institutions such as the Institute for Local Government Studies at Birmingham University and, especially in relation to this study, the Local Governance Research Centre at De Montfort University, led by Steven Leach, then Colin Copus and later Steven Griggs, and also the Urban Studies group led by Jonathan Davies. The work of Mark Sandford, at the House of Commons Library, has also proven to be invaluable. Connections to these centres have been further widened through the Political Studies Association Local Politics and Governance specialist group through the efforts of Peter Eckersley and Joanie Willett. Among colleagues we have also had valuable discussion on the theme of the book with Chris Game and David Wilson, Janice Morphet, Helen Sullivan and Arianna Giovannini.

Former colleagues of the authors, John Kingdom, Ralph Spence and Roger Ottewill, have also helped at various times in developing our ideas within this study. Support for the project was also provided by Lord David Blunkett and Hugh Atkinson. We would also like to add personal thanks to Professor Steven Griggs.

Abbreviations

APSE	Association for Public Service Excellence
BRRS	Business Rates Retention Scheme
CA	Combined authority
CCT	Compulsory competitive tendering
CLES	Centre for Local Economic Strategies
CPA	Comprehensive Performance Assessment
DCLG	Department for Communities and Local Government
DEM	Directly elected mayor
DTLR	Department of Transport, Local Government and the Regions
ESRC	Economic and Social Research Council
EU	European Union
FEA	Functional economic areas
GLC	Greater London Council
HoC	House of Commons
HCLGSC	Housing and Local Government Select Committee
HMSO	His Majesty's Stationery Office
HRA	Housing Revenue Account
ICS	Integrated care system
IFS	Institute for Fiscal Studies
IPPR	Institute for Public Policy Research
JP	Justice of the peace
LATC	Local authority trading company
LBC	London Borough Council
LEA	Local education authority
LEP	Local enterprise partnership
LGA	Local Government Association

LGB	Local Government Board
LGiU	Local Government Information Unit
MATs	Multi-academy trusts
MHCLG	Ministry of Housing, Communities and Local Government
MP	Member of Parliament
NALC	National Association of Local Councils
NAO	National Audit Office
NDP	Neighbourhood development plan
NLGN	New Local Government Network (now New Local)
NHS	National Health Service
NPM	New Public Management
NUL	New Urban Left
ODPM	Office of the Deputy Prime Minister
OECD	Organisation for Economic Co-operation and Development
Ofsted	Office for Standards in Education (now Office for Standards in Education, Children's Services and Skills)
ONS	Office for National Statistics
PCC	Police and crime commissioner
RDA	Regional development agency
RSC	Regional schools commissioner
RSG	Rates Support Grant
UDCs	Urban development corporations
UK	United Kingdom
WHO	World Health Organization

Introduction

Local government in Britain was at the zenith of its political importance and popular regard from the 1880s until the 1940s. The lives of citizens in large cities were substantially ordered and arranged through the auspices of their county boroughs. Many of the vital services necessary for life and personal liberty were governed by their councillors and professional officers. Birmingham and Glasgow can be cited as exemplars of local governments that were 'place shapers' (Hunt, 2004; Maver, 2000). Central to these developments was the town hall, whose magnificence outshone any contemporary buildings in the expanding city boundaries. Decisions and management that were made and nurtured in the town halls directly enhanced the lives of their citizens and the needs of the local economy. Water, sewage, gas and electricity services for businesses and domestic use were provided by the local authority, as was street lighting and road maintenance. The centres of towns were being transformed as slums were demolished and replaced by retail, commercial and cultural centres such as libraries and art galleries. From the 1920s, new houses at affordable rents were being built as homes fit for heroes. Travelling to and from work or for leisure was possible for the many on the trams and buses owned and operated by the local council. Revenue in profit and rents from these productive ventures could subsidise the rate demands to help finance redistributive services for all. In the early twentieth century, families sent their children to be educated in schools governed by local education boards, that were later transferred to the higher tier local authorities. Pupils who showed intellectual promise could often go on to train for professional occupations in technical colleges maintained by their local authority. Law and order and protection from fire and flooding were provided by locally controlled police and fire services. If illness struck, many boroughs and counties provided hospitals developed from the poor law institutions to ensure medical care.

Not only did the municipal local authorities have substantive powers and duties, they were also well connected to both the local economy and central government. Senior policymakers were often industrialists, tradesmen and bankers, and after 1918 the growth of the Labour Party ensured that trade union and other representatives of the workforce of the city were elected to city councils. Mayors and leading aldermen and councillors not only held positions of influence in the private economy of towns, but also became Members of Parliament or even ministers of state. In Birmingham, Joseph Chamberlain began his career as a major manufacturer in the city, became its mayor and effectively council leader from 1873 to 1876, and went on to become a Cabinet minister and a divisive voice within the Conservative Party. In Glasgow the position of mayor was held exclusively from 1833 to 1902 by prosperous manufacturers or bankers, and after 1920 sent former Labour councillors such as John Wheatley and George Buchanan, who were elected as Members of Parliament (MPs), to Westminster. Both Conservative and Liberal industrialists, or, from a different perspective, trade unionists, realised that policies improving the lives of their fellow local citizens were also good for their own business interests. Similarly, in many rural areas the county council began to take on the role of ensuring that central services such as education were open and free to all, while the many smaller urban districts based on small towns, and for villages and hamlets rural districts, had councils elected to provide community-based services such as maintenance of streets or refuse collection. In practice these 'lower tier' authorities took over most of the duties of the community-based parish councils. The district councils and parishes could still be dominated by the election of the larger landowners and their representatives, thus retaining, as in urban areas, a strong connection between the economy of a locality with its major representatives. This was a time when the council and its leaders could be seen to be central to people's lives in novels and plays such as Robert Tressell's *The Ragged Trousered*

Philanthropists (1914), *South Riding* (1936) by Winifred Holtby or J. B. Priestley's *The Inspector Calls* (1947).

What is local government?

The term 'local government' is recorded as being used in 1834 by the Whig economist Colonel Robert Torrens in a parliamentary debate (Chandler, 2007: xi) when supporting an amendment to the Poor Law Reform Bill that 'No rules or regulations framed by the Commons should be binding on any parish without the concurrence of the majority of rate payers' (Hansard HoC, Series 3, 17 April 1834, Vol. 23, Col. 1340). He is reported as saying that 'A good system of local government be looked upon to be the perfection of all government.' According to the late Professor George Jones in a comment to J. A. Chandler, this is perhaps the earliest recorded use of the term. Few accounts of the subject give a clear statement of what specifically 'local government' may mean in practice. It remains a 'weasel' or 'wicked' phrase, widely used, but, as Foucault (Smart, 2002: 19–26) pointed out in his study of the term 'madness', words can carry ideological positions that evolve over time and have several meanings dependent on the point of view of each individual. Peter John (2014) has argued that local government is a great survivor, as the institution is sufficiently malleable to adapt and evolve as required. However, while the name local government may endure the entity that bore this epithet in 1834 is wholly different from the organisations, let alone their attributes, that carry this name in the 2020s.

Cole and Boyne (1996: 91), noting the lack of attempts to offer formal definitions, observe that it is 'no longer clear what the term "local government" means in the contemporary British context'. They express some scepticism as to whether local government, given changes of significance and meanings, could be satisfactorily defined using classifications which hold firm. They nevertheless defined local government as an institution having:

- jurisdiction over a substantially smaller area than that of the national government

- election by the popular vote
- powers of taxation
- genuine discretion over service provision.

At the same time, Loughlin (1996a: 39) provided a similar list defining local government as having characteristics of:

- multifunctionality
- broad discretion
- powers of taxation
- a representative function.

Clearly Cole and Boyne's definition would allow for single purpose/ single service authorities whereas Loughlin's appears to be more in tune with what we traditionally expect for organisations with a range of services. Moreover, Loughlin's definition requires a 'representative function' rather than direct election by popular vote and so could potentially include unelected delegate bodies. John Stewart provides a similar but more specific definition that 'Local authorities are multi-functional authorities responsible for a defined area and constituted by local election' (Stewart, 2000: 5). If we accept the definition of 'local government' within the framework of these definitions then we are referring to institutions that can be termed as being locally based, have powers to govern and are based on democratic control either as directly elected institutions or institutions accountable to local directly elected assemblies.

Governance

By the 1980s, the mainstream view of the value of local government came to be challenged, with the eclipse in many studies of the institutionalised term 'local government' by the concept of 'local governance'. Among the earlier proselytisers of this change, Goodwin and Painter observed that during the preceding 15 years the local government system in Britain had been transformed into a more complex one of local governance in which a multitude of unelected agencies (public, private and voluntary) had become involved in attempting to influence local areas (Goodwin and Painter, 1996). In practice, this phenomenon was recognised in earlier studies of local government that considered the subject from the perspective of community studies and later the ideas of urban studies, communitarianism or social capital. Nevertheless, the development of the term was of considerable value in shifting academic attention to the wider role of local and external forces in shaping communities and subregional institutions.

The popularisation of the term 'local governance' can be credited as a stimulus to debate on where power lay within communities in Britain in the 1980s by focussing on the many organisations external to local government that shaped subnational government. Among the most prominent initiatives in this context was Rod Rhodes's *Beyond Westminster and Whitehall* (1988). The idea was developed into an ESRC research programme, 'To document the transformation of the government beyond Westminster and Whitehall from a system of local government into a system of local governance involving complex sets of organisations drawn from the public and private sectors' (R. A. W. Rhodes, 1999a: xiv). The research initiative produced a number of valuable edited studies reviewing aspects of local governance, and later a few textbooks on the subject of local governance such as Gray (1994) or Leach and Percy-Smith (2001), who argue in their preface that:

> The literature on local government has only slowly, painfully and partially adjusted to the new complex reality of local community governance. The space generally devoted to 'non-elected local government' suggests that it is much less important than traditional local government and it is explored in considerably less depth, and often with a marked absence of community. (Leach and Percy-Smith, 2001: 1–2)

In this study we use both the terms 'local government', meaning the legally recognised institutions of subnational and subprovincial organisations in Britain, and 'local governance' when discussing the many supranational, national and local public, private and voluntary agencies that influence the institutions of local government. Although local governance expresses the many public, private and voluntary agencies that shape local government, we argue that within the definition of 'local government' there is an important distinction in that this refers to multipurpose community organisations involved in overseeing a number of functions – as opposed to, within the development of governance, largely single purpose, stand-alone groups as identified by Hendriks and Dzur (2021) as 'citizen governance spaces' reflecting spontaneous reactions of citizens to external policy impositions.

The present state of local government

The cumulative effect of reforms in the past seventy years has seen local government lose much of its control over key services and become increasingly constrained by central government. Even during a period of growth in terms of service delivery responsibilities, in the post-war welfare state, its independence was diminished as it became increasingly an agent for providing centrally mandated services and ever more dependent on finance from Westminster. The past forty years can only be characterised as a period of intense centralisation. Boundaries have been reshaped and tiers removed by various governments, producing ever larger councils with decreasing connections to local sentiment. Local government's fortunes have waxed, and mainly waned, according to the ideological predispositions and policy prescriptions of successive governments, bound into wider programmes of public service reform and economic management. These have seen it subject to privatisation and contracting out, the removal of services to unelected agencies and diminishing financial independence, leaving it reduced, at best, to just one player among many in an increasingly complex local governance landscape. Local government has been 'seen as part of the problem, rather than part of the solution' (Association of Public Service Excellence (APSE), 2021: 27).

Providing an overarching context for these trends have been macro-economic forces, with councils becoming increasingly weaker in their ability to influence local economies and well-being amidst globalisation. In the period since 2010 these trends have intensified. Firstly, central government-imposed austerity following the financial crisis of 2008–10 left local government in a precarious state, struggling to maintain even core, mandatory services. Austerity served to intensify long-term weaknesses and, more than ever, pose questions as to whether local government, in any meaningful sense of the term, could survive. A relative easing of financial pressures in 2017 and projected future spending still left local government substantially weakened.

The uncertainty which councils now face is indicative of their continued reliance on central funding. There was, after the general election of 2019, if anything an intensification of a pattern whereby central government treats local government as expedient to its own policy initiatives. A much mooted local government White Paper was eventually published as part of a broader government agenda. The *Levelling Up the United Kingdom* White Paper (HM Government, 2022) contained broad commitments to ongoing ad hoc structural reform and 'devolution deals' with unitary and county areas in England. In the meantime the government had continued with a piecemeal reorganisation aimed at producing larger councils via mergers of existing ones. In July 2021, the Secretary of State announced that he had approved the creation of four new unitary authorities; one council, with a population of 618,000, was to replace the existing eight in North Yorkshire, and one in Somerset, with a population of 562,000, was to replace six existing councils. Cumbria, on the other hand, was to have two councils: East Cumbria, replacing four councils, with a population of 224,199, and West Cumbria, replacing four councils, with a population of 274,176. The pattern of restructuring over several decades, its effects and motivations will be discussed at length in Chapter 3, but in this case the criteria used to determine numbers of councils and their sizes appear particularly opaque, and the 'somewhat bemusing' decisions appear to be motivated by party political advantage (Hill, 2020). This, as we will see, is nothing new, but it appeared in the context of a government which seemed intent on consolidating ever more power at the centre, being less shy about revealing its intentions, with Prime Minister Johnson using a speech in July 2021 to suggest that Conservative-controlled councils might get favourable treatment if applying to him for a 'devolution deal'. Adding to this sense of 'pork barrel' politics (Hanretty, 2021; Mabbett, 2021) was the government's agenda to 'level up' the country by focussing resources and attention on 'left behind' areas.

'Levelling up', however, appeared to be a confused amalgam of ideas and potential initiatives aimed at 'red wall' constituencies in the north won by the Conservatives at the 2019 general election (Jennings et al., 2020; Tomaney and Pike, 2020). For a time, in the summer and autumn of 2022, it seemed to have disappeared without trace from the government's agenda, as the short-lived administration of Liz Truss contained no Cabinet minister with overall responsibility for 'levelling up', and relegated the agenda to an adjunct to a broad 'dash for growth'. In an indication of the expedient role local government has played in the political life and governance of the nation – which will be a core theme of this book – weeks later, 'levelling up' and its associated structural changes again became, at least rhetorically, important to the incoming Sunak government. From the outset, it was clear that local government would play, if anything, only a minor role. The Towns Fund, for example, made available an initial pot of £3.6 billion to address urban decline, with all eligible towns able to bid for funding. In the Budget of March 2021, forty-five deals were announced, forty of which were for areas which had at least one Conservative MP. The selection criteria were such that many of the most deprived towns did not get funding, while some more affluent ones did. Moreover, the Fund was to be overseen and distributed by an unelected local board. There were similar concerns expressed about the operation of the Future High Streets Fund, launched in 2019, and two funds intended to substitute for the loss of European Union (EU) funds – the Levelling Up Fund, announced in 2021, to which £4 billion was allocated over four years (Hill, 2021), and the UK Shared Prosperity Fund. Morphet (2021) sets this approach to local government in the context of a government intent on recentralising power and reining back on devolution generally, with ministers effectively 'taking back' control of decisions previously devolved in particular to the Scottish Parliament, under the guise of the legislation to leave the EU. More fundamentally, she sees 'Brexit' as generally having removed EU treaty obligations around subsidiarity and cohesion which had offered protection to the devolved parliaments of the UK and to a lesser extent to local government. Without these obligations the government had 'free rein' to redesign this constitutional settlement.

This increased sense of financial austerity, insecurity, seeming disinterest amongst minsters and heightened sense of a politically expedient, instrumental attitude to local government in Whitehall saw local government, in any meaningful sense of the term, seemingly hanging by a thread onto what powers it had left. However, it can be argued that local government's malaise has even deeper roots. Even leaving aside the relationship of local and central government and the crucial issues of financial buoyancy and service responsibilities, there would be a need to fundamentally readdress the place of local government in the democratic polity, as political and societal pressures seem to work to undermine local government's credibility. Weak electoral turnouts at local elections and increasing attention on alternative forms of political engagement have served to add to the increasing complexity of local governance to create an ever widening lack of congruence between local government and the actual practices and scope of local politics. Questions about the democratic legitimacy of local government are thus related to wider challenges to its basis in 'traditional' representative democracy. Local government's role in the polity is challenged further by increasing and changing demands and expectations from citizens, as new direct relationships with service users are increasingly demanded, and facilitated by new technology. Local government thus sits at the centre of intense political, societal, cultural and economic pressures which pose questions concerning its value and role.

Local governance and chaos: the COVID-19 crisis

All of the above issues were thrown into sharp relief by the COVID-19 pandemic. Indeed, this intense period of activity saw the best of local government, while also both revealing and accelerating its problems. Along with other public services, local government staff and services were vital to the response but they worked under intense pressure. There is widespread evidence of councils responding innovatively, using local knowledge and empathy to continue to provide core services while going over and above the call of duty to provide additional support for communities (Gore et al., 2021). Like other public services, the capacity of local authorities to respond and their preparedness had been considerably weakened by years of cuts and staff reductions over the previous ten years. Neither was the response helped by the need to coordinate the hugely complex network of agencies and private contractors which now populated the local governance arena. Nevertheless, the pandemic highlighted the value of local knowledge and the flexibility of response which local government can offer. The effort of local government staff at the 'front line' of the response was met by high satisfaction levels (APSE, 2020). Arguably, this provided the potential for councils to 'seize the moment' and build on the new working practices and community engagement developed during the crisis.

Unfortunately for advocates of local government, however, the pandemic further exposed the inherent concentration of power in central government and the structural shortcomings of an over-centralised polity (Gaskell and Stoker, 2020). The default position of the government was to bypass local government, especially during the period March to October 2020, accumulating more emergency powers which restricted local discretion (Morphet, 2021). Time and again the government's response was to turn to the private sector or to default delivery back to central agencies. The clearest example of this was the Test and Trace system, delivered nationally through a multibillion pound contract with SERCO, and subsequently subcontracted by them to a myriad of private companies. The local knowledge essential to an effective system, however, lay in the localities, and the devolving of the function to local levels under a national strategy was recommended as the right approach by the World Health Organization (WHO) in 2020 (Morphet, 2021). Public health had been reinstated as a local government function in 2012, and yet decisions were taken without councils being consulted. Local directors of public health were sidelined (Morphet, 2021), and vital data was not shared with local officials. A national agency, Public Health England, at the same time reappropriated to itself powers which had been devolved in 2012. Similarly, a national system of volunteering was rolled out via the NHS, undercutting or replicating many local authorities' own more targeted initiatives.

The centrally driven response was stymied by political blunders and by ideological preference for private sector solutions, and, particularly in England, was marred by long-standing poor relations between central and local government (House of Lords Public Services Committee, 2020). Local leaders pointed out a lack of understanding of their concerns and superficial treatment, leaving a sense of bitterness on their part (Thomas and Clyne, 2021). However, underpinning this was the distrust of local government in the core executive of central government, along with fundamental weaknesses in their operations which had been present for many decades. Here we use the term 'core executive' as used by Rod Rhodes (1995: 12) as 'all those organisations and procedures which coordinate central government policies, and act as final arbiters of conflict between different parts of the government machine'. The pandemic laid bare the predominance of the 'Westminster model' and the 'British political tradition' in which power is concentrated in this central political executive (Warner et al., 2021). UK government overall is both highly centralised and fragmented, with even the structure of local government itself being populated now with a complex variety of scales and types of authority.

In this respect, the pandemic served to underline the fact that there are increasingly divergent systems of local government in the UK. Not only did the Scottish, Welsh and Northern Irish governments often pursue distinct responses nationally, they operated more clearly in partnership with local government, building on existing collaborative frameworks developed over time. This was particularly the case in Wales, where ministers had weekly meetings with all twenty-two council leaders. In England, the mindset was best encapsulated in the decision-making surrounding the system of tiers, or 'local lockdowns', in the autumn/early winter of 2020. Political opportunism came to the fore clearly, as areas held by Conservative MPs, including the then Prime Minister's own constituency, were removed, without scientific evidence, from the highest level of lockdown (Tier 3) while Labour areas were left in Tier 3. In the regions of the north, COVID restrictions effectively became a matter of negotiation, conducted at elite level with elected mayors. The process became one of deal-making, with government adopting a clientelistic approach to local leaders, offering additional resources in return for financial assistance. Most notably, Andy Burnham, Mayor of Greater Manchester, initially refused to accept the government's offer, leading to a stand-off and offering, briefly, a hand-break on the centralisation process, while neighbouring Liverpool quickly negotiated a deal, to the relief of the government. The whole process appeared, from the outside, to be baffling (Morphet, 2021).

The pandemic also placed huge financial pressures on local government, which not only had to respond to increased demands, but also suffered loss of income from trading and commercial activity, increased council tax defaults and loss of business rates. An early exhortation for local government to 'do whatever it takes' and a Treasury promise that they would be fully recompensed proved to be shallow, as additional financial support was given in tranches and seemingly with great reluctance. Financial relief was given but the period also saw the rise of specific, ring-fenced grants and competitive bidding for funds. Councils were left with a considerable shortfall on their COVID-related expenditure and faced a 'fog of uncertainty' as to future funding (Warner et al., 2021), with some councils suggesting that they had been left bankrupt (Pickard, 2021). In March 2021, the National Audit Office reported £9.7 billion of COVID cost pressures, and the Local Government Association estimated an additional £2.6 billion was needed to cover the cost to councils (APSE, 2021). At best, the sum of these pressures culminated in a need for local government to operate in radically different ways. At worst, existential questions are posed for local governments increasingly seen to be but one institution claiming democratic legitimacy amidst a plethora of alternatives.

The aims of this book

In this book we aim to offer a defence of local government as a central pillar for enhancing democracy in Britain. To do so, it is necessary to examine and diagnose the current malaise. How did we arrive at this point? Understanding the history and development of local government, the changing and sometimes enduring theories which have been used to either justify or undermine it, the constitutional context in which it has been set, and the mindsets, ideologies and motivations of the actors involved, all serve to bring into relief both the scale of the task and its importance. A new local government model will not emerge from a blank sheet of paper, and in practice the residue of its history, institutional configurations and understandings of its role will permeate any reform effort. In this sense, it is particularly important to look at recent policy and the dominant attitude towards local government among central government actors, and we pay particular attention to the New Labour years, 1997–2010, and the period since 2010. Although we give a broad overview of other key periods of development, these, particularly the period of the Thatcher administrations, have been well documented and debated in other studies. In particular we focus on the years after 2010. The condition, and indeed survival, of local government has been of major concern over several decades, and there have been no shortage of claims from authors that the threat is even more pronounced at their time of writing. However, since 2010 we have seen, as noted above, key underlying issues intensified, condensed and compressed into ten to twelve years. We cannot, of course, fully predict what may follow; however, we feel that a detailed examination of this period is vital to learning lessons and recognising the underlying issues in play if we are to address them.

Since the 1930s, local governments in Britain have increasingly become less local and less, in themselves, agencies which govern in the sense of determining policies that significantly shape their communities independently of central government and external public and private agencies. Local government is predominantly an expediential agency of central government that administers centrally determined policies. It does retain enduring qualities which, despite all, offer both hope and indications of future directions; however, the scope and ability to exercise these qualities is constrained by central government and allowed only to the extent that they are tolerated. We argue that a central normative rationale for local government is that it should enable citizens to determine the policies that affect them. Many local authorities have fought in innovative ways to surmount the many barriers erected in recent decades to curb their autonomy. We believe that to build on this we must rediscover that there is a right to community-based local government, although this is a necessary but not sufficient right, in that local governments must be subject to universal human rights and duties.

In practice, we recognise that there is a need for a systemic approach which envisages a broad infrastructure of democratic practices at various scales. The 'mending' of democracy requires 'repair' via primary units of local government being connected to a wider democratic framework (Hendriks et al., 2020) such that, for example, defence or dealing with inequality and, importantly, the maintenance of human rights, are dealt with at a variety of scales, including regional, national and global decision-making forums that, due to their size, necessitate more indirect forms of democracy. We appreciate that such restructuring of decision-making is a herculean and far from immediately realisable task. Moreover, models of democracy remain in the domain of theory unless they are operationalised and lived in practice; the prospects for achieving change have to be viewed in the context of the current low levels of interest in local government and the democratic deficits outlined above. However, we argue for the value of setting out such a rationale as an exemplar against which the state of actually existing local government can be measured. This 'local government to come' can serve as an aspiration towards which we should seek to move in what would be, necessarily, a pragmatic fashion.

Local, community and neighbourhood

Throughout the book we will use the terms local, community and neighbourhood in full awareness of the problems of defining them. Each one could easily have been the subject of a book in itself, and we do not have space here to subject them to a rigorous critical analysis. Others have done so, and we draw on some of this literature as we proceed. In various places in the following chapters we identify how 'local', 'community' and 'neighbourhood' have been attached as rhetorical labels both by policymakers and those seeking to resist initiatives imposed from 'outside'. These uses are often contradictory and based on a range of geographical scales. In addition, elusiveness has pervaded theoretical and analytical applications of the concepts. Community, for example, has been at various times articulated in spatial terms, from a small-scale setting for personal interactions, based on fixed geographical locations, to fluid networks of spatially dispersed regional or national global interests, detached from place amidst 'liquid modernity' (Bauman, 2000). In turn it has been used ideologically, across the political spectrum, in support of forms of self-organisation, and by communitarians as providing the basis of self-identification, having a moral foundation which is juxtaposed with excessive individualism. Neighbourhood, similarly, has been the subject of multiple attempts to map it, both in terms of patterns of interaction and shared material resources, and in terms of a collective sense of belonging and emotive attachment (Lowndes and Sullivan, 2008). This does not, however, mean that they are devoid of all significance and cannot be taken up and applied in meaningful ways. Indeed, despite being malleably used by successive governments, as we will see in later chapters, and sprinkled liberally across various policy initiatives, it is also the case that all three terms, generically here taken to indicate 'small scale', continue to be used for theoretical defences and deployed for practical purposes for a range of progressive economic and democratic aims. Thus, later in the book we will briefly mention 'local' economic alternatives, like community wealth building. Interest in the 'local' as a site of democratic potential has also, if anything, enjoyed something of a renaissance, with, for example, the 'communalism' advocated in the work of Murray Bookchin influencing an international 'new municipalist' movement, and 'good neighbourliness' advocated as a moral underpinning of promoting 'everyday democracy' (Rosenblum, 2016).

In this context, it is worth pausing for just a brief reflection on the 'local'. It does, after all, make up 50 per cent of our subject here: i.e. *local government*. The local has moved in and out of fashion in terms of its perceived usefulness as a meaningful unit of analysis (Jones, 2019). What is important for us to note here is that it has been interrogated from a range of disciplines, and notions of it in scaler terms, as a fixed geographical territory, nesting in relation to other 'higher' spatial scales, have been challenged. Such challenges are perhaps best represented in the work of Doreen Massey, where a 'scaler mentality' is replaced with a relational perspective, with localities seen as 'nodes' of interactions emanating from and crossing multiple geographies (for example Massey, 2005); the local here is 'an unbounded mosaic of different elements' (Jones, 2019: 131). As Clarke and Cochrane (2013: 20) note, 'little about this new geography will be straightforwardly local' – meaning effective local politics must operate in multiple spaces, including supra-local ones – a 'politics of place beyond place'. Such thinking, very briefly sketched here, identifies the spaces over which local politics is conducted as highly contingent and fluid, posing considerable difficulty in conceiving of how this could be encompassed by a local administration. These incursions from the disciplines of human and political geography into the domain of public administration and local government studies pose questions about some fundamental assumptions which have been made, and add depth to long-standing debates concerning where and how to demarcate the 'local' in local government. Added to this are warnings against assigning essential democratic qualities to particular scales of social organisation, and calls to avoid the 'trap' of assuming that small scales are inherently democratic (Purcell, 2004).

In turn, however, the more relational perspective outlined above has been questioned by a 'geographical turn' in democratic thought (Barnett, 2014: 6) which has 'led back' relational geography towards an 'institutional imagination' (Barnett and Bridge, 2013: 1024), and by the growing influence of work which stresses the significance of place and location (Agnew, 1987). In other words, as we will argue in this book, living together, making collective decisions about shared environment and resources by democratic means, requires fixity amidst the flow, and an agreed institutional means and set of procedures, with some temporal depth. They cannot be constantly changed, but can be kept under review and subject to democratic scrutiny; this understanding is neither wholly territorial nor relational. We do not seek to reify the local, then, or assume that it is a homogeneous, unified entity; we interpret it as being born out of sharing common ground rather than common identity (Magnusson, 2015). It is the site for 'being in common', in Jean-Luc Nancy's terms, 'a political community [which] does not seek to fuse particular or individual identities into one singular being, but acknowledges plurality and difference, and in that way recognises the impossibility of a "common being", while striving for a "being-in-common"' (Schwarzmantel, 2007: 462). This involves a process of ongoing communication and interaction with others, 'a community consciously undergoing the experience of its sharing' (Nancy, 1991, in Schwarzmantel, 2007: 463).

We also recognise the local as being permeated and criss-crossed with linkages and power relations emanating from a range of sources, recognising the 'global in the local', and notably the macro social and economic environment in which it sits. However, while accepting this, we argue that the local provides us with the starting point in thinking about a reconfiguration of the democratic polity. While the local may not necessarily be the wholesome imaginary of more romantic notions, by the same token it is not necessarily parochial or inward-looking (Tomaney, 2013). Thus, while we cannot offer precise definitions, against the background of the contestation surrounding the concepts, we use local, community and neighbourhood in the 'everyday' sense that these terms convey meanings to most people – that is, they are associated, broadly, with proximity, belonging, a sense of being in a collective association with others and, importantly for local government, the sharing of interests and services. Local government may have resonance, that is, shared memories and emotions which serve to hold together assemblages to form a source of political action, and be an expression of practical solidarities emerging from shared ways of life (Tomaney, 2013). In this sense, Jones (2019) conceives of the local as including both material and imagined coherence. In our interpretation, this equates to the sharing of interest around collective goods and services, combined with a sense of attachment and belonging which underpins a wider democratic ethos. This provides the setting for the protection of interests and the articulation, contestation and agreement on values via collective decision-making. This combination of shared interests and subjective attachment – a recognition among members that political institutions are an expression of themselves – leads us to believe that the local provides the potential for democratic renewal, and is a site for capturing some democratic qualities which other spatial imaginaries do not offer, at least not to the same degree. Such benefits will not of necessity arise naturally from localities, but will be facilitated by an appropriate institutional arrangement which nurtures and sustains them. We argue that government should be 'Local by Default' (APSE, 2021). For us, an underpinning basis for this should be local governments organised primarily on a smaller scale, along with the use of alternative democratic practices. In doing so, we build on the work of J. S. Mill and argue that, in Chandler's (2010: 10) words,

> the moral justification of local government should not be premised on the view that it must necessarily encapsulate a community in the sense of a group of closely interrelated individuals but on the need to reconcile the differing views of individuals sharing common services and experiencing a common environment.

The structure of the book

Chapter 1 provides the background to the development of local government in Britain up to the twenty-first century. It charts the course of local government from its zenith in the early twentieth century as a network of liberal democratic organisations that had significant influence in the shaping of our cities, towns and rural communities, and thus the lives of our parents and grandparents. It will also show how, by the final two decades of the twentieth century, the boundaries, powers and independence of local authorities subsequently declined through cuts in resources, responsibilities and its relationship to locality and community. Local government in Britain, and in some of its former dependencies such as Ireland, is an element of its constitutional settlements that is very different in style and shape from other major liberal democracies. Table 1 in Appendix 1, on the relative population size of local government in Britain compared with the United States and larger nations in the EU, demonstrates one important aspect of this difference. The roots of the different path taken in Britain and Ireland are, as shown by D. E. Ashford (1982), illustrated by the contrasting attitudes to the development of local governance during the eighteenth century in Britain and France, even though they had similar complex and localised systems, as a consequence of differing responses to monarchy, industrialisation and concepts of democracy. Thus, in Chapter 1 we begin with institutional history to explain how local government developed in Britain along a path towards centralisation. The ideological values that underwrote and justified the institutional changes are the subject of Chapter 2, and show the thinking behind undermining a system that facilitated the move from local democracy as in most European and North American liberal democracies, to a system largely steered by and for the interests of central governments.

Chapters 3 to 8 discuss the present condition of local government in Britain by critically analysing the changes that have accelerated the decline of local government, particularly since 2010. The third chapter considers changes to the geographical structuring of local government in terms of the boundaries and framework of tiers of local authorities, and questions the extent to which the label 'local' has been attached by governments to justify the ever increasing size of local governments. The decline of local government is further appraised in Chapter 4, in which we review the losses and gains in recent decades in the duties assigned to local government, and whether the principal units have the resources to effectively discharge their allotted functions and fulfil a claim to be wholly democratic. Chapter 5 turns to the extent to which the decision-making structures in local authorities have changed in recent decades, the extent to which these changes have been forced on local authorities and their impacts on democratic practices inside and outside of the council. Chapter 6 considers the pattern of intergovernmental relations towards greater central control, using a variety of direct and indirect means, in the context of the constitutional standing of local government and the 'operating code' of a Westminster-centric polity.

Despite the restructuring and restrictions placed on local government since 2010, we do not dismiss local governments as wholly impotent agencies. In Chapter 7 we discuss how the system has managed to deal with change and show that local authorities are capable of making innovative use of their powers. In Chapter 8 we consider the observations in the preceding chapters from the point of view of central governing elites, by asking how local government and governance is viewed by the central core of elected executives and administrators. It is argued that within Westminster and

Whitehall there is a strong body of opinion that sees local agencies as largely expedient to the wishes of central decision-makers. An important conclusion from this analysis is that any change in the declining fortunes of local government is currently unlikely, given that restructuring of the system is largely the province of central rather than local government.

In Chapter 9 we carry forward the lessons from the previous chapters to consider a more normative analysis of what local government is for, bringing together 'traditional' and more recent theoretical developments to consider how a framework can be established to ensure an ethical role for local governance which may aid democratic structuring and well-being as a whole. In the final chapter we summarise the position taken by this study and briefly reflect on whether the ideas that have been proposed have any chance of being implemented in the real world. These reflections, we recognise, require a further study in order to fully explore these normative underpinnings.

1

The evolution of the twentieth-century system

We begin with a brief history of local government that shows how radically the system of subnational government has evolved, particularly since the nineteenth century, from a system that has had substantial power to govern localities. Although much of the system was far from democratic until the enfranchisement of citizens, which was attained nationally within a liberal democratic framework, some aspects of the former organic system of local democracy remained through the practice of open vestries in which local citizens could regularly meet and determine policies that affected their communities. It may be argued that the gain of liberal democracy at the national level in the late nineteenth and early twentieth centuries was achieved in Britain at the expense of pockets of direct discursive democracy in some parish and town governments. In comparison with most Western European and North American democracies, Britain and Ireland secured liberal democracy nationally, but at the expense of any deep-rooted and effective democracy at a community or neighbourhood level. The systems of parish and township governance at a direct discursive level were weeded out rather than, as in the United States or France, preserved as an important adjunct of their national liberal democratic political systems.

The evolving systems of local governance in Britain

English local government in medieval Britain was built on the assumption that a landowning aristocracy largely determined the rule of law within their estates. Below the shire or county, as it was recast by Elizabethan times, territory was divided further into hundreds and governed in rural areas by local courts controlled by local landowners who were not always bound by loyalty to the King or his local deputy the Sheriff. In wealthy towns some communities were able to negotiate an arrangement with the monarch or a senior baron to receive a charter allowing them certain powers over their communities. These were often dominated by the merchant or manufacturers' guilds that dominated the economic life of their town. Such communities were commonly called boroughs through charters in the gift of the monarch or Parliament, and conducted many of their affairs outside the arrangements for the counties in which they were situated. The smallest unit of devolved government, the parish, was originally an ecclesiastical division but came to be recognised in England as a civil unit dealing with local matters, and was often referred to as the parish vestry after the meeting room in the local church. Over time the number of parishes varied, but the First Report of the newly formed national Poor Law Board in 1835 reported that there were around 15,600 at that time (Keith-Lucas, 1980: 76). Many parishes and chartered towns were controlled by wealthy landowners or merchants but some were outside their reach and enjoyed an element of democracy as open vestries in which ratepayers determined policy in local meetings (see Chandler, 2007: 1–28; Keith-Lucas, 1980; Webb and Webb, 1906). This pattern of governance was not dissimilar to structures taking shape in much of Europe and the United States where diverse local units of government, often at the size of small parishes or towns, were governed largely by local landowners or, in towns, prosperous merchants, who were able to make local decisions independently of central governments.

The independent territory of Scotland followed a similar Anglo-Saxon pattern of local governments based on shire counties supposedly answerable to the monarch and more independent urban burghs given charters either by the sheriff and their deputy, usually landowners answerable to royalty, or to a clan chieftain if they were not themselves the sheriff. In Scotland parishes were not recognised until 1845 as civil, as opposed to ecclesiastical, divisions, and only became fully elected authorities in 1894 (Whyte, 1925: 25).

Larger than most English parishes, they were converted in 1929 after the loss of their responsibility for the poor law into district councils with limited powers (Poole and Keith-Lucas, 1994: 218). Wales was subject up to the reign of Edward II to control by local landowners cum warlords until forced finally to submit to English dominance and adopt patterns of local government similar to those in England. The question arises throughout this study of why local government in Britain did not follow the reforms that many other liberal democracies have followed to retain parish and township governments as units of democratic governance for determining predominantly local issues.

Stability and the beginnings of uniformity in the English local government systems began to emerge in the Elizabethan period when a relatively long period of peace and prosperity in domestic politics allowed for a stronger central government that enabled the Queen and her advisors at court to pass more effective Acts and raise taxes, subject to Parliament. At county level the role of most senior representative of central government was transferred to the Lord Lieutenant rather than the office of Sheriff. Lord Lieutenant was usually an office held for life, and in much of the country this was entrusted to a prominent peer of the realm with influence in the royal court. Although often too exalted and tied into the politics and society of the central elites, lord lieutenants appointed the justices of the peace (JPs), who were normally prominent landowners with estates in their county who regularly conferred together in the county quarter sessions courts. The JPs had not only judicial but civil duties. They had powers to summon a county militia to put down riots and defend their territory from any foreign invasion. They appointed a high or chief constable to ensure law and order and also to collect taxes. Lesser duties were assigned within each parish to local men of some standing in their community who were persuaded to take on for a time the often unpaid roles, such as that of a parish constable. The parish also gained responsibility in Acts of 1572 and 1601 for what became its central task, that of poor relief. Helping the poor had been a role for the church and its ecclesiastic parish in medieval times, but with the closure of the monasteries the task had fallen increasingly into the orbit of the secular parishes. Elizabethan Poor Law Acts obliged parishes to raise taxes on property to be distributed for the relief of poverty for those born within their boundaries (Webb and Webb, 1927). Towns and boroughs were also obliged to create parishes to forward this policy. Other parish duties included maintenance of roads, often carried out by those receiving poor relief.

Little change then occurred in the formal structuring and customs of local governance in Britain, despite the turbulence of the civil wars in the 1640s, the restoration of the Stuart dynasty under Charles II, and its demise in the 'Glorious Revolution' of 1689. Consequently by the early 1800s the growth of industrialisation and transport and the development of larger urban centres ensured that town and parish governments needed reform if they were to keep up with changing circumstances. The problems and also opportunities for economic growth were met largely through piecemeal changes which bypassed the existing county, town and parish institutions to create ad hoc structures to facilitate new tasks. Many of the reforms of the early nineteenth century were secured by local initiatives through private Acts of Parliament, an arrangement in which wealthy local sponsors of schemes for improvement could, with the support of a number of MPs or Lords, promote a Bill in Parliament to establish a company or trust to force through developments that cut across local authority boundaries. Many canals were built through this legal process, and problems of maintaining major roads began to be resolved by establishing turnpike trusts that collected tolls to improve the roads, from those who used them. Poor sanitation, policing, road maintenance and street lighting in the growing industrialising towns were similarly partly resolved by the sponsoring of private Acts that created improvement trusts, which took over these tasks from parishes and boroughs who could not or would not provide these facilities. Manchester, for example, aided the town's expansion into a major city by creating a Police Commission in 1765 that went on to take control of many additional services such as street lighting, widening roads and even establishing coal gas production and delivery (Webb and Webb, 1922: 256–273).

The Elizabethan poor law also became ineffective as growing populations and uneven economic growth created financial pressures on towns and rural communities. Parishes began to merge their resources and lower their costs by building workhouses which effectively imprisoned the poor, often separating families, and required many of their more able paupers to undertake hard labour to pay for their keep (Webb and Webb, 1929). Further initiatives, largely on law and order, established on a national basis, began to creep onto the statute book. Robert Peel's creation of the Metropolitan Police Force in 1829 was one of the earliest transfers of local authority powers to central government control. Peel also established arrangements to nationally regulate prisons, which had previously been subject to county, town or parish government. By 1877 this responsibility was transferred entirely to central government (Chandler, 2007: 60).

The Liberal 'revolution' after 1832

The 1832 Electoral Reform Act did not create democracy in Britain overnight but it did undermine the influence of the Whig and Tory landed gentry who based their fortunes and powers on the ownership of land. The Act paved the way for wealthy middle-class merchants and industrialists to secure representation in Parliament. One of the first acts of Lord Grey's resultant reforming government was to establish an inquiry into the poor law, whose conclusions were largely the work of followers of the liberal utilitarian theorist Jeremy Bentham, the economist Nassau Senior and pillar of fact-based policy research, Edwin Chadwick. They were sufficiently impressed by the practice in some areas of grouping together parishes into boards that corralled the poor into workhouses rather than giving outdoor relief in their homes. A reformed poor law was accepted without extensive opposition in Parliament in 1834 following their report's main suggestions. This established local poor law unions, usually created through merging several parishes. The system nationally was subject to a national Poor Law Board that attempted to unify regulations for poor relief and appoint inspectors to tour local areas to see that their ideas were implemented. This formed the basis of a formula that was adopted for many other local services during the mid-Victorian years (Chandler, 2007: 39–42). Edwin Chadwick continued his mission to achieve more centralised care of those in need by helping to establish in 1848 local health boards, outside direct parish or town council control, to ensure efficient clean water and sewage disposal systems and hospital care. These were made subject to a central General Board of Health. Transport boards were formed in 1862 to group together towns and villages to deal with communications more efficiently. Boards of education, established in 1870, ensured that all children went to an elementary school until 12 years of age. Burial boards were formed to set up new systems of cemeteries to augment the often overcrowded churchyards.

While this system of ad hoc boards seemed the preferred solution for social reform, leading industrial and commercial interests in larger towns and cities required greater control of services that contributed to productive industrial growth. The post-1832 representation of industrial interests in Parliament led in 1833 to an Act that required Scottish royal burghs to be elected by ratepayers, and this opened the route towards similar legislation for England and Wales. This was secured in 1835, despite considerable Tory opposition in the House of Lords, by the Municipal Corporations Act. Established boroughs with a substantial population were henceforward subject to a local council, whose members were elected on a regular basis by ratepayers. Some hundred small towns in rural areas lost their status as boroughs when they were excluded from the Act. The compromises required to get the Act through the House of Lords did not, however, apply to growing industrial towns, mainly in northern England, that were not chartered boroughs under the old regime. These communities had to petition the Privy Council to be considered as a borough, and if such a request was seriously contested the community had to seek an Act of Parliament to become governed by a municipal corporation. In the following decade some substantive towns were deeply divided over whether to become incorporated, largely due to the extra taxes that may be the consequence. Sheffield only gained this status in 1843 and Bradford in 1847. Initially the powers of boroughs under the 1835 Act were not particularly substantial, but once incorporated most boroughs began to absorb the duties of improvement commissions and other ad hoc ventures that operated within their boundaries. It was expensive but not too difficult for ambitious boroughs to increase their limited powers by securing private Acts of Parliament to enhance their functions.

In London such developments were hampered by the division of the conurbation into numerous smaller boroughs and parish vestries. It was not until the creation in 1855 of a Metropolitan Board of Works that a London-wide institution could tackle the problems of water supply and drainage. This body formed the nucleus of what was to become, through the 1888 Local Government Act, the London County Council, which could take control of many of the capital's conurbation-wide problems. In 1899 the London Government Act created twenty-eight London boroughs by merging the pre-existing vestries into larger units and also attaching to the new boroughs many remaining ad hoc authorities such as burial boards. The exercise was undertaken largely at the behest of the Prime Minister, Lord Salisbury, who was anxious to set up rival local government units to stand up to the liberal, let alone socialist, pretensions of the London County Council (Robson, 1939: 94–99). Excepted from these arrangements was the City of London which, with the financial weight at its command, petitioned to retain its status as a separate borough elected by a complex franchise which ensured that wealthy guilds which represented the financial and commercial interests in the City retained their hold over the square mile by exerting considerable influence on Members of Parliament (Chandler, 2007: 80–83). Elements of this anachronistic arrangement still remain today.

Democratisation and consolidation

In the last two decades of the nineteenth century the overcomplex ad hoc arrangements for local government began to be consolidated into predominantly two-tier structures elected by male, and by 1894 female, suffrage although only one vote was allowed per household. The most important step in this evolution was the 1888 Local Government Act that established elected county councils and ended the civil powers of the magistrates who, as JPs, acted through the quarter sessions. Scottish county councils were created in 1889 with powers and franchises similar to those in England and Wales.

The councils were chosen under a similar franchise as that given to borough councils and their members were elected to represent wards for three-year terms. However, until the major reforms of local government came into force in 1974, a number of long-standing councillors in boroughs and counties were chosen by their fellow councillors to serve as aldermen with a six-year term in office. Initially, little had in practice changed in terms of the source of power in many rural counties, as the landed gentry who served as JPs ensured that they gained election as the sole nominee without any opposition. At the time of their creation, the county councils had relatively few powers. These included repair of major roads and prevention of infections or infestations that might damage local agriculture. The most important responsibility, policing, was shared with magistrates. Over time, however, they gained many of the tasks previously assigned to ad hoc authorities, such as education and social care. Larger cities successfully pressurised the government in 1888 to raise their status to county boroughs, which took on the tasks of both the county and the borough, making them, in effect, unitary authorities (Chandler, 2007: 100–103).

Following the restructuring of county and municipal local government, considerable debate arose over the status of the parish, with a cross-party alliance of Liberal and Tory MPs and Lords proposing that these should form a lower level of community government. In France and Germany small communities were already the cornerstone of the lowest, primary tier of rural government, but such a solution was opposed by other cross-party groups as giving power to areas of insufficient population to be entrusted with government and, for many Tory landowners, arousing fears that an empowered parish may be exploited by poor labourers to impose higher demands on the rates. In 1894 a Local Government Act was passed that created, as a compromise, urban and rural districts within county areas, based on the boundaries of the health boards that had been set up in 1843 and the more recently created highways boards. The new districts undertook many of the tasks that had previously been held by the parishes. Urban districts had somewhat greater powers over street lighting and recreation than the rural districts, where the parishes continued to have a role in these areas (Chandler, 2007: 106–107). Local poor law boards were given fewer powers, with many of their tasks being absorbed by national and county government, and they were finally wound up in 1948. Education boards remained for a time separate from the districts, although after considerable controversy regarding the role of religious denominations in schools they were in 1902 incorporated into borough, county and some larger urban districts. In Scotland education boards remained separate from local government councils until 1918.

The 1894 Local Government Act was at the time popularly referred to as the Parish Councils Act, even though it seriously diminished the importance of the parish, which was left with predominantly discretionary powers to establish allotments or public libraries under existing legislation, and to maintain rights of way and repair ditches and sewers. They became elected bodies, apart from parishes with less than 300 ratepayers, which could be governed by a parish meeting called usually only once or twice a year and open to anyone in the parish who was on the local or parliamentary register. The larger, in terms of population, open vestries, which could involve all propertied ratepayers in an area through ownership of houses, shops or workplaces, became governed by a parish council whose members were elected by all residents on the electoral register (Odgers and Naldrett, 1909: 57–65). The new system had the merit of not being dependent on the men, and the far fewer women, who owned property, but nevertheless in many areas decreased the number of citizens who had an opportunity to take part in discourse with their fellow property holders to determine the policies of their community governments. The attention given to the reformed parishes varied widely, with strongly contested ballots in some areas. But, due to deference to the squire and parson, many parishes had no need of a ballot as local worthies ensured, through behind-the-scenes pressures, that only as many candidates were nominated as to exactly fill the number of seats on the council (Ottewill, 2008). It was not until the mid-twentieth century that local government was fully democratised. From 1894 almost all male citizens who were ratepayers could vote in local elections. A few women ratepayers could vote by 1869 and this was extended to married women ratepayers by 1894, but only one vote was allowed per household. It was not until 1928 that both men and women had equal voting rights. The capacity of citizens to stand for election to a council was initially confined to men who were ratepayers, but by 1907 this was extended to female ratepayers and then became a universal right by 1945. However, anyone labelled a pauper in receipt of poor law benefit was excluded from voting locally until 1945 (Keith-Lucas and Richards, 1978: 18–19).

Restructuring the local government system

It can be argued that throughout the nineteenth and twentieth centuries and to the present day, local government has been a constant work of construction and deconstruction, but by the 1930s it had reached a plateau. It was consolidated into tiers, governed by councils responsible for a wide range of social and productive services, elected through almost universal adult suffrage. However, there continued to be criticism of the system. The development of technology and economic restructuring to create global industries and financial institutions suggested to many politicians that economic growth had to be guided not by city, let alone township and rural governments, but by national and international government and agencies. In this context a particular arena of contention was occasioned by the growth of urban conurbations. The economic and social expansion of the county boroughs was curtailed within nineteenth-century boundaries, as their demands for future expansion were opposed by adjoining more conservative county councils and rural districts. During the Second World War the publication of the Beveridge Report urged major reconstruction of health and social services that after 1945 became a matter of some importance to the post-war Labour government and the Civil Service. The Labour Minister of Health, Nye Bevan, had little faith in the capacity of the existing system of local government to be entrusted with radical reform and, supported by leading doctors, persuaded the Cabinet to exclude hospitals and doctor's surgeries from local government control (Chandler, 2007: 168–170). Bevan went on to push for the creation of a royal commission to investigate the restructuring of local government, and his personal view was that it should be organised as a single-tier structure with far fewer and less locally bound authorities. London, he believed, had an even more urgent need for reform. The Attlee Cabinet did not, however, support Bevan. Herbert Morrison, a former leader and champion of the London County Council with oversight of domestic policy in the Cabinet, led opposition to the proposal (Chandler, 2007: 173–250).

Pressure for restructuring local government boundaries continued into the thirteen years of Conservative governments between 1951 and 1964. Two boundary commissions recommended changes that secured, with some difficulty, some upgrades of larger boroughs to county borough status, but the most pressing problem concerned London. London County Council, created in 1888, covered only the inner boroughs of the conurbation, and the expansion of the metropolis by 1950 had left most of its suburbs in boroughs and urban districts. A Royal Commission under the chairmanship of Sir Edwin Herbert, appointed to advise on possible reform, proposed in 1960 that the London County Council should be replaced by a much wider and more populous Greater London Council (GLC) to deal with strategic transport and planning issues, and that the whole conurbation be divided into second tier London boroughs which would provide most services including education. Following intense debate, most of the Commission's recommendations were agreed although the London County Council's reputation for good governance of education led to the creation of an Inner London Education Authority covering its former area (G. Rhodes, 1970).

The framework for reform laid out in the restructuring of London was taken up by Richard Crossman, appointed as Minister for Housing and Local Government in 1964 to Harold Wilson's first government. Although this portfolio concerned subjects on which the ambitious minister had never expressed much interest, he needed a major task to make his mark and took the opportunity of setting up a Royal Commission to review the structure of local government. He found little opposition to the proposal, as Prime Minister Wilson remarked to him:

> You have no person like Herbert Morrison, Chuter Ede or Nye Bevan ... who really is an authority on local government. In this Cabinet there isn't a single person of that quality and that's why you have been getting away with murder. (Crossman, 1975: Vol. 1, 439)

The Commission was chaired by an Oxford don, Lord Redcliffe-Maud, who had experience of earlier inquiries on health and local government management. A different committee under a leading judge, Lord Wheatley, dealt with Scotland while the newly formed Welsh Office secured the power to forward proposals for restructuring in the principality. The inquiries completed their work in 1969 and all recommended a decrease in the number of principal local authorities. In England these would be based on single-tier authorities with a few exceptions for major conurbations, named metropolitan authorities, which would adopt a system similar to the newly created Greater London. In Scotland, seven regional councils were recommended, with a single tier of authorities below them, and in Wales a similar pattern of five large strategic counties below which were single-tier authorities for managing the more day-to-day local functions. It was recommended that parish councils be retained and differentiated from the larger principal authorities under the term of local councils (Wood, 1976: 64–65). They remained in their existing state in the consequent 1972 Local Government Act, with, for some small towns, the possibility of being termed 'town councils'. In the separate Acts for Wales and for Scotland, they were named community councils.

The Labour government's efforts to frame legislation based on the reports faltered in 1970 with their defeat by the Conservatives led by Edward Heath. The new minister assigned to local government, Peter Walker, was equally sympathetic to the modernising drift favouring consolidation. But he found serious opposition to a single-tier proposal for local government in rural areas from Conservative landed gentry and allied rural interests threatened by absorption of their local councils into new authorities centred on urban areas. The intransigence of this rural lobby, combined with the pressure they placed on their MPs, obliged Walker to retain a two-tier structure of county and district rather than a predominantly one-tier system (Chandler, 2007: 201–205; Wood, 1976). The amendment of the Bill was perhaps one of the last victories of a declining landowning rural influence in the Conservative Party. The structure of the resultant system that came into being in 1974 is summarised in Table 2 (see Appendix 2) but was to be eroded within ten years by an insidious movement to unitary authorities.

The evolution of the twentieth-century system

In 1986, following clashes between left-wing local socialist authorities and attempts to control spending by local authorities, the Thatcher government removed the metropolitan counties and the GLC by transferring their powers to the metropolitan districts and the London boroughs, to effectively make these areas unitary authorities. A more comprehensive move in this direction was then initiated by the Major government through a boundaries commission under the chair of Sir John Banham in 1992 to revise boundaries in the rest of England, with a view to establishing further unitary councils. The initiative, as discussed in Chapter 4, was only a partial success and was wound up in 1996.

New Labour under Blair focussed not so much on boundary changes to local government but made its mark on the unity of the United Kingdom (UK) by regional solutions, establishing devolved government in Scotland and Wales and giving their Parliaments and governments powers over determining the structure and funding of their local authorities. The devolved governments have generally continued the trend towards large unitary authorities inherited from the Thatcher and Major governments. A strategic regional authority in London was brought back as the Greater London Authority in 2000, but established under an executive mayor. An attempt by Deputy Prime Minister John Prescott to create strategic regional authorities for the rest of England came to nothing when a referendum to establish a North-East England region was heavily rejected by the electorate, largely on the basis that this would add to local taxation demands. However, as discussed later, subregional governments have subsequently been imposed in an eclectic fashion in conurbations in England by post-2010 administrations.

Redrawing the internal policy-making structures

By the early twentieth century the internal policy-making structures of local authorities of any size had uniformly evolved into committee-based systems. While all decisions of the local authority had to be sanctioned by a meeting of all its councillors, in practice, subcommittees of the council responsible for specific functions of the authority, such as education or housing, debated issues on these subjects and passed all but the most controversial decisions to the council where they were rubber-stamped usually without debate. In the nineteenth century the chair of the whole council was usually seen as the most important political leader of the authority. The position was in municipalities dignified by the title of mayor, or in cities with county borough status, the lord mayor. During the twentieth century a gradual change was adopted by local councils to appoint mayors and council chairs on a yearly basis as politically neutral referees of debates and as the ceremonial representative of the authority rather than its leading policymaker. The rise of organised mass political parties ensured that in most boroughs and counties serious power lay within the decision-making process of the party that held the majority of seats on the council. Each party group of councillors appointed its leader, and if the party held a majority of seats their chosen councillor would be leader of the council and usually its dominant political figure. Other senior party members were nominated as chairs of important subcommittees and often formed an executive committee of the party group (Copus, 2006: 6). A further officer in each party group, the party whip, had responsibility to inform and persuade their fellow councillors to vote as their party leader and their prominent advisors required.

From the mid-nineteenth century larger local authorities assigned decision-making to separate subcommittees for specific tasks that could at times become semi-independent from control by the whole council of the authority. The committee system remained embedded in local government decision-making structures until the Thatcher and Major governments, when an enthusiast for New Public Management (NPM), Michael Heseltine, urged local authorities to abandon the long-standing committee system. This would involve creating a framework not dissimilar to that of national governments, in which an executive mayor chaired an inner Cabinet of councillors representing large departments, leaving backbench councillors to serve on scrutiny committees with the task of reviewing the work of the mayor and his or her Cabinet. These ideas received little initial support in Conservative governments but were taken up by Tony Blair's New Labour governments, which set about an ambitious restructuring of local government policy-making, ensuring that the new Greater London Authority would be led by a directly elected mayor advised by a small Cabinet of political heads of departments. Attempts to roll out the system of elected mayors to other larger local authorities in the 2000 Local Government Act received little popular support. Local referenda to give some democratic authority to these systems failed in twice as many areas as they were successful (Copus, 2006). Nevertheless, the broad idea of Cabinet governments led by an executive council leader was mandated in the Local Government and Public Involvement in Health Act of 2007, condemning backbench councillors to largely unnoticed roles on scrutiny committees.

The growth of both central and local government from the mid-nineteenth century established a need for a substantial bureaucracy of technical advisors and a workforce of operatives to put policy into practice. The municipal boroughs that came into being with the 1835 Municipal Corporations Act employed few staff of their own and settled legal matters using a part-time solicitor. In large towns such as Manchester the legal officer soon became a full-time town clerk employed by the council, and was regarded as the most senior of the local government employees. By the middle of the twentieth century the larger municipalities and county councils had evolved into substantive employers of labour led by highly trained professionals in a wide range of specialisms. Many smaller authorities were, however, much slower to develop a bureaucracy, and well into the twentieth century many district authorities used the services of a local private solicitor as town clerk to provide legal advice, and for financial matters a local bank manager, and employed local businesses to carry out public works (Chandler, 2007: 84–85). By the 1960s it was becoming recognised that the town clerk or the treasurer often lacked the capacity to bring together all sections of the local bureaucracy to follow a clear, joined-up strategy. A few local authorities, such as Newcastle upon Tyne, replaced the role with a more empowered manager as the chief executive of the council who would chair a board of senior chief officers. The Bains Report (1972), established to review management in the post-1974 local government structures, recommended that the town clerk should be replaced by a chief executive who would have strategic oversight over policy implementation and be the chief professional advisor to the leader of the council. Almost all major local authorities subsequently accepted this arrangement.

Local government powers

The responsibilities of local governments were originally defined for towns in the royal charters that had established the boroughs, or through tradition and precedent. A more uniform approach to local powers began to develop in the 1840s through the legal concept of *ultra vires*. This ruling, originally developed to control the building of railways, maintained that any corporate organisation must be able to show that they had a lawful right to perform a particular activity. This legal restraint remained until the 2011 Localism Act, as discussed in later chapters. Getting round the *ultra vires* ruling was however open to wealthy authorities through their capacity to sponsor private Acts of Parliament to develop new services such as developing clean water and sewage disposal, and later – often profitably – gas and electricity generation. Many of these productive services that provided the groundwork for industrial growth ensured that the middle-class businessmen in a town could rely on the local authority to provide the most up-to-date infrastructure to support their enterprises, as is illustrated in the example of nineteenth-century Birmingham.

However, by the beginning of the twentieth century the role of local government as, in part, a commercial venture raising substantial funds for the public purse began to be seriously challenged by business leaders who feared that the growth of locally subsidised productive services or, increasingly, leisure facilities, would undermine wealth creation by private companies or individuals. The most substantive pressure to curb productive service provision began after 1920 as Conservative domination of central government enabled a backlash against the procedures that allowed local authorities to present private bills to Parliament to enable them to extend their powers. A central battle took place over attempts by Birmingham City Council to establish a municipally owned savings bank. Further development of this idea was opposed by, among others, Winston Churchill, and an inquiry to examine the issue argued that local authorities should not establish services that could be provided by the private sector (Chandler, 2007: 144–147). Few local authority attempts to increase their powers over productive services were acceptable to Parliament from that time. From a rather different ideological perspective, this state of mind continued into the post-1945 Labour governments with the nationalisation of electricity and gas services and the consolidation of water and sewage agencies. Later, under Conservative governments these essential activities, along with bus services, were privatised, thus removing from local governments important and potentially profit-making activities that they had pioneered in the twentieth century. By the 1950s the losses to local governments' portfolio had, however, been offset by the acquisition of redistributive services so that local authorities could still be seen as important agencies for shaping their communities. These new powers were predominantly distributive in nature and were aimed at improving the welfare and opportunities of the poorer sector of society. Among the first of these initiatives were powers for principal authorities to build council housing, low-cost housing for rent, initially to create 'homes fit for heroes' to ensure a better environment for families that had endured the First World War. Social housing, between the 1920s and the 1980s, became a major element of local government responsibilities. In addition local authorities gained powers to regulate the construction of housing and industry through town and country planning powers centred in the principal local authorities.

An increasing concern for the alleviation of poverty also undermined the nineteenth-century attitudes to the poor law as a punitive last resort option for those who could not for reasons beyond their control fend for themselves. Through National Insurance and pensions policies, resolving the problems of those too old or ill to work or facing unemployment through no fault of their own began to become a nationally administered issue. Administration, if not control, of poor law services remained in an attenuated form for a few decades into the twentieth century, with its responsibility transferred to county councils and boroughs in 1929, but soon afterwards in 1931, during what was then seen as the 'Great Depression', poor relief became a national government concern. This left many hospitals under local authority care until 1948 when they were subsumed into the National Health Service, leaving local government with a rather diverse set of social service responsibilities, such as the protective care of children or the elderly, that had originally developed within the reformed poor law system. It was not until after the Seebohm Inquiry, established in 1965 to review child protection, that a structured social service function became a major joined-up portfolio within county and county borough responsibilities. Thus, while some redistributive services flourished as local government responsibilities, the overall picture until the 1980s is one in which central government curtailed productive enterprise among local authorities that competed with private sector provision or was deemed inefficient if not provided through a nationally controlled network. Hence local government was repositioned as predominantly an adjunct to the welfare state. From the early 1980s onwards, welfare services such as social services were, in turn, subject to legislation requiring them to be contracted out to a range of private or voluntary organisations, creating a 'mixed economy' of provision.

The diminution of local government control over many key services cannot be fully detailed here but we will, as an example, highlight the decline of local government control of education, which was for several decades the largest service provided by local government in terms of expenditure. It was always conducted within a framework of national policy, and as such was characterised by Griffith (1966) as a national service, locally administered. Councils, as local education authorities (LEAs), through their education committees, essentially decided how to organise schools and how to allocate funds to them (Wilson and Game, 2011). The powers given to local authorities to independently provide redistributive and welfare services were, however, seriously eroded by successive Conservative governments between 1979 and 1997. The 1988 Education Reform Act brought into being a national curriculum, extended parental choice of school, and introduced Local Management of Schools, which required 85 per cent of spending to be devolved to school governors and head teachers. Effectively, councils were to 'pass on' this money, provided to them in the form of central government grants, directly to schools in accordance with a formula which had to be approved by the centre. Legislation was also brought in to allow schools to opt out of local government control to become 'grant maintained' schools, funded directly by central government, which later led to most schools being managed by not-for-profit trusts. The effect was to 'hollow out' the role of the local education authority (LEA), as powers passed either to school managers, the private sector or to central government. The creation of Ofsted (now the Office for Standards in Education, Children's Services and Skills) in 1992 strengthened the national inspection regime, which was further enhanced by increasing use of nationally determined performance indicators, the introduction of school league tables, and enhanced powers for ministers to intervene in the management of 'failing' schools. In addition, local authorities' role in education was further undermined by the 1992 Further and Higher Education Act, which transferred further education and sixth-form colleges from LEAs to a national Further Education Funding Council, with polytechnics to become self-governing universities. The LEA's role was relegated to that of a provider of certain support services, should schools choose to buy these from them, and as a commissioner of other support services for which they retained statutory duties.

The major responsibility for providing council housing was similarly eroded from 1980 onwards as, under the 'Right to Buy' policy, local authorities were obliged to transfer council houses to their tenants on a discounted purchase scheme, and were consequently left managing only the most run down and unattractive properties. Further legislation allowed whole estates to be transferred to private landlords, often set up as housing trusts, and many local authorities, especially in Conservative areas, gave up their ownership of housing, although all local authorities retained duties to find shelter for the homeless. Building of new council houses was largely discouraged by lack of finance. Further moves to privatise services such as road maintenance, sheltered accommodation for the infirm and even financial management were developed through requiring local governments to compete with private sector suppliers for the task of carrying these out on behalf of the local authority. The later New Labour governments did not add to the scale of privatisation of local authority powers, but did very little to roll back the trend that they should work closely with the private sector for the provision of many of their traditional services. With the return after 2010 of the Conservative Party to government the trend towards privatisation of local services was to be continued, as will be discussed in Chapter 4.

Finance up to the 1980s

Before 1832 local governments were expected to fund their activities through locally raised taxes, particularly the rates, a tax on property including farmed land, or for some boroughs rents from property or service charges. Pressure was, however, growing among the landed classes arguing that new burdens on local resources such as the poor law and prisons were a consequence of central rather than local legislation. Robert Peel gave some concessions to aggrieved landowners, although these changes did not appease rural landowners, who formed an influential pressure group to petition governments to decrease rates on land and increase central government grants to local authorities. Their demands found some favour with Disraelian Tories who in 1874 assigned revenue from national taxes, such as a duty on carriages, to local government. The Salisbury government in 1896 substantially reduced the rates on agricultural land and by 1929 the tax had been removed entirely. This was a victory for Tory landowners in terms of easing their financial burdens, but also acted as a Trojan horse by opening the road for more progressive central governments to use financial means to wrest control over local authorities from landowners. Between 1896 and 1925 some seventeen separate grants were established to aid local governments in their growing portfolio of socially distributive tasks, including major subsidies for the new push for council-built housing (Chandler, 2007: 148). Grants were also consolidated into a Rates Support Grant and weighted to benefit areas in need, so that by 1939 approximately 39 per cent of local government funding came from central government sources (G. Rhodes, 1976: 154.) Following the Second World War the Labour government's policy of ensuring efficiency in energy supplies and health provision, as noted in the section above on the powers of local government, ensured that they tended to favour central grants rather than locally raised rates as preferred by many Conservatives, so that a consensus settled on accepting a compromise between the two forms of funding (Travers, 1986: 191–203).

Central–local relations

In central government, issues relating to the structuring and powers of local government during much of the nineteenth century was divided between the Poor Law Board, the General Health Board and units from the Home Office concerned with the oversight of private Acts. In 1872, under pressure from medical lobbyists to secure better sanitation and water supply, Gladstone created a Local Government Board (LGB), effectively a ministerial department. A battle over the principal focus of the new creation was won by former Poor Law Board bureaucrats, to the chagrin of the medical professionals. This outcome reflected the trend in the Civil Service to place generalists as permanent advisors to ministers rather than professionals, and this also ensured that the LGB was dominated by parsimony and discrimination against the poor rather than public health issues. It was not until the end of the First World War that, under a more liberal coalition, the LGB was reconstructed as the Ministry of Health, with a more supportive attitude to social well-being and alleviation of poverty. Its first minister, a distinguished medical doctor, Christopher Addison, was one of the foremost advocates of establishing the role of local government as a redistributive agency by promoting legislation and resources to create affordable rented council housing to replace privately owned slums.

The differing levels of local government had since the late nineteenth century begun to work together to form associations that would become the preferred representatives of their interests for senior Civil Service bureaucrats, who could not easily negotiate directly with the many separate local governments. Central among these agencies were the Association of County Councils and the Association of Municipal Authorities. There were also important networks formed between professional associations working within local government such as the Chartered Institute for Public Finance and Accountancy. With few disturbances, intergovernmental relations from the 1920s to the 1980s settled into a well worn partnership between secretaries of state and leading civil servants in the Ministry of Health and later creations, such as a Department of Housing and Local Government, and the senior representatives of the local government associations (Chandler, 1988: 78–92). This *modus vivendi* was to be seriously eroded with the arrival in 1979 of a New Right-influenced government (R. A. W. Rhodes, 1986: 376–378). During the late 1970s several cities including the GLC led by Ken Livingstone were venturing into 'local socialism'. During the first years of the Thatcher administrations a serious schism opened up between many Labour-held cities and the government. Central to the developments being pursued was the sale of council houses, schemes to undermine local authority building and maintenance services, and moves to penalise financially local authorities that wished to raise more funding than was targeted by the central government. The initial efforts to curb the level of council rate demands were largely evaded by left-leaning local authorities, and it took some four years for the first Thatcher government to produce legislation in the 1984 Rates Act that effectively allowed them to ensure that local authorities' overall spending was for the first time largely determined by central government.

A number of local socialist councils sought to defy the new law, but a brief stand-off between the government and sixteen local authorities who refused to cap their rate increases ended in capitulation by the authorities, as the councillors voting for unlawful rate demands could be personally surcharged by the courts to repay the cost of the money they were unlawfully collecting. If taken to its final conclusion the rebellious councillors could have been declared bankrupt and, as defaulters, be removed from their role as elected councillors (Blunkett and Jackson, 1987). A subsequent government inquiry on the conduct of councillors conducted by barrister David Widdicombe set out the principle that

> Although local government has origins pre-dating the sovereignty of Parliament, all current local authorities are the statutory creations of Parliament and have no independent status or right to exist. The whole system of local government could lawfully be abolished by Act of Parliament. (Widdicombe, 1986: 3:3: 45)

Prime Minister Thatcher continued her personal onslaught on local government based on the theory that local authority spending could only be controlled if all voters paid equal taxes to their local authority rather than paying in proportion to the wealth locked into their property. At the height of her popularity Mrs Thatcher pushed forward these un-egalitarian principles through the 'Community Charge', which by 1988 became widely known as the 'poll tax'. This became her nemesis as many ratepayers refused to pay the new tax, and it led to perhaps the most serious violent riots over a clear political issue since 1945. Her successor John Major appointed Michael Heseltine to replace the poll tax with a reformed rating system, the council tax, while keeping a major element of the rates on businesses under central government control (Chandler, 2007: 259–264). The council tax, as with the rates, was subject to capping by the government. The rates rebellion, as dealt with by the courts, and the consequent Widdicombe Report as accepted by Parliament, ended any sense of believing local government worked in a mutual partnership with central government and that both institutions should agree policy relating to changes in the central–local system.

During the 1980s public administration was also ideologically being replaced by what was termed New Public Management (NPM). Local authorities were urged by central government to become more exposed to competition from the private sector, in the belief that this would lead to lower costs and greater efficiency. Compulsory competitive tendering (CCT) was introduced by the Local Government, Planning and Land Act 1980 for construction, maintenance and highways work; the 1988 Local Government Act extended this to a range of 'blue collar' services (like refuse collection) and in 1989 leisure services were included in this list. CCT was further extended in England to a range of professional services, beginning with housing management, legal services, and construction and property services in 1994, and information technology, finance and personnel services in 1995. An Audit Commission established in 1982 had been given the task of vetting the efficacy and economy of local service provision.

Micromanagement under New Labour

Under New Labour and especially the Blair governments, as in other areas of policy there was much continuity from the previous Conservative years, and many NPM-style characteristics remained. In practice, this emerged as an acceptance of local government as inherited, following the rather botched boundary changes following the Banham Commission, as an institution to be managed at some distance from Whitehall. In many ways, the NPM techniques were enhanced and new layers added, with central government appearing to act as a partner, rather than, as in the preceding Conservative New Right years, as an adversary. An examination of this period throws light on much of the rhetoric which went on to pervade central–local relations after 2010, and how new techniques for the oversight of local government increasingly began to be overlaid onto the direction of travel which began under the Thatcher administrations. Not only did new techniques emerge, but 'localism' came increasingly to be used in a variety of government agendas; along with the 'localism' of the Coalition and Conservative governments, which we consider in Chapter 7, it is key to getting a clear picture of how in fact local government has been treated by recent governments.

For the Blair and Brown governments a key part of local government's role was to be that of community leader, a key part of which was the facilitation of partnerships. Their steering, management and structuring at subnational level grew in importance in central–local relations. While partnership working, sharing of resources and joint service delivery are fundamental to a range of local government systems across the world, in this case an increasing number of partnerships were mandated by government guidance or statutory obligations. There was an attempt to shift central–local relations such that central government could deal 'holistically' with the full range of service providers at subnational level – something which had been the 'holy grail' of a rational, technocratic managerial mindset for some time. Achievement of this goal was, however, weakened by its very complexity, and the age-old inability to seriously break down departmental, institutional and professional barriers.

The evolution of the twentieth-century system 45

Alongside these aims were initiatives where the control was much more explicit and attached to central government targets. The introduction of Best Value, via the Local Government Act 1999, appeared to offer a new culture of local autonomy and responsiveness (Bartlett *et. al.*, 1999). CCT was replaced with a 'softer' focus on the demonstration of efficiency and effectiveness across all services, thus giving the initiative more of a focus on qualitative issues (Maille and Hoggett, 2001). However, the whole process was subject to a tightened programme of audit and inspection, led by the Best Value Inspectorate in the Audit Commission. Councils, as a result, found themselves swamped in detail (Chandler, 2007: xi; 2009: 60). Further, a new National Performance Framework and a simplification of the inspection regime saw the introduction of Comprehensive Performance Assessments (CPAs). First released by the Audit Commission in late 2002, these ranked councils as poor/weak, fair, good or excellent. The CPAs perhaps represented the clearest example of the use of 'earned autonomy' as a principle in the local government context. 'Packages' of freedoms were available, on a sliding scale, with 'excellent' councils, for example, 'earning' the removal of all ring-fencing of funding apart from grants passed to schools, a three-year inspection 'holiday' and exemption from reserve council tax capping powers. Here, then, more 'subtle' controls were given enhanced status.

The new inspection model included not just assessments of service delivery, but also of each authority's 'corporate' performance, against a template developed by the Audit Commission after consultation with local authorities. The 2001 White Paper, *Strong Local Leadership, Quality Local Services* (DTLR, 2001) made it clear that service delivery failings were related to shortcomings at the 'heart' of a council's political and administrative ethos. Organisational audit was thus extended to cover 'corporate capacity to improve' after making a series of subjective judgements, for example to assess a council's 'ambition' and 'focus'. There was a commitment to replace top-down approaches with jointly agreed priorities. Subsequently, the number of plans to be produced was to be reduced by 75 per cent for all councils, and the national Best Value indicators were reduced by 25 per cent. Central control of local spending was relaxed, with less central government grant being ring-fenced and capital ring-fencing relaxed. This theme was strengthened by the use of Local Public Service Agreements, which had elements of direct control and 'earned autonomy'. Local authorities were invited to negotiate 'stretching' targets with the Treasury, in return for a 2.5 per cent 'reward' grant for achieving the targets in full, along with additional flexibilities, and were also required to choose thirty-five 'local' priorities from a list provided by central government.

The approach in Labour's first two terms was criticised for being too burdensome and restrictive. The agenda from 2001 onwards gave some recognition that a 'high point' had been reached in the number of central targets, signalled in 2001 by the launch of four Principles of Public Service Reform. These included flexibility and choice, together with 'devolution to local leaders', all within nationally prescribed standards. A new balance was to be struck between central prescription and 'local' freedom. Central targets and inspection regimes were to be slimmed down, with the centre increasingly concentrating on setting fewer but more strategic targets, as noted in the Treasury's *Devolving Decision Making* document:

> We know that national targets work best when they are matched by a framework of devolution, accountability and participation – empowering public servants with the freedom and flexibility to make a difference: to tailor services to reflect local needs and preferences, to develop innovative approaches to service delivery and raise standards; and to give greater responsibility to front-line public service managers. And so it is right to consider greater local autonomy, and its corollary, greater local democratic oversight. (HM Treasury and UK Cabinet Office, 2004: Foreword)

This 'new localism' thus had the intention of allowing councils more freedom from the heavy hand of the centre, but in practice, according to Lowndes (2002: 144), it represented 'the intensification of managerialism at the expense of local democracy, artfully disguised in democratic language'. In reality, then, this was more of a 'steering centralism' (Stoker, 2004) or at best a 'managerial' localism. As Wright (2002: 22) notes, 'Earned autonomy is a phrase that would only be understood in a system where the centre calls the shots.' The new agenda thus saw an 'iron fist and velvet glove' approach in which any additional local 'freedoms' remained contingent, were anyway relatively small and did nothing to fundamentally alter the position of local government vis-à-vis the centre (Lowndes, 2002). In addition, the government still firmly controlled the purse strings. In the field of finance there was no fundamental change in the balance of control, and no move to significantly increase the amount of local expenditure which was raised locally. There was relaxation of the universal power of capping of total revenue expenditure for individual authorities, but reserve powers remained. There was also the extensive promotion of the private finance initiative by central government, against what might have been local political choice, and an increasing use of direct payments to schools, bypassing local education authorities.

This 'new localist' theme continued through Labour's third term, with the 2006 White Paper, *Strong and Prosperous Communities* (DCLG, 2006) promoting a further 'loosening' of central control with, among other things, the introduction of Comprehensive Area Assessments from 2009, which had the ambition of measuring the performance of all key public services in a local area. While local government would play the key role in assembling these, the focus was on the broad outcomes of the government agenda rather than local government per se, and on broader indicators concerning the overall 'well-being' of an area.

The report of the Lyons Inquiry (2007) into local government was perhaps the high point of the momentum behind the mooted 'new localism', arguing as it did for a rebalancing of central–local relations, reform of local government finance and a defined role for local governments as 'place shapers'. As Davies (2008) noted, the main focus of the 2006 White Paper had been on quickening the pace of service improvement as a trade-off for a reduction in the number of national targets, but Lyons' recommendations were quickly consigned to the shelf, representing both a continuation of 'control freakery' and 'double dealing'.

> New Labour was determined to keep local authorities firmly tethered to the shore, simply offering to extend the rope – and thus the room for manoeuvre – for the most competent swimmers ... Labour's commitment to localism was always hedged by its desire to retain control

over significant public investments, and to maintain principles of standardisation and equity over and above those of diversity and local control. (Lowndes and Sullivan, 2008: 70–71)

The combination of this control, the dominance of a managerial rationality (Clarke and Cochrane, 2013) with which councils were exhorted to comply and woolly appeals to the value of community suggested that New Labour's localisation in fact masked an attempted depoliticisation at local level (Lee and Woodward, 2002).

Lost opportunities

Throughout the second half of the twentieth century not only were there initiatives from the major parties that in general ensured local governments were more tightly controlled by the national governments and Civil Service, but powers were being centred in ever larger units of local governance. There was little enthusiasm in such institutions to take a path when opportunities arose to provide greater independence for local governments. The Council of Europe provided a framework through the European Charter for Local Self-Government for the 'right of citizens to participate in managing public affairs, the key rights of communities to enjoy autonomy and self-government, elect their local bodies and to have their own structures and financial resources' (Council of Europe, 1985: Article 3:1) The Charter itself is, however, equivocal in key areas and was watered down following lobbying from the UK government to ensure signatory nations could limit local authority fund-raising through national laws. From another, more localist perspective, the various Acts that have restructured local government since 1974 have in many cases made reference to the parishes as a continuing tier in the structure of local government, and even extended the tier to Scotland and Wales as community councils. However, with these changes came no further powers and there was, despite some pressure, no requirement to create civil parishes in county boroughs, and more latterly in metropolitan areas or in London.

In the late 1980s decentralisation became fashionable in a few Labour and Liberal Democrat councils as local authorities divided themselves up into smaller geographical units for implementing services such as housing, and in a few, such as the London Borough of Islington and South Somerset District Council, funding was devolved to these local areas. The London Borough of Tower Hamlets went so far as to split itself as far as was legally possible into seven separate authorities. Hoggett and Hambleton (1987: 238–266) recorded some eighteen authorities pursuing or planning some level of decentralised community organisations. Not all of these schemes were fully implemented and all of them seem to have failed to take root. Financial austerity, the absence of supporting funding and a desire to retain overall control of the councils by the two major political parties were among the several factors blocking these initiatives. Although the Blair government demonstrated some enthusiasm concerning decentralisation in their 1998 and 2006 White Papers on local government, they did little in practice to develop subsidiarity and decentralisation as opposed to restructuring internal democratic procedures. The 2000 *Modern Local Government* White Paper, ironically subtitled (we assume unintentionally) *In Touch with the People,* devoted only four paragraphs to damning decentralisation with faint praise. The 2006 White Paper suggested the possibility of urban parishes, and this was permitted, but not required in the 2007 Act which followed. However, few local authorities have taken advantage of this means to decentralise power. Only one parish in Queen's Park serving 14,000 inhabitants has, for example, been created in London (Rustin, 2020).

Concluding issues

This resume of the development of local government up to the end of the twentieth century does not suggest that at any time in the past its institutions presented some ideal utopia to which we should return. During much of the eighteenth century local government could be, at the primary level, local, although it was rarely wholly democratic. As gradually more citizens were enfranchised, large sectors of the system were correspondingly closely monitored by national agencies. The predominantly Conservative governments of the interwar years could still believe that in rural areas deference to the landed gentry would ensure that small district authorities would be unlikely to deviate into campaigning for more socialist ideas requiring equality in service delivery or in equal opportunities for all. However, they realised that the boroughs and county boroughs using their newly found wealth and powers had the capacity to push for a more socialist, egalitarian society. Thus in the 1920s and 1930s they retained the concept of *ultra vires* to restrict the enterprise of local authorities in developing and supplying potentially profitable local services and opposed any private legislation that increased the powers of local authorities. In contrast, many progressive left-leaning policy shapers believed that the future required direct intervention by the State to ensure equality of access to essential services, in part because local authorities were too small in size and too diverse in ideology to develop the utilities necessary for industry and commerce and to provide for self-improvement through welfare and education. Under a Labour government after 1945, nationalisation of local services began to undermine local authority powers to develop their local economies and moved the focus of local government towards the provision of redistributive services rather than productive innovation. This emphasis in the mainstream of Labour Party ideology on the need for more larger units of local government under close scrutiny by the State was well ingrained in the post-Second World War ideology and continues into the present day. In the wake of Conservative values adapting to accept the need for the welfare state following their defeat in the 1945 general election, a similar recognition dawned on many in the party that larger local government units were required to provide essential services. By 1974 all pretensions to retaining localised service provision at a primary level had evaporated, for somewhat different reasons, in both of the dominant parties. As a consequence, democracy suffered as principal local authorities were becoming too large to enable citizens to experience any semblance of self-government and councillors were becoming detached from their electorate, as opposed to their local party allegiances.

Although both the Conservative and Labour Parties since the 1970s had, for differing reasons, similar views on the size and methods of government in local authorities, they began to differ on the extent to which local authorities, as public sector agencies, should be involved in securing economic growth. The advent under the Thatcher governments of New Right policies, and the reaction to the socialist values of some urban authorities after 1979, underpinned the move towards privatisation of many local services. Experience of the capacity of socialist-leaning local authorities to have the power to use the rates to subsidise local enterprise and assuage local inequality emboldened the New Right governments in the 1980s to further restrict much of the capacity of local authorities for raising revenue and to privatise many essential services such as subsidised housing, care for the elderly or education services. New Labour under the Blair and Brown governments only half-heartedly changed the policy direction set by the Thatcher and Major governments by slowing but not reversing New Right policies and furthering the power of central government to micromanage the performance of local authorities in what powers were now left to them. This period saw the use of revised tactics, devices and rhetoric which have been built on and revised in the period since 2010, to which we will turn in Chapters 3 to 8. However, they remain underpinned by the assumptions developed by the major ruling parties since 1918 which have been outlined in this chapter.

2

Theorising local government in Britain

An understanding of the evolution of local governance in Britain has to be rooted in political theories that provide a justification for the need to promote reform or demand stability within a political system. In this chapter we chart the changes in the dominant values in British political theory that have been both causes and symptoms of the evolving system of local governance. These form an important aspect of the ideas that ought to shape and justify the framework of government and society in Britain. Without such an understanding of political ideas and ideology it would appear that recent developments are little more than accidental whims rather than a product of elite consensus following political divisions around the shaping of the political culture of the nation. These political elites are the dominant shapers of society at any stage in the history of a nation. They comprise the leading politicians and senior bureaucrats, and at a further level, national, if not global, industrial, financial and communication managers who control the press and audio-visual media. These, often conflicting, groups may determine through using the coercive forces at their disposal, such as the police and law courts, or through debate and deliberation in the central institutions of government, some degree of agreement on the dominant framework of political thought. In a stable polity these ideas may be passed down to social groups and individual citizens to become the frequently unrecognised assumptions that create what is often termed the civic culture of that society.

The pre-industrial civic culture and local governance in Britain

In England, until the 1640s Civil War, it had been expected by monarchs and their courts that local issues were the province of the dominant local landowners, or in chartered towns their councillors. Under the subsequent republic in the 1650s, this position was seriously threatened by the creation of twelve regions in England and Wales controlled by major generals appointed by Oliver Cromwell; they had a remit to deal not only with military matters but with 'a wide range of other local government functions' (Durston, 2001: 22) that included church attendance, vagrancy and the poor law. The experiment soon collapsed, and with the restoration of Charles II the polity resumed under the assumption that local opinion should be moulded and upheld by deference to landowners or merchants and manufacturers in the towns. This was despite, or because of, the growth in Britain of popular unrest following the example of the French Revolution and subsequent wars against, firstly, the revolutionary armies, and then the empire building of Napoleon. Many strands of elite opinion in Britain were drawn towards the cautious conservatism of Edmund Burke that eschewed fundamental changes in government and society based on untried rational principles in favour of change by cautious incremental steps. It is such a path that for over two hundred years underpinned the approach to structuring the local government systems in Britain, shown in Chapter 1 to be a system tied in rural areas to the needs and wishes of the squirearchy – that is, the landowners and their extended families – or, in the towns, the interests of merchants and established guilds of manufacturers.

By the late eighteenth century the development of industry and commerce and more extensive systems of communication created a new class of wealthy entrepreneurs who demanded a role alongside the older landed aristocratic elites in forging the direction of national and local policies. The most radical elements within the emerging capitalist middle class began to demand greater democracy based on a wider franchise than that favoured by the predominantly aristocratic landed interests who had dominated the political system since the Glorious Revolution of 1688, which obliged the monarch to follow the rule of Parliament. While these liberal radicals supported a wide but far from universal suffrage at national and local levels, they differed sharply on the extent to which they considered democratic local government should have powers that were local in scope and outside control by a central government and legislature.

Among radical British theorists of the late Georgian period, the most concerted thought given to the rationale and role of local government was developed by Jeremy Bentham, and this was to become the foundation for a more clearly defined path for local governance within the confines of a centrally controlling executive and parliament. Bentham upheld the view that each individual was best able to determine their own interest and should be free to enact their wishes provided they did not harm the freedom of others – if this was inevitable, they should be able to debate on equal terms the policies that needed to be adopted to ensure the least harm to those individuals concerned. Bentham argued that the sovereignty over all matters of difference should be located in a representative parliament for the whole nation, elected by all men over 21 years of age who can read and were not, as he termed it, 'passengers' (Parekh, 1973: 208). Below the legislature the nation should be divided into districts, which were probably intended to be large, county-sized areas. These would be controlled by an elected sublegislature, and below these would be at least one further, more local tier, led by a 'headman'. The subdivisions would be able to create and implement policy on matters not subject to laws passed by the national legislature, and would therefore have a measure of freedom. National Acts passed by the central legislature should, however, be binding on all levels of governance. The 'headman' would act as a servant of the national government, ensuring that laws passed by the legislature or district sublegislature were enacted and also act as a judicial authority with the task of reconciling family disputes, disputes between individuals and local civil disputes between, for example, travellers and local innkeepers (Parekh, 1973: 224–227). This element of Bentham's thinking is perhaps based on the developing constitution of France and the emergence of the prefect and mayor as both local and central government representatives.

Although these ideas were not sketched out until 1823 and only published after his death in 1832, Bentham's influence on his radical protégés and associates such as James Mill and Edwin Chadwick ensured that there were administrators connected to the service of national government who were grounded in the view that the national parliament and its agencies were superior to, and should interfere in, the activities of local governments. James Mill, a senior administrator in the Indian Office and a close confidant of Bentham, proposed in an influential essay on government (James Mill, 1828) a wider male franchise, but also argued for the sovereignty of a national parliament. Government should be by the 'community', by which he referred to the national male adult society, as this was superior to a monarchy or an aristocratic oligarchy that would use their powers to take from the community whatever gave them pleasure. A government elected by the community for a limited term in office would not be inclined to plunder the property and well-being of those they represented. Despite his use of the term 'community', James Mill assumed that such a body could not all gather in one place to allow everyone who wished to debate an issue. Hence popular government must be representative. James Mill followed Bentham's implication that such a legislature must be omnicompetent in that it should develop policies on every issue including those affecting localities.

Bentham and his contemporary followers such as James Mill, Edwin Chadwick, Joseph Parkes and Nassau Senior were, however, not wholly in agreement with other radicals outside this circle, who also demanded some form of democratisation of the State. Radical polemicists such as Thomas Paine (1969: 224–225) and William Cobbett (1834) criticised the system of local government largely in relation to its disenfranchising the lower middle class and rural smallholders. These differing voices, which welcomed, at least in its early days, the revolution in France, were by no means in agreement on how, if at all, change should be initiated in favour of the disenfranchised majority in Britain. Paine criticised the borough corporations for taking away the rights of their inhabitants – as opposed to the few who, by being property holders, had the right to vote in local and national elections. Similar views were supported in the eighteenth and nineteenth centuries, often for very different reasons, by radical Parliamentarians such as Colonel Torrance, who argued for the right of citizens to control parish governments in an open vestry (Chandler, 2007: 33). In contrast, luminaries such as William Cobbett (1834) or the poet William Wordsworth (Gill, 2020: 485–487) found much to their displeasure at the despoliation of the countryside by industry, and supported rather different paths to democracy – in Cobbett's case, by seeking to open up rural parish governments to control by the smaller tenant and yeomen farmers. From the perspective of the landowning squirearchy, as shown in the following outburst by the young Disraeli during a debate on the renewal of the Poor Law Act in 1841, there was much opposition to increased centralisation and concern over the growth of utilitarian liberal policies that could be seen as attempts to control rural government from Whitehall and Westminster:

> Government did not institute the system of national education – did not institute the Universities – did not create our colonial empire – it did not conquer India – it did not make our roads or build our bridges. It did not, even now that it was interfering with everything, make our railroads. In the case of the Poor Law, however, the government did interfere, and they terminated the old parochial constitution of the country. It was certainly impossible, although it might not posses the individual interest of what was called a political revolution, to conceive a political revolution which exercised a greater influence on the people at large. (Disraeli, Hansard, HoC, Series 3, 8 February 1841, Vol. 56, Col. 377)

These various strands of opposition to ad hoc local governance for specific purposes under the guidance of national agencies crystallised opposition into an Anti-Centralisation Union. The most active leader of this movement was Joshua Toulmin Smith, a lawyer born in Birmingham and practising in London. In relation to the wellspring of moral values and individual liberty there is little difference between Bentham and Smith, although in his major works Smith does not mention Bentham and had few dealings with Bentham's protégé John Stuart Mill (Chandler, 2008: 361). Where they diverged was in how individual differences should be reconciled.

Smith could not be said to be a theorist of philosophical precision and founded many of his views, in part, on interpretations of historical myths and legends. These included a strong humanitarian belief in individual and communal liberties that he believed were rooted in an idealised impression of Anglo-Saxon Britain and Norse legend. Smith argued that common law, as agreements evolved over time within open communities, was being undermined by inferior national decisions made by interests that dominated Parliament. The national legislature was, argued Smith, insidiously overriding the rights and privileges of the many in favour of the interests of wealthy elites. Decisions made by governments such as open vestries, in which all members of a community could express their views and reach conclusions largely through mutual understanding, tolerance and compromise, were superior to ideas implanted by the special interests that had little connection with anyone but their own class. Local self-government provided a moral justification as well as an effective practical base for policy-making.

> Local Self Government is that system of Government under which the greatest number of minds, knowing the most, and having the fullest opportunities of knowing it, about the special matter in hand, and having the greatest interest in its well-working, have the management of it, or control over it.
>
> Centralization is that system of Government under which the smallest number of minds and those knowing the least, and having the fewest opportunities of knowing it, about the special matter in hand, and having the smallest interest in its well-working, have the management of it or the control of it. (J. T. Smith, 1851: 30)

People would, argued Smith, have common empathy and concern for each other, especially if they frequently interact and debate their views and interests in local assemblies on matters specific to that community. They would, through such meetings, reach the most morally satisfactory policies and should have powers collectively to implement their conclusions. If individuals did not use their responsibility to develop their lives but were merely followers of political institutions in which they had little or no involvement, they would become incapable of developing views that are supportive of their own advancement or the advancement of others. In this context Smith might have much to say about the development of populist support for demagogic 'super star' politicians.

Smith based his idea of local government on the preservation of parish governments that were increasingly under attack from poor law and health legislation and the growth of municipal boroughs. Through open debate among freemen who had the right and even the duty to express their opinions:

> they shall thus be able to understand the opinions of others ... and the wisest and most statesmanlike policy is that which most effectually tends to make it part of the habitual business and regular and unevadeable duty, of every freeman, so to know and understand and give utterance to opinion. (J. T. Smith, 1851: 80)

Freedom and national independence could never be assured 'unless true local self-government is fully and freely exercised in every district throughout the land' (J. T. Smith, 1851: 31). The powers of such districts, according to Smith (1851: 31), should extend to 'all matters of general management, police, public works, taxation, and every class of administrative arrangement whereon the common welfare of a local community depends'. The basis of the districts ought to be founded on Anglo-Saxon arrangements of local assemblies, which were interpreted as folk moots. These could at one level be based on civil parishes or boroughs, but could refer more general, substantive issues to meetings in the ancient county divisions, the hundreds, and above that to the county assemblies (J. T. Smith, 1851: 217–233; 1857: 1–40). There should be no interference by any central authority on how these powers specific to the community were decided and carried out. Smith did accept that there are general matters such as foreign affairs that must be decided at a parliamentary level, but that body must be representative of local districts and their representatives should not act as if they were individuals empowered, as the eighteenth-century Whig politician and political theorist Edmund Burke maintained, to put their own opinions into national policy (J. T. Smith, 1851: 70–88).

Smith was, however, far from being a socialist, condemning 'communism' if 'it means the abolition of all property, and therefore the cessation of all effort for its individual accumulation' (J. T. Smith, 1851: 349). In this context Smith, like some of his contemporaries such as perhaps Disraeli, supported parish government even though the power of landowners over the local economy in many rural areas ensured an attitude of deference to the aristocratic elites who dominated Parliament and the localities in which they had an economic interest. Smith recognised this problem but fell back on his romantic view of England to argue that, from Anglo-Saxon times to his own time, land was more widely distributed among numerous freeholders than in most other countries (J. T. Smith, 1851: 387–393). Smith's concept of democracy also would today be subject to serious limitations. The freeholder who should be free or even have a duty to participate in community debates is defined by Smith (1851: 243) as 'Every grown man who maintains himself and his immediate family upon the results of his own freely disposed means of effort', and adds that 'this definition excludes every man who lives on alms, every man who will not use his powers in accordance with the duty and responsibility he owes to society, and every criminal' (J. T. Smith, 1851: 244). Modern critics would also object to his habitual use of the term 'men' so that the regiment of 'freemen' excludes women, whose role is not discussed in his work.

John Stuart Mill and the balancing of local and central government

The differences between centralists such as Bentham and the supporters of decentralised local government such as Smith were to a degree reconciled in the second half of the nineteenth century through the popularity accorded to the writing of John Stuart Mill, the son of Bentham's confidant James Mill. John Stuart Mill was a highly gifted prodigy as an economist, statistician and supporter of women's rights, as well as arguably the most influential theorist of his time on representative democracy. Following the conclusions of James Mill, his father, Mill developed in his essays on liberty and representative government a more substantive and balanced theory of freedom and government which may be argued to be the most important rationale promoting the development of liberal democracy in Britain, condemning Smith's ideas to at best a footnote in English constitutional history. Mill's arguments on the role of local government are largely established in chapter 15 of his *Considerations on Representative Government* as a precariously balanced discussion that can fall on the one side on Smith's bottom-up conception of a democratic constitution or, on the other, a top-down position in which the state is dominant over localities. Mill's several arguments for local government are largely, in essence, expediential justifications that place local governance as a counterweight to the power of national government or as simply a means of resolving the administrative problems faced by a large organisation. Local government has for Mill undoubted value in that:

- Central government cannot not do everything.
  'It is but a small portion of the public business of a country which can be done well or safely attempted, by the central authorities' (Mill, 1975: 363).
- Local representatives know better the issues affecting their community.
  'I need not dwell on the deficiencies of central authority in detailed knowledge of local persons and things, and the too great engrossment of its time and thoughts by other concerns, to admit of its acquiring the quantity of local knowledge necessary even for deciding on complaints, and enforcing responsibility from so great a number of local agents. In details of management, therefore, the local bodies will generally have the advantage' (Mill, 1975: 376).
- Local government is a means of educating individuals in the values of liberal democracy.
  'I have dwelt in strong language ... on the importance of the operation of free institutions, which may be called the public education of citizens. Now, of this operation the local administrative institutions are the chief instrument' (Mill, 1975: 365).
- It provides a basis for political stability.
  'Let a person have nothing to do for his country, and he will not care for it' (Mill, 1975: 181).

Following Bentham and his father, Mill believed that a representative national parliament should be dominant over the structure, resourcing and policy output of local authorities. In this context the utilitarian position differed significantly from the idealised views on human nature and understanding that underlay

Smith's ideas. Mill not infrequently pours cold water on the pretensions of the unintellectual lower classes to make just decisions, and looks favourably on ideas that representative agencies such as the Poor Law and Health Boards or the Metropolitan Board of Works, which included a minority of unelected professionals and JPs on their governing bodies, should guide the less well informed (Mill, 1975: 366–367). In complete disagreement with Smith's views of the competence of centralised government, Mill maintained that

> in the comprehension of principles even of purely local management, superiority of the central government, when rightly constituted, ought to be prodigious: not only by reason of the probably great superiority of the individuals composing it, and the multitude of thinkers and writers who are at times engaged in pressing useful ideas upon their notice, but also because the knowledge and experience of any local authority is but local knowledge and experience, confined to their own part of the country and its modes of management, whereas the central government has the means of knowing all that it is to be learnt from the united experience of the whole kingdom, with the addition of easy access to that of foreign countries. (Mill, 1975: 376–377)

A well-documented concern in the late nineteenth century that troubled debates on widening of the franchise was that such a democratic system may lead to a 'tyranny of the majority', which would in their general ignorance support reckless spending to relieve their poverty, to the detriment of the knowledgeable and educated minority who understood the realities of establishing a just and also practical economy. Mill's answer to the problem was to exclude from the franchise individuals who were illiterate or subject to receiving aid from the poor law machinery (Mill, 1975: 277–281) while maintaining a belief that effective local government would be a means of educating voters on the complexities and moral duties required to make decisions in the long-term interests of themselves and the society on which they depended. Many aspects of the cautious and balanced approach to Mill's conclusions on the value of local government are a response to the French writer Alexis de Tocqueville (1994), whose writings on democracy in the United States he much admired if not always fully accepted

(Brogan, 2006: 303–304; Jardin, 1988: 234–236). Mill reflected in his *Autobiography*, first published in 1873, that both centralisation and decentralisation could encapsulate 'evils' on both sides and hoped that he had steered a middle way between the two positions. However, in relation to decentralisation his main concern was that there was 'too often selfish mismanagement of local interests, by a jobbing and bornè local oligarchy' (Mill, 1969: 163–164). It is a matter of conjecture whether Mill would in the times of Trump and Johnson have been as confident that in liberal democracies the central government would necessarily be the best fount of probity and proven understanding, but, as should be apparent in the previous chapter, his view has carried the day in Britain. Mill thus concluded that:

> The authority which is most conversant with principles should be supreme over principles, while that which is most competent in details should have details left to it. The principal business of the central authority should be to give instruction, of the local authority to apply it. (Mill, 1975: 377)

The practical application of this conclusion for Mill, and where he significantly distances himself from the conclusions reached by Smith, was that central government should have ministers and civil servants who could inform and advise local governments on good practice and where necessary pass legislation to ensure that principles were uniform throughout the nation (Mill, 1975: 377–379).

Nevertheless, as Chandler (1989: 604–612; 2010: 5–21) observes, it can also be shown that Mill's doubts on the logic of utilitarianism, as espoused by Bentham and his father, can be used to present one of the most important, meticulously grounded ethical justifications for the value and limits of local government in liberal democratic society. In his essay *On Liberty*, published in 1859, Mill argues that an individual's freedom should only be curbed if a person's liberty causes serious harm to others. This principle he confers not only on individual but also on collective conduct, observing that

> The liberty of individuals in things wherein the individual is alone concerned, implies a corresponding liberty in any number of individuals to regulate by mutual agreement such things as regard them jointly, and regard no persons but themselves. (Mill, 1975: 125)

And in 1861, in *Considerations on Representative Government*, Mill observes that this position also applies to local representative institutions that should ensure that policy affecting a community is only dealt with by its citizens.

> The very object of having a local representation, is in order that those who have any interest in common, which they do not share with the general body of their countrymen, may manage that joint interest by themselves. (Mill, 1975: 368)

We can infer from arguments drawn from J. S. Mill and Joshua Toulmin Smith that in so far as an individual has the right to pursue interests that affect themselves alone then a local community has a similar right and, if organised as a democracy, such as in de Tocqueville's (1994) depiction of government in New England, that local governments also have a right to exist at a neighbourhood level such that each individual has a right, should they wish to use it, to help shape the self-regarding policies of their local communities. Chandler (2010: 18) has presented this conclusion as an essential moral right for the establishment of local institutions for community government:

> Local governments ought to determine and implement those policies that do not infringe the interests of those outside their area and represent the views of that area to other agencies where its policies may affect others.

The proposition on the right of citizens to be involved in participative local government at a primary level is a necessary right but is far from being a sufficient right. A democratic society in any of its many possible varieties is contingent on the rights of freedom of assembly and speech and the determination of policy either by consensus or at least the views supported by the majority of those citizens who involve themselves in a political system. This right, to be operationalised in practice, gives rise to issues as to the extent of interests which are held in common, and to competing claims as to who may or may not share a legitimate interest in a joint concern, and therefore the size, scale and nature of the polity which would be implied. In practice, as we note later, this would necessitate democratic debate involving negotiation and settlement of disputes over the boundaries of such interests and the appropriate extent of their reach.

Justifications for local government following Mill

Even if Mill maintained some balance, succeeding theorists of the ethical status of local government have veered increasingly to the top-down thesis. Liberal values partly prompted by Mill also began to change in relation to the role of the state and private means of self-help. Thomas Hill Green, who was both an Oxford don and a member of the city's education board, established in his lectures the concept of liberalism as requiring not only freedom of the individual to develop themselves and the good of society, but also the duty of the state to enable a measure of equal opportunity for all to achieve such a goal. Unfortunately, Green's thoughts on the status of local governance are far from clear. While he believed that people in his position should involve themselves in local politics, his major studies refer to the role of the state rather than its many subdivisions. It may be argued that the status of local government in Britain may be, as with T. H. Green and succeeding liberal writers such as L. T. Hobhouse, due to an absence of trust in the efficacy of small communal actions as opposed to the capacities of larger representative institutions. This position is also fortified by a view that the rights of all individuals can only be nurtured by a beneficent community of the well educated, who can rationally understand the value but also the limits of personal liberty in a developed society. In his mature writing, Hobhouse spells this out in an evolutionary view of the formation of political societies, starting with small hunter-gatherer groups progressing to tribes governed by a chieftain in which:

> The village elder, a simple and well meaning man, knowing his neighbours, and familiar with the customs of the countryside, may doubtless administer patriarchal justice under his own vine and fig tree, but summon him to the elaborate and artificial system of law and, unless he is a genius, he must break down. (Hobhouse, 1904: 149)

Hobhouse puts forward a view that communities advance by developing themselves on a greater scale in terms of population, 'by efficiency – the adequate apportionment and coordination in the service of an end, whatever the end may be' (Hobhouse, 1924: 78), by freedom given to its citizens, and by mutuality between its members in achieving and serving agreed ends. Hobhouse saw the eventual end of these developments as some form of world governance, but in practical terms this formula, while admirable in the hope for a common morality of mutual understanding and respect for individual freedom and coordinated help for the more downtrodden or less morally literate, can be translated as, for geographical local communities, the bigger, the wiser and therefore the better.

The emergence of widely held social democratic values was consolidated in the growth of the Labour Party, nurtured in part by theorists such as Sydney and Beatrice Webb. The husband and wife extensively researched and supported local government as both a practical necessity and a means of widening democracy and political literacy and competence, and added a further argument for central controls on the grounds of securing economic and social equality. From a socialist perspective, a measure of freedom and experimentation to secure social equality was to be encouraged at the level of local government, and for the Webbs local government should not be the only policy agent at community level but work alongside cooperative ventures (Webb and Webb, 1975: 147–168). Nevertheless, the socialist ethic of equality was not just concerned with opportunity, but also equality with reference to need. This required a superior government to that presiding over a locality, to ensure that all sections of a polity received equality of outcomes. Delivering social justice required implementation of social egalitarian policies for the whole of a polity, and thus in practical terms for mid-twentieth-century Britain, the dominance of the national government over local government.

Later mid-twentieth-century writers such as G. D. H. Cole (1947), Hermann Finer (1945) and W. A. Robson (1954), writing specifically in support of local government, may have imbibed the liberalism of J. S. Mill, Green and Hobhouse and the ideas of Fabian writers such as the Webbs and began, perhaps unintentionally, to further erode the localist element in local government. There is little evidence in their works to show that liberal or egalitarian philosophy had any great relevance to their arguments, even though their political values do not differ radically from those of their preceding utilitarian generation. It might be speculated that their political values were to be taken for granted for their supporters and, for their more conservative opponents, deliberately hidden from view through arguments based on practicality and economy rather than moral and political principle. For theorists such as Robson and Cole, local government was an agency that, if properly managed for social change, required larger local authorities dominated by urban areas which could become a powerful counterweight to the centralising tendencies of predominantly Conservative administrations of the 1920s and 1930s. Both Robson and Cole supported the social democratic values of the Attlee governments, including Aneurin Bevan's moves to promote larger local authorities on the grounds that they would also be able to deal more adequately with issues of communication, transportation or water supply. Cole (1947) campaigned for the creation of a third tier of regional authorities to deal with the problems that were not confined to smaller authorities. Robson (1954: 7) argued that since the first edition in 1931 of his book on local government, 'local authorities are being denuded of their functions' and that 'accompanying the curtailment of functions is an immense increase of control over the remaining duties of local authorities'. To reverse such a trend he proposed that

> the primary elements of the municipal structure which is contemplated will consist of county councils and county borough councils. These bodies will be grouped together for various purposes into a number of combined authorities, whose areas will vary according to the function to be carried out. (Robson, 1954: 211)

Successive governments accepted his argument for larger local authorities but ignored his central concern that democratic accountability should remain at the local level.

Later mainstream writers on local government have continued with more expediential lines of thought. W. J. M. Mackenzie (1961: 14) rather conservatively observed that 'Local Government is justified because it is a traditional institution' even though its traditional position was subject to rapid change. He further observed that

> It is justified because it is an effective and convenient way to provide central services. It is justified because we like to think that our central

government needs the kind of qualities, which are best trained by local self-government.

L. J. Sharpe (1970: 174), taking a rather different but nevertheless expediential angle, defends local government as

> a coordinator of services in the field; as a reconciler of community opinion; as a consumer pressure group, as an agent responding to rising demand; and finally as a counterweight to incipient syndicalism, local government seems to have come into its own.

Jones and Stewart (1983: 10) maintained that the case for local government is that it embodies:

- diffusion in power in a society which cannot afford concentrating power in one central location;
- diversity in response in a society which cannot afford the centralist risk of single solutions which may go wrong;
- economy in resource utilisation in a society which cannot afford the waste of national standards unrelated to perceptions of need;
- localness in knowledge and response in a society which cannot afford the remoteness, rigidities and limitations of centralised bureaucracy;
- democracy and self government in a society which cannot afford to entrust control over bureaucracy to only twenty one ministers and 650 MPs.

As W. Hardy Wickwar (1970: 60) observed:

> The problems of local administration in the twentieth century are so multi faceted and so interlocking that no responsible thinker would dare claim that Local Government as such offers either a simple means or the best means of finding solutions ... It is perhaps for these reasons that one can no longer identify any one clear current of legal or socio philosophy that today is demonstrably moulding the law and structure of Local Government.

While within their own parameters such arguments have considerable weight and rationality, they present, as does Mill's account, more an argument for local government as a valuable expedient for better governance nationally rather than the nineteenth-century views of early Disraeli or the arguments of Smith that maintained that local government was to be valued in its own right as a means of securing local freedom and democracy. Robson, Sharpe and Jones and Stewart, for example, place less emphasis on democracy than on the efficient provision of public services. Thus the difficulties in ever larger authorities being a basis for democracy is, in many established academic arguments in Britain, never sufficiently considered or resolved. Following the restructuring of local government from 1974 there were few studies arguing that a different path was possible, apart from within radical liberal and liberal democratic thought, as in the 1970s (Hain, 1976), or Hadley and Hatch's (1981) critique of social welfare provision in Britain. Such studies gained little recognition in mainstream politics and never developed a comprehensive theoretical basis for local government being local at the neighbourhood level, let alone as a means of enhancing a direct rather than representative system of government in Britain. This was not, however, the case in the United States, where the beginnings of a critique of the theories of representative liberal democracy developed by Schumpeter (1943) and Dahl (1961) began to emerge through the writings of Benjamin Barber (1984) and communitarian thought through theorists such as Amitai Etzioni (1993, 1996) or Henri Tam (1998), while the American historian Douglas Ashford (1982) provided a very convincing analysis of how France had retained a more localised structure than Britain.

In Britain it could be argued that these ideas, and particularly communitarianism, were an influence on New Labour, although this was more in theory rather than substance in Blair's thought (Hale, 2006). More generally, there was within this genre in a more British perspective, as noted by Tam (1998), a continuing suspicion of the role of political institutions, whether at a central or local government level, as tending to undermine individual rights and freedoms. The post-2010 onslaught on local government by the Conservative-dominated governments from Cameron to Johnson has however awoken a substantial literature that is critical of the demise of local government. Chisholm (2000) and Chisholm and Leach (2008) are important in emphasising the need for being local in its traditional meaning of relatively small-scale in terms of population. Copus presents in his more recent writing an emphasis on securing greater democratisation in governance through the role of localised government, but is not detailed on the ends which ethically should be achieved by allowing greater freedom for democratic decision-making at a local as opposed to a national level. Wilson and Game (2011) cover the range of restructuring of powers, democracy and central–local relations in the early twenty-first century with reference to ethical concerns, although they do less to resolve the varied issues around conflicting views of what local government ought to be rather than presenting strong critiques of what it has become.

Innes Newman (2014b) presents more of a contribution to resolving the travails of local government with a consideration of the democratic and further ethical issues that need to be highlighted by local authorities. She considers (Newman, 2014b: 99–100) referencing dilemmas related to the more general questions raised by fashionable contemporary theorists Sandel (2009) and Sen (2009), as to whether social justice should be established via the capacity of local government to be a means of ensuring greater equality and fairness in the distribution of goods, services and opportunities. However, it is also a problem, recognised by Newman, that there are further ethical issues of what social justice may entail, for example in reconciling claims of rights of ownership with the need to use resources most effectively for all in need. In particular, there is a question of whether ethical issues such as fair distribution of property and services could be better developed and practised by a central government that is designed for society as a whole. If this is the case, the commitment to underwrite the dominance of national over local government is in tension with Chandler's (2008, 2010) argument, as summarised in this chapter, that local government should have a shared role in ensuring continued deepening of a democratic culture within British civic culture. The question arises throughout this study of why local government in Britain followed the reforms that many other liberal democracies have eschewed and did not retain parish and township governments as units of democratic governance for determining predominantly local issues for its members.

In conclusion, in the absence of strongly rooted arguments and conventions in British political culture to underpin the value of local government, there was up to 2010 an insidious move towards a more centralised state in which local government has gradually lost some of its capacity to be regarded as local in any meaningful sense, or to have substantive powers to govern independently of the centre. In the following chapters we show that, despite claims to the contrary by successive governments, these trends have continued and were further accelerated with the creation of fewer but ever more populous local governments, leading to less accountability and democracy in the structuring of local policy-making. Moreover, despite the appearance of providing greater autonomy in the powers of local government through the 2011 Localism Act, this was in practice accompanied by greater powers of control at the centre and a dramatic decline in resources available to local authorities in the interests of financial austerity.

3

Changing the boundaries

We have seen in Chapters 1 and 2 how the structure of local government has developed, reflecting the way its role has been perceived by successive governments, amidst changing social and economic circumstances, and how it has been perceived through the lens of differing ideological views of welfare and service delivery. These developments have been enabled by local government's particularly fragile normative foundations in Britain, summed up by Mackenzie's much-quoted statement that 'There is no theory of local government. There is no normative general theory from which we can deduce what local government ought to be' (Mackenzie, 1961: 5). However, Mackenzie's point that local government is 'tolerated' as a 'traditional institution', noted in Chapter 2, is important in explaining both its survival and its structure. Successive reorganisations have attempted to grapple with the tensions involved in marrying efficient and effective service delivery with a vague sense of 'traditional' local government, reflective of 'communiy' sentiment, with local government units that could be deemed 'local' in democratic terms. As noted earlier, 'community' and 'local' are malleable concepts, open to interpretation across a range of criteria and to suit a range of desired ends. Similarly, the perceived scale of operation needed for the efficient and effective delivery of services has varied in line with changing methods of calculation, administrative/managerial fashion, and political and ideological preference. The way in which these issues have been addressed and settled across time, then, tells us much about the prevailing attitudes towards, and influences on, local government and its place in the polity.

The reorganisation of the mid-1970s, noted in Chapter 1, was essentially a political compromise which attempted, in the context of the times, to resolve these tensions by largely maintaining a two-tier structure. Doing so led to the retention of historic counties as local government units, which represented some recognition of traditional place attachment. On the other hand, traditional units of local government, such as the Ridings of Yorkshire, were replaced with a mixture of newly created metropolitan counties, in this case Humberside, and second tier districts created from the amalgamation of existing urban and rural district councils, and remaining cities and towns in shires outside of the designated metropolitan areas. The reorganisation produced a structure based on compromise and perceived party political advantage, resulting in a mixture of some units which bore relation to historic attachments and others, mainly second tier authorities, created mostly, and often quite hastily, by amalgamations of existing councils as a matter of expediency. This produced what Copus et al. (2017) have called 'compass point councils', 'and councils' and 'non-existent councils', as judged by the names given to them – for example, *North East Derbyshire*, Hammersmith *and* Fulham, and the 'made up' *Three Rivers*. Here there was little, if any, consideration of a link between the unit of local government and a recognisable community or locality, with an 'imagined' community being constructed once the approximate size of the council had been determined. Once the framework of the two-tier structure had been agreed, consideration of boundaries was dominated by assumptions made about minimum and maximum sizes to secure the efficient delivery of their allocated functions. To the extent that the democratic basis of these units was considered, it was related to an instrumental view of democracy associated with the perceived capacity to deliver services effectively and secure the implementation of decisions.

A process of piecemeal change began almost as soon as the new systems had been implemented. The Labour governments of 1974 to 1979 were pressured by several cities, which had been reduced in status from county boroughs to district authorities under the 1972 Act, to be given the status of metropolitan boroughs. The Thatcher government, only ten years after the formation of the two-tier metropolitan counties, legislated to abolish them to create single-tier structures in the large conurbations and, more controversially, also abolished the GLC. The policy was justified as a means of saving resources by removing unnecessary tiers of government, but can alternatively be interpreted as jettisoning large authorities that were predominantly Labour-controlled (Young and Rao, 1997: 211–213). The incremental march towards the Redcliffe-Maud vision of a single tier of local authorities was continued by Michael Heseltine, who joined John Major's Cabinet as Minister of the Environment on condition that he was free to engineer an overhaul of the structure, finance and policy-making machinery of local government (Crick, 1997: 362–363). He established the boundary commission led by a former director of the Confederation of British Industry, John Banham. The Banham Commission in the 1990s began with an assumption about the technical superiority of unitary authorities, and was influenced by Heseltine's desire to move towards a pattern which more accurately reflected 'functional economic areas'. The actual process proved to be messy and the process was left essentially incomplete, with the creation of forty-six new unitary, single-tier authorities between 1995 and 1998.

The 'failure' to complete the project can to some extent be attributed to the Commission's inability to reconcile unitary councils with the opposition it found among the public to their creation, and to the fact that assumptions about the universal benefits of unitary councils did not stand up to scrutiny (Banham, 1994: 67–79). The result was to add to the complexity of local government structure, creating a 'dog's breakfast' (Wilson and Game, 2011: 69–70) of varying types of council. This complexity is not to be, per se, necessarily viewed negatively, of course; we might expect, and value, local governments which reflect varying collective interests, attachments and perceptions of the 'local' not to follow a uniform pattern of sizes, in population or geographical area. However, the resultant complexity was more a result of the culmination of successive reorganisations in which considerations of efficiency and associated scale predominated, along with a lack of political will to complete the task on even these terms. This point can be most starkly emphasised, perhaps, by the creation of thirty-two unitary councils in Scotland and twenty-two in Wales, implemented by the relevant secretaries of state in 1996 without any independent review.

The Major government here faced less political opposition from within its own ranks and could push the unitary project through quickly and in complete form. Not only did this leave a variety of differing types of council in England along with divergent systems in Scotland and Wales, but also indicated that reorganisation had, more than ever, become a matter of expediency and political opportunity rather than underlying principle.

However, with hindsight, the willingness of governments to assign to local government sufficient importance to launch a comprehensive study of structure, size and functions can be looked on with some incredulity. The Banham Commission represented the end of decades of debate concerning local government structure, which it was assumed an overall review, based on some underlying principles, was required to address. Admittedly, such reviews had been determined, as we have seen, in favour of its fit with changing functional capability, administrative efficiency and patterns of economic activity. At least, however, competing considerations of the democratic characteristics of local government had been a factor; the investigations had taken place in the context of the recognised tensions and perceived necessary trade-offs between democratic and managerial/administrative logics, however the recommended solutions had been arrived at. The pattern of local government was deemed – from the establishment of the Herbert Commission on the future of local government structures in Greater London in 1957–60, until at least the initial to mid stages of the Banham Commission in the 1990s – to be a matter worthy of weighty consideration and interest. What has followed has rather been born out of the legacy of the 'unfinished business' of the 1990s restructuring in its ad hoc, piecemeal nature. Again, there is nothing wrong, per se, with an evolutionary approach to local government reform. Indeed, incremental adjustments to the realities of changing collective identities and interests could be seen, ideally, to be more appropriate than taking a top-down 'blueprint' approach in sweeping overall reorganisations, which might tend towards a 'one size fits all' outcome. The reality, however, has been that the ad hoc nature of reform has intensified in the context of continuing central control and oversight, and of financial pressures from central government, which have driven, in particular, mergers of councils to meet centrally determined criteria. The piecemeal approach, we would argue, is indicative of the waning importance of local government generally, with fundamental questions concerning its make-up occupying the thoughts of senior ministers – even those with responsibility for its oversight – less and less, rather than it being a thoughtful, incremental approach to change.

Thus, New Labour governments continued with a rhetorical commitment to unitary structures and assumptions about their superiority, couching their support in language which resonated with their desire to 'modernise' local government. The White Paper *Strong and Prosperous Communities* of 2006 claimed wide support for the view that 'moving to unitary structures would be the best way [to] improve accountability and leadership, increase efficiency, and improve outcomes for local people' (Wilson and Game, 2011: 73). However, the approach now was to invite proposals from councils in shire areas, which would be assessed on criteria laid down by ministers. The outcome was the creation of a further nine unitary councils, including five covering whole shire county areas with average populations of over 400,000 (Wilson and Game, 2011: 74), and an overall reduction of 1,321 councillors. The White Paper's concern that local government structures should reflect a natural sense of place proved to be purely rhetorical; in fact the reorganisation was a deeply flawed process with the outcome displaying a bias in the application of the criteria in favour of unitary councils, justifiable only on some tenuous grounds of greater efficiency, bringing the scathing reaction from Chisholm and Leach (2011: 20) that 'it is difficult to imagine how a disinterested observer could reach any conclusion other than that the Government has been persistently and deliberately dishonest'.

New Labour's Local Government and Public Involvement in Health Act of 2007 did, however, establish the procedure for the creation of new councils in England, by the invitation of proposals from single or groups of councils, based on differing criteria as determined by the Secretary of State, which continued to provide the basis for ad hoc restructuring. In practice, councils could submit proposals prior to a formal invite. A separate procedure allowed for the merger of two district councils where, on the request of the Secretary of State or a council, the Local Government Boundary

Commission for England would conduct a review which could abolish a local government area, create a new one or divide one part of a council from another (Sandford, 2020a). Indicative of the expedient nature of the approach was the limitation that proposals could not alter existing county or unitary authority boundaries. This process was to work with the existing map, and was to be completed, if at all, with the minimum disruption to existing administrative arrangements.

Restructuring the boundaries post-2010

The importance of structures and boundaries was to be even more diminished in the successive Coalition and Conservative governments from 2010 onwards, as such issues became subsumed amidst a wider agenda of austerity and the creation of new subregional governance institutions. The financial crisis and the subsequent decision of the Coalition government to pursue a stringent programme of austerity had a deep impact on the financial viability of many councils. In particular, many second tier district councils had no option but to intensify what had been an emerging trend towards providing services via contracts shared with neighbouring councils. For many, already responsible for delivering a diminishing number of services, this amounted to a de facto merger, with key long-term service-related decisions being taken jointly. In 2019, according to the Local Government Association (LGA), there were 626 such arrangements (LGA, n.d.). Moreover, as Copus et al. (2017: 101) noted, 'the unitary battle [was] once again raging across the two-tier shire areas of England', with proposals for unitary authorities being submitted by districts, groups of districts, and county councils, each replaying familiar arguments about delivering efficiency and service delivery, and putting their case with respect to the democratic credentials of the resulting mergers.

This seemingly strange phenomenon of 'turkeys voting for Christmas' can only be explained in the context of drivers emanating from central government policy. Firstly, austerity required cuts to council budgets to the extent that senior officers and councillors, particularly in smaller district councils, feared for their financial viability, and the main drivers were claims of cost savings and more joined up delivery of services to customers (Sandford, 2017). Secondly, council leaders and senior officers sought to reposition their authorities in the emerging subregional structures, and the economic logics driving that agenda, which favoured 'strategic' leadership and scale. For county councils, it was necessary to seize an opportunity to protect their position amidst the ongoing subregional devolution agenda, and stake their claim to be the key strategic players outside of city region areas. Although merger proposals could emanate from the 'bottom up', that is, the councils themselves, this was very much in the context of central government pressures which were seen to offer no alternative, and was conducted according to central government rules. Councils had no power of veto over the decisions finally taken by the Secretary of State, and the criteria informing the creation of the new bodies was not clearly set out.

This ad hoc process, which Leach and Copus (2021) called a 'reorganisation by stealth', produced a number of proposals, sometimes but not always with the consent of all the councils affected. For example, Suffolk Coastal and Waveney District Councils, in Suffolk, agreed to merge to form East Suffolk District Council by 2019. In Somerset, Taunton Deane voted to merge with West Somerset District Council in July 2016 and West Somerset approved the plan in September 2018. A merger between Forest Heath and St Edmundsbury District Councils, to form West Suffolk District Council, took effect from 2019. In Buckinghamshire, a unitary county came into being in April 2020, and the four district councils were abolished. A similar proposal from Leicestershire County Council, based on what council leader Nick Ruston called the 'perfect storm' of 'financial pressures, [the] national funding situation and growing service demands' (Leicestershire County Council, 2018), on the other hand, failed to gain support from the district authorities. In 2019 two new unitaries in Dorset replaced the county and six districts; four districts in Suffolk were merged to create the two new second tier districts of East and West Suffolk; and two districts were merged in Somerset. Most controversially, proposals for the creation in 2021 of two unitary authorities from the existing county and seven districts in Northamptonshire followed the appointment of two commissioners, in May 2018, by the Secretary of State to take over the running of Northamptonshire County Council's affairs following its declaration of bankruptcy. By November 2018, the lead commissioner had been able to reach the conclusion 'that Northamptonshire County Council was not able to put in place a recovery package quickly enough to avoid negatively impacting upon residents' and that therefore 'local government in the county should be reorganised: instead of the current two-tier system of the county council and district/borough councils, there should be single-tier authorities being responsible for delivering all of the local government services to its residents' (Ministry of Housing, Communities and Local Government (MHCLG), 2018: 6). Notably, it now seemed that Northamptonshire conveniently had no east or south, as two new councils of North, and West, Northamptonshire were created. People in the previously named South Northamptonshire district now found that they were in fact in West Northamptonshire, as it is to that unitary council that they were allocated. This seemingly bizarre conclusion provides in one example the extent to which considerations of expediency have triumphed.

Underpinning this process of reform has been a continuing preference for unitary structures, as evidenced in ministerial statements after 2016, without any seeming clarity of purpose, direction or sense that the process may be informed by fundamental considerations of the role of local government. While being open to unitary bids and mergers, Secretary of State James Brokenshire stated that 'the Government does not support top-down unitary restructuring' and would only look favourably on bids which were 'locally' requested (Marinko, 2019). Note that 'locally' here meant being requested by two or more councils, rather than by the public in those areas. Ministerial approvals then seem to have been made on a case-by-case basis, on criteria which were largely kept guarded. Indeed, for a period from 2016 to 2019, the Secretary of State, via provisions of the Cities and Local Government Devolution Act 2016, removed the need for local unanimity, so a move to unitaries could take place without the consent of one or other of the affected tiers of local government. The Act also permitted new unitary authorities to be created that crossed the boundaries of existing unitaries

(Sandford, 2020a). There was no published guidance as to what criteria were to inform ministerial judgements, but what information was available indicated the predominance of efficiency and service delivery considerations, along with assumptions concerning size and scale. Thus the guidance for the Northamptonshire review stated that the object was to produce a solution with 'a credible geography consisting of one or more existing local government areas and having a substantial population that at a minimum is in excess of 300,000' (Cusak, 2018), while Dorset County Council had a number of guidelines indicated to them, including the statement that the 'optimum size for a unitary council is 300,000–700,000 residents. These are not absolute rules, but the government will ask searching questions of proposals of fewer than 300,000 and more than 700,000 residents' (Dorset County Council, 2016). The council also received a clear indication that a unitary solution would meet with a more favourable 'devolution deal' in future.

Decisions in 2021 saw the creation of large unitary councils in North Yorkshire, Cumbria and Somerset, as the ad hoc process continued. Having abolished the county council and created two unitaries, it was then suggested that a Cumbria-wide combined authority (CA) may be necessary to deliver social care – seemingly an admission that the county authority was required after all. Once more, local government's future was subject to the machinations of various competing interests and opinions at the centre of government, as delay in the production of a long mooted White Paper served to create further confusion and in-fighting among local authorities, who took their cue from ministerial statements and strong hints in favour of larger unitary councils. Incrementally, the creation of new, larger unitary councils became entwined with preparations for bids to central government for devolution deals (see below for more on these deals and CAs). Councils were invited, in the summer of 2021, to submit further reorganisation plans and bids for devolution deals, while receiving varied and sometimes contradictory messages as to whether these would require the adoption of a directly elected mayor (DEM). Thus, in England, county and district councils either agreed or argued over possible mergers, as the rules of the game shifted beneath the feet of local government without any principles for direction. A variety of geographical models were proposed, and in turn opposed, by competing local interests. For example, Hampshire County Council discussed a devolution deal covering a 'Pan-Hampshire' authority, instigating a backlash from several of the district councils which would be covered (Kenyon, 2021a). Leicestershire County Council proposed a deal based on the county area, whereas in December 2020 a proposal from district councils in Leicestershire for an East Midlands Combined Authority had been supported by the then Secretary of State, Robert Jenrick. Thus, various geographies were imagined and constructed by local actors keen to follow what they took to be the government's intentions.

The *Levelling Up* White Paper, when it appeared in February 2022, at least sought to address the issue of complexity in England by providing what the government saw as a new, clear devolution framework, setting out guidance for devolution in and beyond metropolitan areas. There was to be no 'imposition' of any structural reform on local government, and the incremental approach, based on agreements between authorities, was reiterated. However, the result of the incremental moves towards larger unitary authorities, deal-making and CAs resulted in the issue of local government structure becoming increasingly merged with and tied to the machinations of devolution deal-making and requirements in terms of expected scale and size, with shire county areas coming to the forefront as the preferred institutional basis outside of metropolitan areas. The clear 'winners' were the county councils; devolution deals would be available for county areas but not for combinations of districts, although adjacent districts could be included if they wished and made up a 'sensible' geography, particularly if they were part of the same functional economic area (FEA). 'Sensible' geographies were deemed to be either FEAs or shire counties, seemingly, in a combination of economic logic and political compromise with the county council lobby, putting paid to decades of research and debate concerning the extent of community sentiment and belonging. Indeed, the White Paper invited nine 'pathfinder' combined county areas to submit proposals for devolution deals. Bids could only come from county councils; the involvement of district councils was encouraged, but they were to hold no veto over proposals. As would be expected, the White Paper contained the usual rhetorical commitments, it being 'important that new devolution deals are based on geographies that are locally recognisable in terms of identity, place and community, as well as being sensible economic areas that join up where people live and work' (HM Government, 2022: 137), but this was somewhat undermined by the firm stipulation that any councils seeking devolution must have a combined population of at least 500,000, without providing any justification for this specific figure, and despite it being considerably higher than the 300,000 which appeared to be appropriate in 2018.

The White Paper thus sought to get some control over what had become an increasingly complex and ad hoc process, setting out a direction of travel intended to give every area of England which requested one a devolution deal by 2030. However, there would remain a complex picture of unitary and two-tier councils, together with various subregional arrangements. The clear trend was further towards unitary councils based on arguments of efficiency and effective service delivery, which mirror the assumptions made by the government at the outset of the Banham Commission, and for which Banham was unable to establish any universal case or support.

These incremental changes have brought England more into line with the unitary systems in Scotland, Wales and Northern Ireland. In Scotland and Wales, despite the creation of devolved assemblies with responsibility for local government, a unitary structure is now in place although a Local Governance Review began in Scotland in 2018. In Northern Ireland, twenty-six unitary district councils were merged into eleven larger ones in 2015, albeit with the new councils gaining some powers over planning matters. In Wales there have been successive attempts to further reduce the number of councils, and the process is again enlightening regarding the status of local government. It started with the recommendation of the Williams Commission in 2014 that the twenty-two councils be merged into ten, eleven or twelve, while the following Bill, published in 2015, proposed options of eight or nine councils, created by merging existing ones. In an indication of the expediency of the process, the councils were not at this stage given names. Following widespread dissatisfaction, the plans were dropped, replaced in 2017 by a White Paper which proposed the creation of regional bodies to enable greater collaboration between existing councils. In turn, this was superseded by a Green Paper, *Strengthening Local Government: Delivering for People*, in 2018, which again made the case for the creation of ten councils, but this time via three possible pathways: a system of voluntary mergers, a phased approach with authorities merging in either 2022 or 2026, or a comprehensive system of mergers to occur in 2022. Unlike in England, voluntary proposals for merger were not forthcoming, and the structure remained unreformed, with the Local Government and Elections (Wales) Act 2021 holding out the option for councils to pursue voluntary mergers if they wished.

English subregionalism

Since 2010 in particular, it has been policies directed at institutional reform at the regional and subregional levels which have had most impact on local government; local government structure has been increasingly driven by these and the associated 'devolution' agenda, based on deal-making. Issues of democratic local governance were subsumed into the rescaling of economic subnational governance, which in turn was largely justified by a political economy approach and the calculation of political benefit by successive governments. A much vaunted agenda of 'devolution' of powers to local areas was deployed in an effort to achieve 'a functionally efficient means to achieve agreed policy outcomes' (Ayres et al., 2018). As Shaw and Tewdwr-Jones (2017: 213) state, this saw a range 'of overlapping and even competing "spatial imaginaries" being proposed for subnational governance ... communities and localities, cities, city regions, county subregions and even pan-regions'. Debates surrounding local government's place in a wider hierarchy of subnational governance, in particular its relationship with or correspondence to regional or subregional territorial settlements, was in itself nothing new. Governments ever since the 1945 Attlee administration established water and electricity boards have designed various institutional devices at this level, reflecting a variety of geographical areas. In the post-war period considerations of local government structure were influenced by the associated debates concerning scale, identity and economic functionality, as reflected clearly in Derek Senior's recommendation for councils based on city regions in his Memorandum of Dissent to the Redcliffe-Maud Report. However, the process of subnational institution-building since 2007 has had significantly more direct impact on local government structure and powers than had previously been the case.

Various 'spatial imaginaries' have been deployed by governments at subnational level, driven by changing perceptions of economic rationality. Labour's preference for regional planning was overtaken in the 1980s by the Thatcher government's favouring of private sector-led, specifically urban, regeneration, via urban development corporations (UDCs). In turn, the creation of Government Offices for the Regions in 1992–94 reflected the growing impact of the need to coordinate bids for European Structural Funds on a regional basis. New Labour governments initially had a preference for regions, driven by the agenda of Deputy Prime Minister John Prescott, and established regional development agencies (RDAs), and 'regional chambers' which brought together local government leaders and regional stakeholders. The ambition to introduce directly elected regional assembles for the first time was abandoned after rejection of an assembly in a referendum in the north-east in 2004. Significantly, with the replacement in 2007 of the regional chambers with 'local authority leaders' boards', the city region, or subregional, scale became the predominant spatial imagery. This was driven by the 'new economic orthodoxy', set out in the *Review of Sub-National Economic Development and Regeneration* (HM Treasury, DBERR and DCLG, 2007), which stressed the importance of city regions as 'engines' of economic growth, influenced by research stemming from international bodies (Morphet, 2016), and which placed a new emphasis on FEAs. Local government personnel did have some influence on this change of direction, which was strongly advocated by the leaders of the increasingly influential Core Cities group of councils. However, issues of identity and a sense of 'local' attachment were now, more than ever, explicitly secondary considerations, despite rhetorical commitments to the contrary, to solutions based on calculations of economic rationality (Tomaney, 2016).

New Labour initiated rescaling at city region level and thus began the journey into 'scaler messiness' (Harrison, 2012: 1255). The Local Democracy, Economic Development and Construction Act 2009 allowed for subregional collaborations of councils in metropolitan areas (multi-area agreements) to be consolidated into new formal entities called combined authorities. Unlike previous approaches to subnational governance, a variable geometry was used (Shaw and Tewdwr-Jones, 2017). Contrasting with the 'traditional' 'one size fits all' approach, this was promoted as allowing for flexibility and locally agreed solutions which could meet local economic circumstances. In turn, however, it initiated a pattern of filling the subregional 'vacuum' with a system based on bids and contractual relationships with government, favouring those who were able to demonstrate their capabilities and display the deemed qualities of 'leadership'.

The approach was taken up by the following Coalition and Conservative governments, keen to be seen, politically, to be addressing issues of economic growth and spatial disparities, by particularly focussing on deals in the north of the country. The Coalition government made an early commitment to this, stating 'We will take a bespoke approach, agreeing on a case-by-case basis the spatial level at which decisions should be made, and the governance structures that need to be in place' (HM Government, 2011: 8). They were able to portray this as being in line with both a distaste for the over-heavy bureaucratisation of regionalism and the commitment to 'localism', which rhetorically underpinned their wider agenda for local government. Thus, after 2010 came a continuation of the concentration on larger cities and wider subregions, in what was to produce a 'patchwork quilt' of initiatives, further adding to the complexity of local governance. Again, complexity and diversity according to local circumstances are characteristics which can and perhaps should underpin local government, and we could perhaps identify in this approach 'a strategy that not just tolerates, but actually celebrates, local variation, and also allows for future iterations as contexts and priorities change' (Lowndes and Gardner, 2016: 363). However, in this case the extent of 'local variation' is determined by central government, is highly prescribed and monitored, and local initiative is 'tolerated' to the extent that it is in line with central government policy.

The subregional direction of travel since 2010 has involved three main policy and institutional initiatives. Labour's RDAs were replaced with thirty-nine subregional local enterprise partnerships (LEPs) designed to 'better reflect the natural economic geography of the areas they serve and hence cover real functional economic and travel to work areas' (HM Government, 2010a: 2). LEPs were to be unelected, essentially voluntary bodies, established by invitation from the government to business and local authority leaders. They were initially unfunded, until they were subsumed into the wider subregional programme, and led by business interests, with their boards also containing appointed representatives from the local authorities they covered. Each LEP was granted a 'local growth deal' which was tightly controlled by central government (Morphet, 2022). Shaw and Tewdwr-Jones (2017: 216) noted their 'insufficient powers and resources to achieve their aims, variable arbitrary and transitory territorial boundaries that have at least as much to do with political "fixes" as economic analysis, and their lack of long-term vision and dynamism'. For example, from 2018 local authorities could belong to more than one LEP, showing a fast-and-loose approach to boundaries, loyalties and 'sense of place'.

Following this, the Localism Act of 2011 initiated the creation of City Deals, which consisted of a contractual arrangement whereby English cities and their surrounding areas, which could have varying geographies (some coterminous with LEP boundaries, others more tightly constrained to a smaller number of councils), were granted some additional powers in exchange for delivering growth, in line with their agreement. As an 'asymmetrical devolution' this would deliver differing powers to different city-based subregions. The first wave of deals covered the eight largest cities, followed by a wave of twenty further agreements, including some smaller city regions. The process was flexible, at least for the ministers involved, who could offer a selection of different additional responsibilities from which the cities could choose.

The third initiative was the further consolidation of Labour's creation of CAs, which continued to be created after 2010 under the provisions of the 2009 Act. These added a new layer of complexity, as the LEP, City Deal and CA areas in some cases had the same boundaries, as in Greater Manchester, while in others they did not. The first CA, Greater Manchester, was created in 2011, gaining economic development, transport and health duties and covering ten council areas. This was followed by five more CAs in 2014, with a total of ten created by 2019. The new Conservative government from 2015 extended the approach by announcing additional 'devolution deals', via the Cities and Local Government Devolution Act 2016, allowing existing CAs to bid for additional responsibilities while also allowing areas outside of CAs, including shire counties, to make bids. The Act also allowed the Secretary of State to transfer statutory duties from other public bodies to CAs. These deals, then, had an extended 'menu' of possible additional duties, involving housing, transport, skills, control over fire and rescue services, and taking over the work of police and crime commissioners, while also potentially retaining the surplus from business rate growth. These may seem like considerable powers, but this has to be seen in context, as these concessions were made by central government, were subject to 'performance' on agreed goals and could be removed. The Local Government Finance Act 2018 gave a number of further powers for mayors to raise small amounts of additional funding, including the ability to levy an infrastructure supplement on non-domestic ratepayers, resulting in what Sandford (2019) called a 'menu with specials', with each deal containing unique elements.

The deals came with an important proviso, however; to get a deal, it was a requirement that the CA must accept the introduction of a DEM. The policy was driven by the close personal interest of the then Chancellor of the Exchequer, George Osborne, and his desire to be seen, amidst austerity, to be 'doing something' particularly about economic regeneration in the north of England, and in the context of yet more spatial 'fixes' at a pan-regional level. Thus, the 'Northern Powerhouse' was followed by the 'Midlands Engine' as a means of coordinating the various subregional bodies. The insistence on elected mayors was seen by many in the local government community as a huge sticking point which stymied the progression of bids, particularly in shire areas, where this 'imposition' was resisted. Osborne was adamant that, while he would not impose the mayoral model, he would not 'settle for less' in granting a deal. Despite hints that this requirement might be dropped during the May administration of 2015–19, it remained and was not covered in the Conservative manifesto for the 2019 general election, only later being addressed in the *Levelling Up* White Paper. There were six CA mayoral elections in 2017, one in 2018 and one in 2019.

By 2022, there were eleven agreed devolution deals, some of which sprang from new combinations of councils which emerged to 'rescue' bids following previous failure to agree (Morphet, 2022). Osborne's invitation had sparked a flurry of interest in securing deals from outside of city region areas, with shire counties and districts quickly organising to create new spatial imaginaries from proposed mergers of the shires – for example, the bid for a merged CA formed from Derbyshire and Nottinghamshire County Councils, 'D2N2', and supported by all the district councils covered. To add further to the complicated picture which emerged, in one case, Cornwall, a devolution deal was agreed with a single authority, in this case a unitary county council which was not a CA and which did *not* have an elected mayor. In another, West Yorkshire, which *was* a CA, was initially allowed to have a deal without having an elected mayor (one was later elected in 2021), while the non-mayoral North East CA remained in existence but had no deal, being formed from the 'rump' of councils left in the CA after the formation of a North of Tyneside CA in 2019. One CA with a deal and an elected mayor, Cambridgeshire and Peterborough, was created from a combination of shire county and district councils in a non-core city area. Adding additional layers of confusion to this picture was the government's approach throughout 2020–21, referred to above, which saw individual counties, once committed to combination, now seeking their own devolution deals, for example in the cases of Durham and Derbyshire.

CAs, the associated deals and the manner of their creation, then, give a good insight into the status of local government and the dilemmas it faces. On the one hand, the 'devolution agenda' was embraced in key sections of the local government community, being considered for its potential to, perhaps, lead to further enhancements of powers and a more concerted move to 'localism'. CAs and deals represented important additional sources of authority and leeway in decision-making which could have significant impact on service delivery in the areas concerned. On the other hand, the 'offer' was conditional and the deals were the 'only game in town'; amidst austerity councils could be forgiven for seeking every ounce of additional leeway they could grasp. This precipitated rounds of negotiations, mainly among local leaders and elites, as they sought to create entities capable of finding favour with the government while at the same time satisfying local political interests. Amidst this, notions of place and locality were being drawn on and constructed to support proposals based on varying geographies, which played 'fast and loose' with any consideration of community sentiment. 'Subregional' geographies were shoehorned into combinations of existing council areas, themselves often already the product of expediency, to create areas approximating the desired coherent economic geographies – if indeed such things are possible to fit into meaningful administrative areas.

Several cases from the bidding process illuminate the point. For example, the 2016 Act allowed for non-contiguous areas to combine if they had strong reasons based on economic geographies, such as shared travel to work areas or housing market areas. This allowed for the possibility of 'exclaves' that for the first time allowed a council to join together, as part of a statutory body of local governance, with others with which it did not share a boundary. This gave rise to the case of Chesterfield Borough Council and Bassetlaw District Council proposing in 2016 to become constituent members of Sheffield City Region. The move was challenged in court, with respect to Chesterfield, by Derbyshire County Council, which sought to 'keep' Chesterfield in the historic county, leading to the eventual withdrawal of their applications by both councils. The districts, like others, can and do remain as 'non-constituent' members of the city region. The story of the attempt to create a Yorkshire-wide CA met with similar political machinations, where eighteen of the twenty councils agreed to a 'One Yorkshire' devolution bid in January 2018, with Sheffield and Rotherham dissenting and preferring a 'South Yorkshire based' solution. The bid was rejected by the government in January 2019, leaving the existing Sheffield City Region CA and the West Yorkshire CA to continue, but with Barnsley and Doncaster, while being in the

Sheffield CA, refusing to ratify the city region deal until May 2019. The One Yorkshire bid was resubmitted, with the intention to move towards One Yorkshire on an incremental basis, with councils being able to leave the Sheffield CA after 2022 to join another if they wished.

In the north-east of England, a proposed devolution settlement for a CA was cancelled after Durham, Gateshead, South Tyneside and Sunderland Councils withdrew their support in 2016, leaving Newcastle City Council, Northumberland County Council and North Tyneside Council to agree a deal as the North of Tyne CA in 2017. The north-east thus acquired a complex set of governance arrangements which in turn gave rise to alternative proposals, with Durham County Council arguing for its own devolution settlement, others arguing for uniting the two CAs (Smulian, 2021) and the government indicating in its *Levelling Up* White Paper of February 2022 that it would be seeking to join the parties back together in a single North East Combined Authority.

Further evidence for the domination of expediency over local identity was provided by the government's 'rationalisation' of LEP boundaries in 2018, when LEPs were requested in July to submit proposals for reform based on 'geographies which best reflect real functional economic areas' by September (MHCLG, 2018: 23). The *Levelling Up* White Paper of 2022 suggested that LEP functions would be subsumed into the areas covered by devolution deals. The huge complexity of the resulting institutional landscape can hardly be said to be congruent with clear understanding by the public, and serves to make accountability more opaque. While geographical coherence for public service delivery has long been an elusive holy grail, the resulting 'jumble' has produced new heights of complexity, and made it problematic to devolve more duties to the subregional levels covered by CAs, deals and LEPs. For example, other than in Greater Manchester and the West Midlands, the areas covered by CAs were smaller than the footprints of the sustainability and transformation partnerships and integrative care systems developed between the NHS and councils (NAO, 2017). In addition, Scotland, Wales and Northern Ireland are now covered geographically in full by Growth or City Deals, agreed directly between cities and subregions and the Westminster government, adding an additional level of complexity, particularly in Scotland, to their nationally devolved administration by providing the government in London with an additional form of influence.

As noted, the *Levelling Up* White Paper represented an attempt to address this complexity in England by setting out 'a clear and consistent set of devolution pathways for places' (HM Government, 2022: 136). The 'menu' of incentives offered was slimmed down and consolidated into three levels of devolution. Level three was the government's preferred option, involving the most powers and functions, in return for which the bidding authorities would accept a DEM. Naturally, level two involved fewer 'goodies' but did not require an elected mayor, while level one consisted of less formalised joint working. Level two and three deals were open to either county council areas, including any unitary authorities within their boundaries (for example, Derbyshire County Council and Derby City Council), or 'sensible' FEAs, with in either case 'a single institution in place across that geographic footprint' (HM Government, 2022: 137). Neighbouring authorities could also be considered if they wished to join. Thus, counties would be eligible for deals without being an FEA, while in other places covering, or part covering, an FEA. The government therefore addressed the elusive search for geographies which were both meaningful in terms of identity and sense of place while also being 'sensible' in economic terms, and came up with the answer (to paraphrase): either shire counties, or FEAs or perhaps both. Clearly, this response represented a compromise, promoting the subregional and 'levelling up' agenda while not being seen to be imposing a wholesale 'top-down' reorganisation, by also conveniently accepting the current structure of existing county councils and their boundaries outside of the metropolitan areas.

As noted earlier, the progress of the agenda was held up by the political turmoil and changes of prime minister in mid to late 2022, and given, for a short time, an added complication in the proposal by Liz Truss to create investment zones, with boundaries to be determined. In late 2022 the Sunak government appeared to put things back to square one, or at least to where they had been in February of that year. And by the end of 2022 it appeared to be 'a bit of mess' (Hill, 2022a) – perhaps an understatement.

Derbyshire and Nottinghamshire and their respective cities agreed a level three deal, forming a CA and accepting an elected mayor, in August 2022. A level three deal for Cornwall was held up by disagreement over accepting the mayoral model, while a similar reluctance held up the creation of a CA consisting of Hull City and the East Riding of Yorkshire. In Leicestershire, talks descended into a 'dog's breakfast' (Hill, 2022a), with the government's insistence that the FEA included neighbouring Rutland, which refused to join, along with Leicester City. Adding to the growing complexity was the creation of a CA, with mayor, combining York City and the newly created North Yorkshire County Council in a level three deal, meaning that the prospect of 'One Yorkshire' from just a few years previously was now effectively ended for the foreseeable future. In a further twist, by mid-2022, Durham had decided that it did indeed wish to be part of a bid for a new CA for the northeast and had opened discussions to this effect. In the round, this complicated story sees local governance in many cases manipulated according to the changing strategic calculation at both council and national level; the very complexity, twists and turns and about-faces involved speaks volumes about the nature of local governance, particularly in England.

To an extent, the resulting institutional picture from the cumulative effect of these reforms is path-dependent, arising incrementally out of existing regional and subregional fixes, working pragmatically with existing local government boundaries (Rees and Lord, 2013). On the other hand, it has represented in many areas a rapid and ad hoc approach which has had little concern for principles of democratic local governance, reaching new heights of expediency with respect to boundaries. This 'scalecraft' involves a constant invention and reinvention of structures and has produced highly imbalanced and inequitable outcomes, having been concentrated on Core Cities and leaving the 'rest' of local government essentially scrambling to gain 'crumbs from the table'. There was for some time an assumption that the interests of the larger cities were to be foregrounded, downplaying the economic difficulties of 'free standing' towns and mixed urban–rural areas. For Haughton et al. (2016: 356) this was merely one example of a wider set of highly debatable economic assumptions that 'privilege large global cities as generators of economic growth' despite evidence that 'economic growth rates are higher in many of the smaller cities of the UK and elsewhere in Europe'. This had a destabilising effect on the remaining system of county councils, evidenced in the extensive lobbying efforts of the County Councils Network for the creation of unitary counties. The Johnson government, via the *Levelling Up* White Paper, sought to assuage these concerns, but it indicated only a continuation of what Tomaney (2016: 550) observed was 'a patchwork of deals and fixes with no clear underlying principles of local governance', representing an 'idiosyncratic, uneven and highly centralised form of multilevel government ... only approved if it meets the criteria of central government and selected business interests'.

Overall, reorganisation by 'deal-making' has been at best an opaque, confusing and seemingly chaotic and informal process, with for the most part no clear framework or published criteria, and with 'rewards going to those who can dance most credibly to the tune of central government' (Haughton et al., 2016: 367). The financial arrangements themselves have no legal basis, being in this sense 'fuzzy' modes of governance whereby government incentivises subregional actors; CAs are not subregional local authorities, like the Greater London Authority, but are *sui generis,* each one having an individually designed basis (Morphet, 2022). Despite the more 'clear' framework set out in the *Levelling Up* White Paper, such is the system of governance and the extent of political, legislative and financial control at the centre, that in practice all such bidding processes looked set to be conducted in the same vein. In considering the 'devolution' process in England, Bailey and Wood (2017) note how central government has used tools of metagovernance to retain control 'at a distance' of increasingly complex governance networks, including framing and designing the institutional settings of networks of actors, and the shaping of rules and norms. The government thereafter also retained a tight grip with respect to monitoring through more 'traditional' means of control. There were requirements for monitoring CAs via Local Assurance Statements, devolved investment funds, scrutiny from an external 'expert' panel and five-yearly 'gateway reviews', with further funding being dependent on Treasury satisfaction that all objectives had been met. The White Paper of 2022, with its proposal for a new Performance

Framework (see also Chapter 6), indicated that this scrutiny would continue, if in a different format. As for the amounts of finance which have been available via deals, Sandford (2020b: 42) argues that they 'would barely register on any of the standard measures of fiscal devolution', adding to the picture of the process representing 'centralisation on steroids' (Hambleton, 2016).

Richards and Smith (2015) thus identify the agenda as being in 'the British political tradition', and the 'Westminster Model' of administration, whereby the centre retains control through elite–elite central–local negotiations. They refer to this as a 'Whiggish' approach to change played out through the 'court politics' of a few key actors, resulting, in the case of CAs, in the 'micro' reproduction of Westminster models based on closed, negotiated settlements between national and local political elites. This approach also had the advantage of further allowing central government to use 'devolution' as a smokescreen, deflecting blame for the effects of austerity by engaging in 'scaler dumping' (Peck, 2012: 647) to mask the scale of cuts, and incorporating local elites willingly into their implementation, while creating the larger administrative areas favoured by the private corporations looking for economies of scale in their public service contracting operations.

Economic growth, high-profile leadership and quick wins have thus been at the forefront at the expense of democratic engagement, with an emphasis on uncontroversial, consensus-based policy over addressing local concerns (Sandford, 2020b). Mayors or leaders who can facilitate consensus among subregional business and public service elites are required to make CAs function, and these attributes have predominated at the expense of wider democratic engagement of the public in the process. For Tomaney (2016: 550), this is 'a form of devolution in which "business" exercises a direct and indirect veto over the preferences of citizens' and is indicative of a 'post-democratic' polity which governs in the interests of a small elite. A survey of public discussions on devolution involving central government, local government, think-tanks and civil society groups between 2011 and 2015 highlighted that 41.6 per cent focussed on achieving economic growth as the main justification for devolving power, while only 12.9 per cent of arguments made the case for devolution in terms of shifting power, strengthening democracy or increasing citizen involvement in decision-making (Lyall et al., 2016).

The emphasis on elite consensus resonates with critiques which set state spatial restructuring in the context of broader processes of neoliberalism and, drawing on the work of Harvey (1989), 'urban entrepreneurialism', whereby the primary concern of urban political leaders is economic 'attractiveness' to investment and the 'enabling' of economic enterprise. This 'neoliberalizing urbanism' (MacLeod, 2011) is held by some to have become hegemonic, dominating states' attempts at reform as they adjust their spatial geographies according to the changing requirements of largely transient capital. Etherington and Jones (2016) argue that this requires the constant making and remaking of governance arrangements, in a constant 'churn' of reforms, with each iteration representing a 'sticking plaster', as governments seek to deal with the deep-seated economic problems and inevitable contradictions thrown up by capitalist development.

Such lines of argument see local governance arrangements as having increasingly been prey to the 'unchallenged ascendancy amongst elite actors of neoliberal ideas about economic development' (Deas, 2014: 2302) and a seemingly rational, 'post-democratic' and neutral set of assumptions about its benefits. Subregional spatial reform, the creation of CAs, deals and LEPs and the associated knock-on effects for local government can thus be interpreted in this light as a form of statecraft which seeks to insulate decision-making 'beyond the direct control of elected politicians' (Flinders and Wood, 2014: 135), and in the context of a longer-term process of depoliticisation, characterised as a form of governance 'without politics', in which decision-making is 'cleansed of ideology and cleansed of burdensome responsibilities which detract from the single-minded pursuit of economic growth' (Deas, 2013: 75). This produces an apparent managerial-technical 'common-sense' consensus, shared by elites, which forecloses the genuinely political, which, in contrast, involves dissent and conflict, and offers the possibility of more egalitarian and inclusive outcomes (Swyngedouw, 2018). The economic logic which has underpinned much of the agenda and the manner of its implementation certainly displays such characteristics. At the same time, there has remained a pragmatic adherence to some existing structures due to political expedience and the lack of will, or perhaps even interest, in government circles for wholescale reorganisation, mooted as unpopular and potentially expensive amidst a harsh financial environment. As we have noted, the White Paper of 2022 seemed to represent this more complex statecraft, using as it does the economic logic alongside a politically pragmatic adherence to existing counties. As Werran (2022) notes, the approach 'allows government to wash its hands of any need to go about the messiness of a top down restructure of local government in the shires', the implication being that 'political nature will take its course'.

Conclusion

We have seen that, over the years, the debate around local government structure has been dominated by considerations and assumptions concerning technical efficiency and effective service delivery, with, at times, concessions to 'community' and 'local' sentiment, and a rhetorical commitment, even amidst reorganisations which do not reflect it, to the value of democratic local government. The issue of congruence between local government areas and functional economic geographies has been present throughout; as definitions of the scope of these areas has changed, so too have the perceived implications for local government. However, restructuring, as in the major reforms of the 1970s, historically tended to settle on some form of compromise between these demands and local sentiment and attachment. As noted in this chapter, there are good reasons for now thinking that an economic rationality has become dominant. Setting local government reform in the context of the wider political economy can thus highlight a move from the settlement of the 1972 Act, which still perceived local government as an instrument for the delivery of welfare services, more towards the 'growth-first neo-liberal' nature of later reforms (Macleod, 2011: 2212) which are sugared with the rhetoric of localism and still, to an extent, tempered by the remnants of the historic system in the form of the shires.

'Local' government, in this context, has meaning only in the extent to which it can find any space for agency amidst what are considerable constraints. However, in turn, we need to be careful that we do not assume that *no* such space remains, and look at the reactions of councils and newly elected mayors, for example, to see how these new arrangements are working in practice and whether, perhaps, they are able to exploit 'cracks' in the new arrangements and from there widen them into 'wedges' which open up further possibilities (Wright, 2004, in Ayres et al., 2018). Sweeting and Hambleton (2020), for example, looking at the working practices of the mayor in Bristol, found evidence of depoliticised, consensual leadership, but also space for greater political agency. It may be that we can find, even now, reasons to believe that the 'local' refuses to remain silent and that this provides us with hope on which to build, at least pointing us in the direction of alternatives. This is a theme to which we will return in particular in Chapter 7, but is also in evidence, as we see in the next chapter, in the way many councils have responded to much diminished service responsibilities and financial constraint.

4

Can local governments govern? Powers and resources

The capacity of local governments to make a significant difference to the communities that they serve is dependent on the extent to which they are given powers and resources by central or federal governments to provide services, and their capacity to act independently. In Britain the decline and occasional gains in powers to provide local services independently of central government up to 2000 have been outlined in Chapter 1, but have been still too numerous in the last two decades to discuss in full, and so are summarised here through the larger services. Moreover, lists of powers and responsibilities in themselves cannot convey a full picture of local governments' power of governance, which is vacuous unless accompanied by the resources to effectively operationalise these responsibilities. Later in the chapter, we will discuss how the agendas of recent governments have further weakened local governments' ability to do so.

At face value the development of local governments' capacity to govern independently of the centre paradoxically appeared to have been given a substantial boost by the 2011 Localism Act that ended the constraints imposed by the principle of *ultra vires* by giving local governments, including parish and community councils, a power of general competence to undertake any activity that was not prohibited by statute and common law. According to the then Secretary of State for Communities and Local Government, Eric Pickles,

> The Bill pushes power out as far as possible into communities and neighbourhoods, into the hands of individuals and community groups. (Hansard, HoC, Series 6, 17 January 2011, Col. 562)

The reference to 'individuals and community groups' is an indication that the Act was, however, as much about removing power from local government. The Localism Act thus appeared to give local government a long sought-after power to secure whatever they thought best for their areas. In practice, however, these gains were established in the context of other legislation and restructuring which led to the further marginalisation of local government in key service areas, with more emphatic central government control established by an overarching environment of fiscal austerity.

Schools

The successive removal of responsibilities for school education from local authorities provides perhaps the clearest example of a weakening of local government's role as a service provider, brought about by successive governments since the early 1980s. Since 1997, policy in England has been dominated, under governments of various hues, by the promotion of academy schools, self-managing their own budgets and directly funded by central government. The New Labour governments initially ended the capacity of schools to opt out of local control, but later returned to a more interventionist strategy and further eroded the local authority role in a process of 'academisation' (Ball, 2018). This included the 2000 Learning and Skills Act, which allowed schools deemed to be failing to be established as non-profit making academies under the guidance of trusts outside local authority control, and after 2006 further legislation allowed schools whether failing or not to opt for education trust status. Funding for schools was ring-fenced as the Dedicated Schools Grant was mainly provided directly to schools. This was replaced by the national funding formula in 2018, with the transition to direct funding of schools via this mechanism, to replace local funding formulae, to start in 2022–23 – a further move in the direction of centralisation.

Devolution to national assemblies has created a greater divergence both in level and type of service, and indeed in management, structure and decision-making by local authorities. There are in effect four systems in the UK, although in Northern Ireland local government has no responsibility for education. Scotland and Wales do not have academy schools. In Wales, local authorities decide to allocate funds to schools, via their own schemes, subject to guidance. In Scotland, there is the Devolved School Management Scheme, introduced in 1993 and subsequently enhanced and extended in 2019. This still leaves more of the budget in the hands of Scottish councils than in England, and overall in Scotland and Wales local government has retained more powers than in England.

Under the Conservative and Liberal Democrat Coalition government an Academies Act 2010 and an Education Act 2011 made it possible for all local authority maintained schools in England to become academies, directly funded by central government through the Education and Skills Funding Agency, and independent of local authority control. The Department for Education could require poorly performing schools and those 'eligible for intervention' to become academies or be closed. The 2011 Localism Act introduced a presumption that any new school would be an academy. Fast-tracking of academy status was extended to 'outstanding' schools while other schools could become academies, but only as part of a chain or with a sponsor. Multi-academy trusts (MATs) containing between 2 and 100 schools increasingly governed chains of schools. Also introduced was a new form of academy, free schools, which could be established by parents, teachers, charities, universities, business, community or faith groups in response to parental demand.

By January 2018, 27 per cent of primary schools and 65 per cent of secondary schools in England had become academies. As West (2015) notes, the presumption in favour of academies was important, as it signalled that a key function of the local authority, as the main provider of schools, was being further curtailed, while the power of central government increased. In addition, regional schools commissioners (RSCs) were established in 2014, as unelected bodies not bearing any relationship with local authority boundaries, to take decisions on applications for academy status, and to monitor the performance of non-academy maintained schools. Ball (2018: 216) noted that 'RSCs mark a further move in the almost total displacement of local authorities from education policy responsibility while mimicking some of their previous roles.'

The diminishing of the LEA role, however, did not leave schools 'free' to manage as they saw fit in accordance with local wishes or preferences; as Ball (2018: 230) observed:

> Despite the deregulation of provision and greater institutional freedoms offered to some schools, all schools are subject to targeted, systemic and partial, disparate and uncoordinated, and repetitive interventions from government.

What developed was a complex maze of organisational forms and 'tangled webs' of accountability. Councillors and parents found it difficult to scrutinise and hold MATs to account. For example, the Wakefield Academies Trust failed in 2017, leaving its twenty-one schools to be 'rebrokered' by the Secretary of State to other providers. The Trust, the local authorities, the Schools Commissioner and the Department for Education each attached blame to the others. While local authority schools were inspected by Ofsted, MATs and their governance were not. Regional schools commissioners provided oversight but again had no powers of inspection over MATs. Further complication was added by the promotion, since 2010, of school improvement partnerships involving clusters of schools. A complex variety of overlapping geographies thus became the order of the day, with governance styles including both the promotion of competition and collaboration between schools and providers.

Further, the fragmentation of the schools system and acceleration of school financial independence led to patchy council provision in a range of discretionary services that were once universally provided. This was consistent with the move to contracting out such services and to the creation of mixed markets of service deliverers from which schools have freedom to choose. These include, for example, support services for teaching and learning, extracurricular activities and facilities management (APSE, 2020). Local authorities continued to offer music and outdoor education, ICT, human resources and legal support to maintained schools, but encountered intense competition from the private sector. Similarly, their stake in the provision of free schools meals, property and grounds maintenance, caretaking and security was much reduced. Thus APSE (2020: 15) noted that 'the consequences of this reduced demand is that local authorities are finding it increasingly difficult to balance the books. The less buy-back income they receive, particularly from the larger and more cost effective secondary school market, the more difficult it becomes to make service provision financially viable.' Some ceased to provide these services, others retained a direct labour organisation or trading arm which competed for business and others pursued other models such as the creation of arms-length trading companies or outsourcing to private contractors. As such, this picture provides a good representation of the position local government found itself in generally.

However, councils continued to have a role with respect to schools. 'Upper tier' councils in England, and all councils in Wales retained an overall responsibility for children's services along with a legal duty to ensure that every child achieved his or her educational potential. In England, since the Children Act 2004 these duties had been carried out within Children's Departments, now variously named, which aimed to integrate education and social services for children to promote a 'joined up' approach to their well-being. Their duty was to ensure that there were enough school places available in their area, but without the power to require academies to expand, and increasingly needing to work in partnership with them to this end. Councils set the admissions policies and catchment areas for community schools and coordinated all schools admissions in their areas, while continuing, for example, to provide free school transport for children between the ages of 5 and 16 who attend schools more than two miles from their home, and having a range of responsibilities to support those with special educational needs.

Housing

Local government's role in housing reveals a similar, continuing trend towards residualisation, accompanied by some gains in duties and an increasingly localised response to utilise any new and remaining powers. The reduction in local government's role started in 1980, with council housing stock being sold under the 'Right to Buy' policy of the Thatcher and subsequent governments.

There were 6.5 million council homes in 1980 in England, Scotland and Wales, compared with 2 million in 2019 (Kentish, 2017). Councils were increasingly left with the housing which was in most need of repair, with decreasing capacity to upgrade it. This, together with caps on local authority borrowing to build social housing or repair their stock, and central government retention of receipts from sales, left councils a long way from being the major player in social housing that they once were. In 1970, 136,000 houses had been built by councils; in 2000, only 60 were built. In 2017/18, more than six times as many houses were sold under Right to Buy than were built by councils, with only a fifth of the 70,000 homes sold since 2011/12 being replaced (LGA, 2019b). Councils were allowed, in 2019, to retain only a third of receipts from sales despite a government commitment in 2012 that all homes 'lost' in this way would be replaced on a one-for-one basis. However, again providing an example of divergence, Right to Buy was ended in Scotland in 2016 and in Wales in 2019.

The period after 1980 saw local authorities become at best one player within a range of social housing providers. From 1988, housing associations and other providers were able to take over council stock following a ballot of tenants (Wilson and Game, 2011: 146). Under New Labour governments, from 2000, councils, lacking the funds or ability to borrow to manage and repair homes, had the option of transferring their stock to a housing association or other registered social landlord, contracting out the management of their housing to the private sector or continuing to manage it themselves, albeit via a semi-independent arms-length management organisation and accepting the limitations on borrowing which that entailed. Subsequently, many councils over the years divested themselves voluntarily of all of their housing stock, with 1.3 million homes transferred in this way to housing associations between the late 1990s and 2012. Any local housing authority which still owned 200 or more dwellings was required to account for them within a ring-fenced Housing Revenue Account (HRA), funded from rents and charges, to be spent on building and maintaining property. By 2019, of 326 housing authorities, 161 did not have a HRA. Councils faced restrictions on what they could borrow within this account, which were only lifted, after intense lobbying, in 2018. However, in December 2019 the Treasury made use of this additional freedom more difficult by raising the interest rate on loans from the Public Works Loan Board, at a time when councils were hoping to increase house building from this source (Merrick, 2019). Councils could, however, gain grants from a central funding body, Homes England, to 'kickstart' housing developments.

Again, since 2010 councils have used their much diminished powers to address as far as possible the substantial issues in social housing, and through various means have re-entered the field of social housing provision and indeed building. These efforts have been documented by Morphet and Clifford (2021) and are dealt with in more detail in Chapter 7. While there is no disputing the extent of local government's demise in this area, from being the dominant provider of social rented accommodation in the 1970s, local councils continued to provide a source of innnovation, and a desire to address social issues based on local knowledge.

Police and emergency services

Management of law and order was, as shown in Chapter 1, a central concern of county, borough and parish government prior to the nineteenth century, and with democratisation by the twentieth century was a responsibility shared by magistrates with local councils. After 1945 subsequent restructuring led to the role being confined to larger ad hoc police authorities, based, outside London, on shire county areas and, after the abolition of the metropolitan county councils in 1984, on their subregional scale, with representation from local councils and magistrates, which had powers over the resourcing of the police rather than on legal and criminal policies, which were increasingly in the hands of central government. The 2010 Coalition government maintained that the system was by this stage out of touch with citizens and replaced the police authorities with an elected police and crime commissioner (PCC) outside London, where the Metropolitan Police had become the responsibility of the Greater London Authority. Scotland established a nationwide police authority in 2013, answerable to the

Scottish Assembly. Thus, policing ceased to be a local authority service, although many of the forty-three forces in England and Wales retained some connection with local government boundaries in being congruent with shire county boundaries, while others were subregional amalgamations. The Mayor of Manchester CA took over policing, fire and rescue, and the Mayor of West Yorkshire CA policing, responsibilities in their areas. For the most part, local government input is confined to councillor representation on local police, fire and crime panels, and local fire and rescue scrutiny committees.

By 2022, fire and rescue services also retained only a measure of connection with local government. Top tier councils retained control of the service in the case of fifteen of the forty-five fire and rescue authorities in England and Wales. As with policing, others covered combinations of areas, either of county and unitary urban councils, or were subregional bodies, although not in all cases consistent with police authority boundaries, and, as with policing, the Mayors of Greater Manchester and London had responsibility for the service. The three Welsh authorities are subregional combinations, and Scotland has created a single service responsible to the Scottish Assembly. The ambulance services in England had since 1946 been under the control of county and borough councils, but were transferred in 1974 to National Health Service regional or area health authorities, and after 2006 to thirty-one ambulance service trusts; after 2012, further mergers led to the creation of ten regional bodies in England and one in Wales. These services have not for some time been part of local government's core activities, and together they paint a picture of a system increasingly distant from local government structures and of a variety of spatial imaginaries which are driven by considerations of efficiency. Thus, for example, Devon and Somerset fire authorities were merged in 2007, and Dorset and Wiltshire in 2017. The latter case was driven by the perceived need for savings and efficiencies as a result in particular of austerity and financial restraint imposed across public services after 2010. Indeed, the effects of austerity led to calls for widespread amalgamations of both police (Deloitte, 2018) and fire authorities (Knight, 2013).

Social services

Social services is perhaps the great survivor from the 1990s in terms of the responsibilities of local government, although its control is firmly allocated to the top tier authorities rather than the districts, and many aspects of the service, especially care of the elderly, have been contracted out to the private sector since 1990. Indeed, since the early 1980s, local government's role has moved to that of 'enabler' more than direct provider of services. The 1990 National Health Service and Community Care Act explicitly sought the creation of a 'mixed economy of care', with a range of care providers – public, private and voluntary – being commissioned by councils via competitive tender, and regulated through contracts (Wistow et al., 1992). In practice this led to a major shift in the provision of care for adults, which became heavily dominated by the private sector and highly fragmented. By 2012, local authorities and the NHS provided only 6 per cent of residential or nursing home beds, falling from 64 per cent in 1979, while 93 per cent of domiciliary care, or 'home help', was provided directly by councils in 1993, falling to 11 per cent in 2012 (Hudson, 2018). The House of Commons Health and Social Care Committee (2020) noted an increasingly unstable market, with growing numbers of care home providers going out of business, and an estimated one in three of providers making a loss. Larger providers became more dominant, with two going into administration – Southern Cross in 2010 and Four Seasons in 2019. Concern has been raised about 'debt-fuelled' private social care provision (Blakeley and Quilter-Pinner, 2019: 2), dominated by private equity ownership, with 'astonishingly complex corporate structures' (Blakeley and Quilter-Pinner, 2019: 7). The COVID-19 pandemic served to further focus attention particularly on adult social care and councils' ability to meet intense pressures, including staffing shortages and low pay in the sector, and growing demand from an ageing population.

Services less attractive to competitors as profitable, such as dealing with children in care, retain a somewhat greater local authority input, while in general, as noted above, the focus in children's care after 2004 was on integration with education, itself increasingly fragmented and at arm's length from local government, and on protecting welfare in partnership with other agencies, in England through statutory safeguarding partnerships, in Scotland safeguarding committees, and in Wales via regional safeguarding boards. Increasingly, partnership became the dominant model of service delivery here as in other areas of local governance. The most controversial aspect of children's care, however, was the encroachment of outsourcing and the use of the private sector in an area which had hitherto been relatively insulated from this trend. The House of Commons Health and Social Care Select Committee (2020) recognised the increase in children's homes being provided by the private sector – 1,712 in 2019, with only 418 provided by local authorities and 163 by the voluntary sector. By 2021, many councils were outsourcing Special Educational Needs Assessments to the private sector.

The move to commissioner rather than provider of care was also accelerated by the development of direct user involvement in decision-making. Since 2008, local authorities had been required to allocate personal budgets to those in receipt of care, based on a needs assessment, which could be taken in the form of a direct payment, a trend strengthened by the 2014 Care Act. Recipients could use this direct payment to commission their own care from a range of providers. Along with this 'enabling', a parallel theme was aimed at achieving greater integration of health and social care by introducing new partnership configurations, which again are not always consistent with local government boundaries. Thus, in 2016 in England, local sustainability and transformation partnerships were established in an attempt to coordinate all health and care providers in forty-two 'local' areas, of 500,000 to 3 million population. These developed into integrated care systems (ICSs), with the Health and Care Bill of 2021 setting these out as the key local delivery mechanism in England, while the Greater Manchester Combined Authority was given 'devolved control' of the health and social care budget in its area. In Wales, this integration was sought through seven regional partnership boards, while in Scotland integration joint boards were introduced in 2016, mostly congruent with local authority boundaries and with the option of the local council being the lead authority. In both Scotland and Wales, in the case of both education and social care, there is more use of joint working or consortia arrangements across councils. However, moves towards integration with health services, and continuing questions about long-term funding brought the long-standing issue of where responsibility for social care should lie more sharply into focus. Increased pressures on hospital services caused by 'bed blocking' by patients unable to be discharged due to lack of adequate social care added to this. In 2021 the Scottish government proposed a National Care Service which would remove the oversight of social care from local authorities, effectively taking it into the control of the national government. In England ICSs were, with a few exceptions, planned to be coterminus with the boundaries of local authorities or combinations of them, but they were also to be governed by boards which could have only one member from a local authority, who would not necessarily be an elected member.

'Joined-up' provision of health and social care has been a long sought-after goal, thwarted as the various attempts at partnership working have been held back by administrative barriers and issues of organisational and professional culture, and not least by the financial pressures. There have for some time been suspicions that the mechanisms for seeking such integration will increasingly involve the NHS becoming the more dominant player in social care provision. At the same time, councils have experimented over time with a variety of local integrated delivery models which predate the ICS initiative. For example, 'St Helens Cares' 'is unique as it is much broader than just health and social care, it also includes services and support such as housing, education and arts and culture' (St Helens Cares, n.d.). In other areas, post-2010, councils took services previously outsourced to 'arm's-length' management companies back in-house, as in the cases of children's services in Doncaster and South Somerset. Innovation persisted, then, but in reality social services provides the most stringent test for any argument that local government has a significant part to play in the delivery of vital public services in the future.

Public health and welfare

While there have been many losses and restraints on local services, in a few sectors there have been some gains. Coordinating strategies for public health was in the nineteenth century attached to health boards, but this became a local government task in 1894. Much of this was submerged into the orbit of the NHS in the period after 1945, but it has been revived through legislation that became operative in 2013 giving responsibility for public health to local authorities through the formation of health and wellbeing boards in all upper tier authorities, with the proviso that this would be undertaken with the cooperation of other private and public interests. Thus local government gained important responsibilities for funding and commissioning public health, including tackling obesity, smoking and substance misuse and the provision of sexual health services. However, the finance for this came via a ring-fenced government grant and councils did not have discretion as to how this income was allocated to the various branches of these services. Funding for the service was then reduced by 14 per cent between 2015 and 2020, a fundamental restriction on councils' ability to develop this new service as they saw fit. Significantly, as we outlined in the Introduction, the reality of the fragility of the 'gains' made by local government in the public health field was exposed by the COVID-19 pandemic, with central government simply choosing to ignore their involvement and take powers back to itself.

Councils also 'gained' the administration of certain welfare benefits. From 2013 to 2014 they were given responsibility for funding and designing schemes to help those with low incomes pay their council tax bills and, through the Homelessness Reduction Act 2017, duties to find shelter for the homeless. However, given the overall context of financial restraint, these additional duties were somewhat of a poisoned chalice. For example, despite the virtual collapse of local authorities' capacity to build houses for rent they nevertheless still retained a duty to house the homeless, and thus risked being used as a scapegoat for the inadequacies of centralised policy-making. Seven out of ten English councils overspent their homelessness budgets in 2018/19 by a combined total of nearly £115 million (Housing Maintenance and Management, 2020).

As noted in Chapter 3, some of the CAs created since 2010 gained some service responsibilities through the various deals offered by the government. Most notably, the Greater Manchester Health Authority has responsibility for an integrated health and social care budget, managed by the Greater Manchester Health and Social Care Partnership. As we saw, however, such deals are subject to considerable central oversight and are given at the discretion of the centre. The Greater Manchester CA also announced in 2021 its intention to take control of bus franchising, with subsidised fares, from 2023. As noted earlier, the *Levelling Up* White Paper held out the possibility that councils, or new CAs, might gain from a 'menu' of potential additional responsibilities, depending on which level of devolution was opted for. The government's preferred Level 3 thus contained the possible 'carrots', for example, of bus franchising, adult education, rail partnerships and possible control of PCCs, so long as their boundaries aligned. Again, these would be conditional on nationally laid down performance criteria, and of course subject to the financial limits set by the centre, leading Travers (2022), like many commentators, to the conclusion that there was actually 'very little real devolution on offer, simply a chance (subject to central agreement) for more places to become like existing areas with mayors, CAs and devolution deals. Levelling up will continue to be run from SW1.'

The consequences of austerity

The Coalition government from 2010 was able to portray the 2008 recession as a consequence of public spending. Chancellor George Osborne's initial plan for economic recovery involved an ambition to reduce the national deficit within four years, leading to 'the most significant period of fiscal retrenchment since the 1920s, with a time frame for deficit reduction that was ten years faster than the OECD recommended' (Slay and Penny, 2013: 10). Despite several extensions to the date at which austerity was to end, this financial tightening continued in the Conservative administrations from 2015 to the 'give away' Budget of January 2020, which was in turn subsequently overtaken by the impact of COVID-19 and followed by the impact of lower economic growth, high energy prices and inflation in 2022.

There are a number of calculations of the extent to which local government had lost funding due to austerity after 2010. The National Audit Office, in their submission to the House of Commons Housing,

Communities and Local Government Committee (HCLGSC) report into local government finance and the 2019 Spending Review, highlighted a real terms fall in government funding of local authorities of 49.1 per cent from 2010–17/18, equating to 'a 28.6% real-terms reduction in "spending power"' (HCLGSC, 2019: 7). Gray and Barford (2018: 553) found that between 2009/10 and 2016/17 the average reduction in service spending for local government in England was 23.7 per cent, in Scotland, 11.5 per cent and in Wales 12.1 per cent. This was mainly due to a reduction in Revenue Support Grant, from £15.4 billion in 2013/14 to £2.1 billion in 2019/20, meaning that central funding overall fell by 37 per cent per person on average. In Scotland and Wales the reductions were less sharp, at around 11 to 12 per cent, but still substantial. Devolution to Scotland and Wales gave those governments more discretion over where the impacts of austerity fell from within the block grants given to them by the Westminster government. Thus, cuts to local government in Scotland and Wales were not as extensive, nor did they proceed as quickly as in England, although this divergence began to narrow after 2015. In both countries, the impacts were spread more evenly geographically, although some urban areas like Glasgow were hard hit (Gray and Barford, 2018: 553).

In England, there was a 'patchwork' pattern of impacts. The actual level of cuts varied considerably from authority to authority, ranging from 46 per cent to 1.6 per cent. Gray and Barford (2018: 553) noted that 'the impact of reduced funding is likely to be most severe in areas with high concentrations of people who need local government services'. This was obviously related to politically motivated choices by the Coalition and Conservative governments to direct more resource to their own areas of support, at the expense of the largely Labour, and poorer, urban areas that are more dependent on the needs-based government grant, which was cut universally. These areas also have lower property values and lower council tax bases, and their local economies were less amenable to the sale of council assets (APSE, 2021). The New Policy Institute (2018, in APSE, 2021: 60) found that

> 97 per cent of the reduction in spending by English local authorities on services for adults and children facing disadvantage in the

five years from 2012 took place in the most deprived fifth of local areas, notably metropolitan and other urban areas concentrated in the North and Midlands, as well as coastal districts across England, where there are more demands for support.

Thus 'the more deprived areas tend to correlate with bigger cuts in service spending; in the less deprived areas service spending cuts tend to be smaller' (Gray and Barford, 2018: 554). The COVID-19 pandemic 'amplified such inequalities, laying bare the uneven distribution of resources and life chances across the country' (APSE, 2021: 13). Overall, these financial shocks saw councils increasingly use their reserves to balance budgets, leading to reduced financial resilience; in particular, smaller district authorities have been able to 'bounce back' and provide services, albeit at a lower standard, but with little leeway in finding additional scope to 'bounce forward' by improving and changing working practices (Coyle and Ferry, 2022). In 2020/21, nine councils required 'exceptional support' from central government in the form of 'capitalisation directions' allowing them to use capital funds to meet day-to-day revenue, which required, in each case, government approval – for example, Luton LBC was allowed an extra £35 million in 2021. The October 2021 Budget, however, left councils still facing the need to make cuts to services (Kenyon, 2021b). The councils of Croydon (in 2020) and Slough (2021) followed the earlier example of Northamptonshire in declaring bankruptcy by issuing a notice under Section 114 of the Local Government Act 1988, and the Public Accounts Committee in July 2021 warned of the dangers of a wave of bankruptcies, with Peterborough and Wirral Councils also facing the threat of Section 114 notices in November 2021.

Financial controls by central government have also been implemented through other means. With respect to schools, the new national funding formula, essentially a needs-based equalisation, was introduced in 2019/20, aimed to reduce further the remaining vestiges of council influence over funding by removing the discretion to pass on Dedicated Schools Grant according to a locally agreed formula. In some key service areas, then, there was a re-emphasis on centrally determined overall funding, coupled with fiscal equalisation aimed at delivering a consistent national standard of service

(Phillips, 2018). Central control was also tightened by the limitation of thresholds on council tax increases. At the same time, the intended path set for local government finance indicated by the Business Rates Retention Scheme (BRRS) and Fair Funding showed the tolerance of wider diversity in funding and service levels, in order to give greater incentives for promoting revenue growth and, in theory, greater accountability to local taxpayers. This is discussed further in Chapter 6. The incentivisation stance seen in the BRRS was also evident, for example, in the New Homes Bonus, introduced in 2011, by which government doubled the council tax local authorities received from new homes for several years after their completion (Wilson et al., 2017), and the Community Infrastructure Levy, which gave councils as planning authorities increased powers to negotiate financial contributions from developers. In yet other areas, there was some, if limited, increased discretion, for example over levels of business rate relief.

The 2019 Budget contained a 'relaxation' of austerity and additional spending for local government, adding to some extra support for social services. As will be discussed in Chapter 6, there was a growth in enthusiasm indicated in the May and Johnson governments to end austerity and also rebalance central–local relations by giving local authorities more capacity to fund services through their own means rather than through grants from the centre. In England, councils had been given the power from 2015 to raise an additional council tax precept of 1 per cent for spending on adult social care, which, together with additional government grants, increased spending, but still left it £0.4 billion below the 2011 level. The Johnson government of 2020–22 provided a series of budgets and spending settlements which loosened the financial constraints and provided local government with some much needed relief from the high point of austerity. This was partly the result of a change in the political landscape, with the government now, as part of its 'levelling up' agenda, keen to divert additional funding into certain local authority areas where they had won seats in the 2019 general election, in the form of targeted pots of funding. However, as outlined in the Introduction, the COVID-19 pandemic threw both council finances and central funding into uncharted territory, with funding streams being provided which still failed to meet the increased pressures councils faced. Austerity had left local governments ill-equipped to face the challenges posed by the pandemic, with inevitable consequences for the effectiveness of their response (Arrieta, 2022).

For local government generally, the 2021 Autumn Budget and financial settlement provided an extra £8.5 billion, with £4.8 billion of this to come from new grant funding, and the rest to be raised locally through council tax. However, this was not sufficient to meet existing demand for services (APSE, 2021); councils were able to keep services at 2019/20 levels, but would fall short by more than £1 billion by 2024/25 (LGA, 2021). In particular, funding would continue to be insufficient to meet rising demand for adult social care. The headline figure of an average 3 per cent increase in spending power became only 1.8 per cent once funding for proposed adult social care reforms was accounted for – an amount which would not come close to restoring the damage to other services due to austerity. The comparative relief from austerity, however, proved to be short-lived, with energy prices rising rapidly in 2022, and councils also having to deal with high inflation and wage demands. The 2022 Autumn statement saw the Sunak government deliver a better than expected settlement for local government, with core spending power assumed to rise by 13 per cent, including increased amounts raised from council tax and business rates, mostly channelled into social care. This assumed that councils would raise council tax, and now allowed up to 5 per cent total rises without the need for a local referendum, 2 per cent of which must be ring-fenced for social services for relevant authorities. Given earlier decisions and inflation, however, this would not be enough to return spending to pre-pandemic levels; and again, the least deprived councils would see a greater increase in spending power, and the most deprived the smallest (Pope et al., 2022), while also key difficult decisions about public spending were delayed until at least 2024.

For council services, then, the period of austerity represented a permanent reset, with a new norm for levels of service and funding. Moreover, the dependence on council tax for extra funding meant that again the biggest increases in spending would not necessarily go to the areas most in need. Suggested reforms to funding of adult social care in 2021, using money from a rise in National

Insurance contributions, were intended to raise £5.4 billion over three years, but were shelved pending further review, along with any long-term plans for social care reform, in the 2022 Autumn Statement. The LGA estimated that a recurring £1.5 billion per year was required to keep services at 2019/20 levels. Again, raising these sums would put an increasing burden on council tax and disadvantage the poorer areas (LGA, 2021). Widespread disappointment was expressed from the local government community and observers that the *Levelling Up* White Paper, in turn, contained no new funding commitments associated with the possible devolution deals (Werran, 2022) and that 'money in general [was] something of blind spot' (Carr-West, 2022).

The impact of cuts on services

As noted in the introduction to this chapter, local government's ability to provide its diminishing suite of services depends on having adequate resources to secure their implementation. Here we will deal with the financial effects of austerity on service delivery, returning to broader issues of the central–local balance of financial control in Chapter 6. There is no doubt that councils have met the requirements to make the extensive cuts without any overt resistance. Lobbying against the financial pressures from all types and sizes of council, of all political persuasions, and from the LGA and others, has been intense but councils do not have the freedom to rebel that they once had within the current legal framework.

Hastings et al. (2015) observed that three strategies had been used to meet the reduced budgets, which together serve to bring into stark relief the scope for meaningful local government autonomy. Firstly, councils increased efficiency, achieving savings from 'back office' functions, including staff reductions, redesigning services, making more use of digital technology and seeking to reduce costs with external providers. As a consequence, higher proportions of revenue spending went into social care. Thus, between 2010 and 2019, councils' net expenditure on planning and development and housing services had been reduced by over 50 per cent, on highways and transport, cultural and leisure services, including libraries, by more than 40 per cent, while spending on adult social care services had been cut by just 5 per cent and spending on acute children's social care services increased by around 10 per cent (IFS, 2019). Council planning departments had cut spending by half by 2018 (LGA, 2018a). Generally speaking, councils made cuts to discretionary services in order to protect mandatory ones, particularly social care services. As Hastings et al. (2015) noted, there was a limit to how much councils could 'squeeze' their operations to find efficiency savings, and some discretionary services, like libraries, were identified as 'early targets' for cuts.

This financial stress came on top of rising demand across services. The number of children in care in England, for example, increased by 27 per cent from 2009 to 2019 (HCLGSC, 2019). Between 2010 and 2019 the number of children with a child protection plan rose by 31 per cent and there were 108 per cent more referrals to children's social care services (APSE, 2021). Local authorities faced other cost pressures, such as higher National Insurance contributions, an apprenticeship levy and the National Living Wage (NAO, 2018). Councils also bore the consequences of cuts to other parts of the welfare state, with people needing housing support, for example, following council tax support reductions and a benefits freeze. A rise in homelessness required increased spending; there was a 71 per cent increase in households in temporary accommodation between 2011 and 2018 (HCLGSC, 2019). The rising cost of energy in 2022 and the increase in fuel poverty created extra pressures on councils to provide support and, in many cases, 'warm hubs' in public buildings. The impact also extended beyond personal services. In 2018 the Local Government Association (LGA, 2018a) estimated a backlog of £9 billion in pothole repairs for roads.

As the space for finding efficiency savings became ever smaller, councils had to focus on a second strategy: retrenchment. For example, local authority spending on children and young people's services fell by £536 million between 2010 and 2018, a 6 per cent reduction, and spending was increasingly taken up by statutory services and social care, such that social care now accounted for 57 per cent of local authority spending. Money was transferred from other, discretionary, areas of spending to support young people in crisis, with a shift away from early intervention and prevention towards late and crisis intervention (APSE, 2021; Gray and Barford, 2018). Retrenchment was implemented via a range of methods, including simply reducing the range of services, reducing the level of services and more specifically targeting them. One in ten libraries were shut between 2010/11 and 2016/17, and subsidised bus transport was cut by half, while 'hundreds of parks and playgrounds ... have also been shut' (Arnold and Stirling, 2019: 3). Councils increasingly used capital receipts from the sale of assets, ranging from town halls and historic buildings to open spaces, to meet the costs of staff redundancies and other savings. Between 2014 and July 2018, a total of £2.8 billion was raised in this way (Hancox, 2019). Other methods included increasing charges, or charging for services previously provided free of charge. Elements of 'self-help' or co-production of services also became more prominent as a range of service users were encouraged to make best use of their own resources and networks of family and friends, and 'civic responsibility' was called on more to make up for reductions in services (Hastings et al., 2015).

The third strategy saw an acceleration of investment, with opportunities now more widely available through powers given in the Localism Act of 2011. Councils sought to raise income and reduce the demand on services by encouraging economic growth, investment for capital growth or 'preventative' revenue spend. Examples include investment in assisted living technology to promote independence and reduce care costs, and in areas which were covered by them, councils signed up to growth deals, city and devolution deals designed to promote economic growth. However, more widely and controversially, councils turned to investments not only to facilitate growth but to generate revenue. The National Audit Office (NAO, 2020) reported that commercial property acquisitions by councils, including shopping centres, office blocks and hotels, increased fourfold from 2016/17 to 2018/19 compared with the previous three years, with 38 per cent of these acquisitions being outside of their boundaries. Warrington MBC's commercial portfolio, for example, reached a value of £500 million in 2021. External borrowing by local authorities had increased by £14.3 billion. Alongside this trend, councils resorted to more short-term borrowing and inter-council lending, moving from cash deposits to investment in money market funds and credit extension (Dagdeviren and Karwowski, 2022).

All of this was controversial, in terms of risk, and seemed to many simply inappropriate and 'not what councils are for'. Rob Whiteman of the Chartered Institute of Public Finance and Accountancy, in evidence to the Housing, Communities and Local Government Select Committee in 2019, noted that there had been some 'excessive' borrowing and gave the example of Spelthorne District Council, which 'had a £30 million turnover ... [and yet] borrowed £1 billion in order to invest commercially'. Such concerns were borne out in some cases as the COVID-19 pandemic impacted on commercial activity and thus income. The year following the pandemic, 2021, saw a 41 per cent reduction in commercial investments by councils, and property investment company assets fell by £12 million. Concerns about the scale of council investment led the government to change the rules for access to loans from the Public Works Loan Board and to change the Prudential Code governing borrowing, closing down the option of borrowing primarily for financial return, and in 2022 they closed a 'loophole' by which some councils sought to use receipts from selling assets to their arm's-length companies. The *Levelling Up* White Paper contained provisions for the government to require councils to sell assets or reduce borrowing levels.

The warnings of risks have proved to be accurate in several cases. 'Brick by Brick', an arm's-length housing company set up by Croydon LBC, accounted for over half the council's £66 million deficit in 2020/21. Spelthorne Council saw its commercial property portfolio decline in value by more than £100 million in the three years to 2022 (Hill, 2022b). A seemingly imaginative scheme by which Bournemouth, Poole and Christchurch Council was to sell its beach huts, effectively to itself, via a special purpose vehicle was prevented by the Minister for Levelling Up, Housing and Communities. Surrey County Council saw the value of two retail investments made in 2017 fall by more than half by 2022 (Rudgewick, 2022), while Thurrock Council in November 2022 'admitted [that] a series of disastrous investments in risky commercial projects caused it to run up an unprecedented deficit of nearly £500 million and brought it to the brink of bankruptcy' (Butler, 2022).

Some investment vehicles used by councils to secure developments were particularly controversial, one of the most high profile being the proposal by Haringey Council to build 4,600 new homes via a company, the Haringey Development Vehicle, in which the council owned a 50 per cent share, together with developer Lend Lease. Opposition to the proposals centred on the inadequate provision of affordable social housing and the displacement of existing tenants, and caused them to be dropped, leading to the resignation of the council leader in 2018. This is one of a number of new types of mechanism used, especially by London councils, to regenerate areas, which Beswick and Penny (2018: 612) labelled as

> speculative council-owned special purpose vehicles (SPV's) that replace existing housing stock with mixed-tenure developments, creating ambiguous public/private tenancies that function as homes and the basis for liquid financial assets.

The imposed austerity resulted in not only cuts in spending, but also changes to the organisational configuration of councils, including, as a result of enforced losses of staff, internal restructuring to create fewer departments, creating amalgamations of services and much reduced management teams (APSE, 2019b). In addition, it led to new organisational forms and ways of working via alternative 'arm's-length' arrangements which are indirectly related to the usual democratic oversight by councillors and more opaque with respect to accountability. Ferry et al. (2018) refer to this process as 'corporatization': the creation by councils of wholly or partly owned corporate entities. From 2010/11 to 2016/17, they found an increase from 400 to 600 of such companies, covering a range of trading concerns, with the number of companies limited by shares increasing from under 200 to 300, arguably leading to a 'field-level' change in the landscape of local governance (Ferry et al., 2018). This led in turn to a 'marketisation of income' (Taylor et al., 2021), with funds generated by trading activity increasingly supplementing council budgets. Again the risks of such reliance were exposed in some cases by the loss of trade during the pandemic. For example, North Yorkshire County Council's commercial subsidiaries, covering a spectrum from legal services to waste disposal, forecast losses of £640,000 for 2020/21. Councils which ventured into gas and electricity supply through the ownership or part-ownership of energy companies also found themselves at the mercy of market volatility, particularly as global gas prices increased in 2021 and 2022 (for example, in the case of Two Together, 50 per cent owned by Warrington MBC), or broader issues relating to the competitiveness of the market, as in the case of Nottingham City Council's Robin Hood Energy.

One other impact was that the smaller, second tier district councils, in particular, began to jointly commission services at an unprecedented rate. The LGA estimated in 2018 that £805 million of efficiency savings had been made through 550 shared service arrangements across a range of different services (LGA, 2018a). These involved joint contracts for back office tasks, administrative processing and IT infrastructure and maintenance services, and the sharing of personnel such as joint chief executives and senior officers. As seen in Chapter 3, at the same time a momentum was building for council mergers. In effect, many district councils were showing their inability to survive in the financial climate, paving the way for future mergers. While there is nothing inherently wrong with councils choosing to provide services jointly, these decisions were clearly driven by cost pressures imposed by central government rather than by local choice.

In addition to the immediate impact on services and the organisational impacts, austerity also served to refocus attention on the broader question of the financial relationship between local and central government. The decreased financial support went alongside a desire by central government to increasingly make local government dependent on locally raised funding, while at the same time restricting the ability to raise council tax beyond the centrally set limit, as will be seen in more detail in Chapter 6. However, there was a change of heart on this after 2020, which serves to illustrate clearly the expediency with which local government is treated by central government. For electoral purposes, the government now wished to direct more money towards some poorer areas and belatedly 'called time' on the previous approach which would have left those areas increasingly under-funded. Local government now found itself within the ministerial remit of the newly named Minister for Levelling Up, Housing and Communities, who reversed six years of government policy by telling the House of Commons Housing, Communities and Local Government Committee that moving to more dependency on local finance 'works against the process of redistributing money to those who need it most particularly in the wake of COVID-19' (Hill, 2021). Thus the issue of local government funding, it was clear, remained 'an annual football' (Carr-West, 2022) to be played with for party political gain.

Conclusion

Over time, then, local government's service responsibilities and financing have been see-sawing according to the overall direction of central policy, changing ideology concerning welfare and state provision, and straightforward political expediency. The period of austerity appears to have left an indelible mark on local government, what it provides and how it is structured and managed, which is, we would argue, as significant as the years of the Thatcher governments. The debate over the effects of a cumulative loss of services and of austerity outlined in this chapter, however, serves to further underline fundamental questions about the role of local government in the polity. We have seen that local councils had to adjust to new, often severely diminished service delivery responsibilities, and to implement the cuts, but at the same time they largely did all they could to mitigate their effects. This underlines the reality of local government's contradictory position at the 'nexus' of state and civil society, and as a locally representative body which is also embedded into the state welfare system as a delivery agent. The freedom to manoeuvre for local governments is highly constrained; many of the options for overt resistance to central government or for pursuing a distinctly divergent path have been closed down by legal and financial constraints. However, there will always be some space, even in the seemingly most inhospitable of climates, for local agency, discretion and resistances, even if they appear small in the context of the size of the challenges. Again it seems that during recent years the 'local' in local government has been buffeted further but has endured, and continues to resonate and to provide at least a tentative basis for distinctive political trajectories.

What, then, has been the effect on 'government' at local level? As we have seen, recent years have seen the continuation of a reduction in the role of local government in key services for which it once held major responsibilities – notably education, housing and social services. Remaining statutory powers have been further diminished, in particular since 2010 by austerity, while non-mandatory services like leisure, parks, culture and libraries have borne the brunt of the cuts. Without being able to secure the goods and services the public wants, and which significantly impact on the lives of its populations, local democracy lacks a substantive aspect and becomes emptied of effect. This raises the question of whether local government can be reimagined in democratic terms if it becomes effectively devoid of responsibilities for services.

It is possible to theorise a local government system which provides no, or very few, services, but acts as a conduit of local opinion to central government. This could still meet democratic criteria, with local government primarily functioning to reflect the local will to other tiers of government, and existing as an independent political entity (Denters et al., 2014). Here, while there is a clear political role, local government has few or no decision-making powers, and cannot therefore be deserving of the title 'government'. Alternatively, it could act as a 'hub' in a range of networks, being a local 'metagovernor', facilitating the search for democratic agreement, resolving conflict, orchestrating, facilitating and coordinating the activities of other agencies and a range of service providers, a role in which local government and local service delivery may or may not be aligned (Sullivan, 2011). However, in practical terms, local government, despite its efforts, remains too weak to perform these roles. Moreover, as Scharpf (1999: 6) notes, there are 'two faces of democratic self-determination': democratic decision-making requires procedural aspects involving participation to ensure that decisions reflect community preferences, but it also implies efficacy and the means of operationalising those preferences. There is a need for system capacity, which in practice cannot be secured through the 'soft power' of facilitation, but requires responsibility for the services which affect everyday life and which are the subject of local political contention.

This recognition brings us full circle, back to debates about how 'best' to marry democratic identity functions with technocratic and service delivery ones. This ideal, which Davies (2008) has called the 'holy grail' of practitioners and academics alike, is usually in practice portrayed as a trade-off, particularly in the discourse of policymakers and elites, as noted by, for example, the Widdicombe Committee, which was of the opinion that 'the more local authorities provide services that are central to people's lives, and seen to be so, the less realistic it becomes that they can be autonomous in the provision of those services' (Widdicombe, 1986: 54). We know that it is very difficult to reconcile democratic and technical functions, yet if we detach them we are left with weak local government (Stoker, 2011b). On the other hand, if local government is to be purely the best way of technically delivering services according to national criteria, then why should we bother with it as a political unit?

We would argue that a local government must have both 'local' and effective 'governmental' attributes, but that they will always remain more or less in tension. As already noted in the discussion of structures and scales in Chapter 3, the search to align effective service delivery, or capacity, with a scale conducive to democratic decision-making and a sense of locality has been at the heart of debates about local government for decades, and remains a tension for which there is no fixed solution. How small or large are the areas over which there should be capacity to act, and to what extent do they vary, issue to issue, or service to service? Our argument is that these are essential, perpetually valid questions, and that seeking to answer them will lead to settlements which will always be open to contestation as debates concerning the balance afforded to each of the 'two faces' wax and wane. However, we argue that often dubious evidence concerning system capacity and technical efficiency has dominated this settlement, and that addressing this balance in future requires starting from a different place. These arguments will be expanded in later chapters.

5

Restructuring democracy within local authorities

Local government in its present form rests fundamentally on elected councils. Representative democracy remains the key mechanism for collective decision-making and the, albeit indirect, expression of local preferences. Elected councillors are thus key to its effective functioning. However, restructuring of local government has led to a significant reduction in numbers of councillors, leaving 'Fewer councillors on Super-sized Councils' (Bottom and Game, 2012). In 1978/79 there were 23,141 councillors in England and Wales, each representing an average population of 2,139 (ONS, n.d.). Notably, these losses continued after 2010 without there being any major national reorganisation; in 2010 there were 21,300 councillors (Wilson and Game, 2011) and Game (2019) noted a 'quiet revolution' in the local electoral landscape, with a loss of 500 councillors since 2014 due to council mergers. By 2018 there were 18,904 councillors, each representing on average 3,117 citizens (LGA, 2019a; WLGA, 2015).

The increased workload for councillors from larger wards has added to long-term concerns over the decreasing attractiveness of standing in local elections, and further exacerbated difficulties in recruiting, retaining and motivating elected councillors, particularly among younger and more socially diverse candidates (Copus and Wall, 2017). Austerity also added additional stresses to the role, requiring constant hard choices, with less discretion, over cuts to services, while simultaneously further diluting the influence of the 'average' councillor over services which are shared, outsourced or now run at 'arm's length'. Councillors not involved in strategic decision-making have found themselves increasingly in the dark concerning the details of contractual arrangements which directly impact on their wards and which may be in place for twenty-five years. As Parker (2013: 16) has put it, 'The move towards service commissioning cuts councillors out of much day-to-day decision-making, while the move towards slicker customer contact centres means that citizens can increasingly resolve their problems directly with the council.'

A notable further challenge to the status of councillors, however, has been an associated focus away from formal representation to alternative forms of political engagement, and the rise of new and more informal types of activism and modes of participation. Sweeting and Copus (2012) noted that local democracy by that time was a mixture of forms of local representative, participatory, market and network activities which posed questions for the role of councillors. Attempts at participatory innovation had become more prevalent as a result of local government initiatives, for example in the use of citizens' juries, and more generally through the growing desire to supplement representative politics with more deliberative mechanisms. 'Market' democracy arose through the growing emphasis on the direct input of citizens into local services by enhancing choice from a range of providers, while 'network' democracy, or 'governance driven democratization' (Warren, 2009), is identified as the outcome of the growth of partnership, collaboration and co-production, stressing the inclusion of all knowledgeable and interested parties.

The role of the councillor, then, has been under severe pragmatic pressure and appears to be on increasingly shaky theoretical ground. There have been many attempts to categorise the types of representative roles councillors have played, including the classical categories of trustee, delegate and party representative, and it is true to say that there has never been a unified role model for the councillor as representative (see Copus, 2008). Given this, it may be that persisting in arguing for councillors' core role in underpinning local democracy may be the equivalent of 'flogging a dead horse' (Richardson, 2012). On the other hand, others have laid the blame for this increasing lack of relevance at the door of councillors themselves. Sweeting and Copus (2012) noted councillors' unwillingness to accept or adapt to demands placed on them by the diversity of political activity taking place in their localities, and in particular being unwilling to take seriously citizen-based participatory initiatives, arguing that by so doing they were ensuring their future irrelevance. Copus (2010) similarly noted that councillors retained an attachment to traditional 'Burkean' notions of representation, focussing on output democracy via decision-making at the expense of input democracy through citizen involvement, and that they continued to see themselves as trustees for their electorates rather than delegates. These debates about the place of the councillor in the local democratic mix thus go to the heart of what we mean when we discuss local democracy, what forms it takes or should take, and how those various democratic practices fit together. These themes will be discussed further in Chapter 9.

In line with the areas of service responsibilities and finance which we have discussed in the previous chapters, concern with councillor behaviour reflects an expedient attitude towards them from central policymakers and a long-standing desire to ensure that councillors comply with expected forms of behaviour. These expectations have waxed and waned according to the dominant thinking among central actors, and in particular following the changing fashions in management theory. For more than five decades, government White Papers, select committee and expert inquiries, not to mention think-tank reports and sundry media representations, have sought to address the perceived inadequacies of councillors, either through institutional reforms or through exhortations to change behaviour through processes of socialisation and training. The Redcliffe-Maud Commission (1966–69) (Redcliffe-Maud, 1969) and the report of the Maud Committee on the Management of Local Government (Maud, 1967) identified the professionalisation and managerialisation of local councillors, together with an increase in the size of local councils, as key to the management of now expanded responsibility for welfare services. The qualities deemed to be required were derived from the managerial and professional skills associated with the corporate planning and associated coordination then popular in the business world, with leading councillors needing to become more technocratic and 'managerial', and less 'political' (Barnett et al., 2019).

As time went on, the managerialist blueprint developed in line with neoliberal thinking. In the 1980s and into the 1990s, corporate planning came to be seen as an expensive overhead, and the logics of competition, efficiency and contracting skills now required councillors to develop the commercial or 'enabling' skills of the New Public Management. Again, organisational reforms were suggested to facilitate the development and practising of these skills, and to limit councillors' roles to more 'strategic' matters, with them meddling or 'interfering' less in detail and encroaching on the managerial domain of officers. The Audit Commission (1990) thus recommended separating out policy-making and 'operational' roles. Council leaders were now encouraged to focus on strategy, while others got on with the more 'day-to-day' business of representing their wards (Barnett et al., 2019; DoE, 1993).

The New Labour governments built on this legacy of promoting the latest fashionable management theories and undertook institutional reforms intended to facilitate their take-up. More emphasis was placed on indirect methods aimed at bringing about the desired change in councillor 'quality' and on hopes that councillors would internalise the appropriate behaviours (Hale, 2013). Training programmes delivered by an Improvement and Development Agency, and via in-house council training, coupled with the promotion of a strategic, 'visionary' outlook through the Comprehensive Performance Assessment, aimed for both compliance with the government's agenda and the development of particular attitudes and dispositions towards it (Barnett, 2003). As Hale (2013) notes, these attempts to encourage 'self-responsibilisation' became increasingly prescriptive, evolving into role descriptors, councillor contracts and performance reviews, such that the language of management now permeated the democratic 'world' which councillors occupied. Labour's modernisation agenda also emphasised a new managerialist rhetoric, emphasising leadership skills, associated with a strategic executive core, which would 'steer, rather than row'. In addition, the fragmented local governance environment was now deemed to require – in line again with in-vogue managerialist thinking – the 'soft skills' of partnership and networking. As Barnett et al. (2019: 784) note, the 'neoliberal mk2' councillor was 'to be a risktaker, entrepreneur, innovator and facilitator, characteristics that were consistent with the popular "excellence" school of managerialism'.

Executives and scrutiny

The most comprehensive attempt to reform and clarify councillor roles was undertaken in England and Wales via the Local Government Act 2000, which for the first time formally recognised different types of councillor. Ostensibly, this was to help with the 'democratic deficit' in local affairs, making council leadership more visible, and bringing greater accountability and transparency by the separation of the roles of executive and scrutiny. It sought to formally recognise what had in fact for several decades been the reality, that most councils had a leadership team made up of the ruling party, and was also a reflection of growing dissatisfaction at the centre with the amount of time councillors were spending on 'detail' in committees. As Rao (2000: 164) noted, the committee system had been for some time 'local government's most criticised feature', with the Redcliffe-Maud, Maud and Bains Committees in the late 1960s and early 1970s all lamenting its faults and calling for a 'rationalisation' of the division of work between officers and councillors.

Viewed in an alternative way, reform represented an enhancement of interference in the affairs of local councils, which now extended to directing them on how to organise their political management internally. The Act did give councils some leeway, offering them the choice of adapting three systems: a DEM and Cabinet; a leader and a Cabinet/executive; or a DEM with a council manager. A council manager was adopted by only one council, Stoke-on-Trent, but was removed as an option in the Local Government and Public Involvement in Health Act 2007. Authorities with populations under 85,000 were allowed to keep an 'enhanced' committee system (Stewart, 2003: 61). Initially, an elected mayor could only be adopted following endorsement in a referendum, proposed by the council or requested by 5 per cent of the electorate, or at the discretion of the Secretary of State. The requirement for referenda was also removed in the 2007 Act, leaving the decision in the hands of the council.

In practice, the proposals were resisted in local government and the 'line of least resistance' (Stoker, 2004: 127), a leader and Cabinet/executive, was almost universally adopted, save for a handful of councils which adopted a mayoral model. In fact, this reflected closely what was already the norm, with a de facto executive being formed by the chairs of the main committees and overseen by the leadership of the majority party. This pattern shows the institutional resilience of existing practices, pointing to the path-dependent nature of the changes, particularly given the local choice which was allowed (Gains et al., 2005) and the 'triumph' of local contexts over national prescription (Ashworth and Snape, 2010). Suffice to say that there was disappointment in central government at the lack of enthusiasm for what was seen as a potentially significant reform. There was some tentative support for the changes; Gains et al. (2005) noted some evidence that councils with clearer executive leadership had started to show signs of better than average performance, and were developing new styles of 'facilitative' leadership. However, the most significant changes were felt by councillors who were not part of the executive, and no longer had their traditional role as committee members. These 'backbench' councillors were instead to take up scrutiny roles.

Overview and scrutiny was promoted as the means by which the executive could be held to account, with scrutiny committees being free to challenge the executive and suggest areas for investigation. In practice, the now more formal recognition of executive roles, and the loss of decision-making powers which they had on committees disempowered non-executive councillors, leaving local decision-making even more of an 'insider game' (Fenwick et al., 2003: 29) and in effect creating 'two tribes' of councillors, one of which felt increasingly left out of council decision-making (APSE, 2014). This malaise has been attributed to persisting institutional factors, with scrutiny not being supported and resourced properly and failing to become embedded culturally as part of the ethos and practices of councils (Ashworth and Snape, 2010; House of Commons Communities and Local Government Committee, 2017). The executive core of councils also became more prominent due to austerity. An existing managerial trend towards fewer, more strategic council departments was accelerated by a need to find savings by slimming organisational structures and having fewer chief officers – who now found themselves with large portfolios covering a range of council services, with titles like 'Director of Place' (APSE, 2019b). Inevitably, and despite the best efforts of council officers, less time was then available for senior staff to deal with councillors outside of the executive leadership team.

A prominent line of criticism has been that the division of responsibilities was in itself a good idea which had potential to reinvigorate local democracy, but it was out of step with the reality of local government, dominated by party politics, which remained the 'elephant in the room'. Simply, for such critics, councillors remained in the 'grip' of parties, and were thus unlikely to criticise their leadership in public (Copus, 2010). Leach and Copus (2004) thus pointed to the intransigence of party group discipline which was thwarting the development of effective scrutiny. Councillors remained stubborn and wedded, according to this interpretation, to 'old' and 'traditional' ways. Overall, the fate of the scrutiny role is perhaps best explained by the fact that no real serious thought was given to the role of the majority of councillors in practical terms; the focus in the agenda was to create a number of easily identifiable leaders, and scrutiny was 'more an afterthought in a reform agenda primarily focussed on different goals or performance' (Cole and McAlister, 2015: 235).

A new role for councillors?

Along with the oversight and scrutiny function, in England and Wales 'backbench' councillors were encouraged to forge a new role for themselves. New Labour portrayed their reforms as an opportunity for councillors to fully develop as 'community champions' as part of a broader 'democratic renewal' agenda. This was to involve a measured balancing of interests and a democratic and developmental role with regard to active citizenship and community engagement. Councils would be involved in 'developing means for users and local people effectively to challenge councils when things go wrong in individual cases and collectively in the face of persistent poor performance' (ODPM, 2004: 18) . This 'democratic facilitator' role was increasingly being envisaged at neighbourhood level (ODPM, 2005) with councillors becoming 'mini mayors', or champions of neighbourhoods. The White Paper *Strong and Prosperous Communities* (DCLG, 2006), and the subsequent Local Government and Public Involvement in Health Act 2007, contained several initiatives aimed at strengthening both the accountability of local authorities and their role as nurturer of democracy. These included empowering councillors to raise issues with overview and scrutiny committees, providing new powers to review and scrutinise the actions of key local public service providers, and the establishment of local involvement networks to 'ensure local communities have a stronger voice in the process of commissioning health and social care and can influence key decisions about the services they use' (DCLG, 2008a). Specifically, the Act placed on local authorities in England a new duty to inform, consult and/or involve citizens and communities in local authority services, policies and decisions.

Continuing the theme of community empowerment, the 'Empowerment' White Paper, *Communities in Control: Real People, Real Power* (DCLG, 2008a), trailed the introduction of a new duty to promote democracy. The subsequent Local Democracy, Economic Development and Construction Act 2009 sought 'to make local authorities the democratic hubs of the locality, encouraging involvement including taking civic roles' (DCLG, 2008b: 10). Although this requirement was dropped by the incoming Coalition government and 'democratic renewal' was less of an explicit theme in the following Conservative administrations, the rethinking of roles along these lines continued in discourse in and around local government.

The Coalition, May and Johnson governments

The governments after the 2010 general election were less concerned with formal consideration of councillor roles. The Coalition government bowed to pressure for the reinstatement of the committee system, allowing its readoption in England via the Localism Act of 2011. However, a rhetorical commitment to revised roles was maintained, with some elements of their programme arguably requiring an associated change in the orientation of councillors for them to become 'community champions' (Shapps, 2010). The Localism

Act sought to devolve community assets and services to community groups or service users, with councillors to aid the process by connecting them to the council and to other sources of advice. In fulfilling their role, the Minister for Housing, Communities and Local Government called in July 2016 for councillors to be 'practical and pragmatic, not doctrinaire' (Clark, 2016). An apolitical neutrality was again envisaged, to enable councillors 'to adequately and successfully build their relationship, work and reputation with the whole community they have been elected to serve, not just their political supporters' (LGiU, 2018). By 2022 most councils in England and Wales operated the leader/Cabinet/scrutiny model, with some choosing to return to committees, while in Scotland and Northern Ireland most councils, having a choice, continued with the committee system. While not arousing widespread public interest, these arrangements have on occasion provoked controversy. In Sheffield, the committee system was reintroduced in 2022 after a referendum held in the previous year, following popular opposition to the Council's decision-making procedures when approving the contract which had resulted in a contentious tree-felling exercise in the city.

Overall, a vision of the '21st Century Councillor' (Mangan et al., 2016) as facilitator repositioned the councillor as 'advocate for everyone – including people from different backgrounds, cultures and values ... a conflict broker' (James and Cox, 2007: 22). This resonated with broader discussion of local government's role amidst competing claims, not just for resources, but for democratic legitimacy in their areas, to which we will return in Chapter 9. Taking such positions would place councillors 'on the boundary' between the formal setting of the council and a range of types of participation and political practice outside of it, requiring them to act as 'dual intermediaries' (Hendriks, 2006), providing a link between various publics and the 'hard' institutional decision-making of the local authority. Councillors, like local government generally, do have a place in both worlds. They are a part of the formal system of decision-making, but are themselves largely laypeople and amateurs, and as such offer a source of a 'loose coupling' between informal sites of deliberation and the 'hard' decision-making institutions of local government. The councillor as facilitator may also claim democratic credence as a metagovernor or guardian of democratic health, ensuring fair access and 'managing the mix' of formal and informal public discourses in a locality, as suggested by 'second generation' governance theorists who recognise the importance of elected politicians in providing legitimacy and democratic 'grounding' for this role (Sorensen and Torfing, 2005).

For some, however, councillors appeared to remain 'stubborn' and in particular 'tend to display a lukewarm, unenthusiastic attitude towards many participation mechanisms' (Sweeting and Copus, 2013: 121). In most places, roles remained unchanged. The reasons for this reluctance may be institutional and context-specific. Karlsson (2013) found that 'party soldier' councillors, more resistant to such changes of role, were more common in larger local authorities in Europe, and especially in Britain given its comparatively large councils. Similarly, councils whose role has traditionally been more focussed on service delivery than interest mediation may be reasonably assumed to contain councillors with a more instrumental than facilitative orientation, and this service delivery/instrumental model would certainly seem to fit Britain (Vabo and Aars, 2013), which belongs to a model of local government which emphasises efficient service delivery at the expense of community engagement, therefore making any move away from an established 'traditional' model more difficult (Plüss and Kübler, 2013). It seems that fundamental changes to councillor roles are irrevocably tied to wider issues concerning local government's position in the democratic 'mix' of the polity and the principles which underpin it.

In practice, dealing with the day-to-day issues raised by constituents has long been the meat and drink of the work of the councillor, who on average spends 6.2 hours per week engaging with constituents, surgeries and enquiries, and 4.1 hours with community groups, as opposed to 8.1 hours taken up with council meetings (LGA, 2018b: 5). However, for non-executive councillors a major issue remains their lack of impact on decision-making. The evidence shows that councillors generally consider themselves to be quite uninfluential when it comes to decisions on local affairs, and most do not share the optimism that the loss of some powers may be compensated by 'new', broader political roles as 'leaders' or 'orchestrators' (Egner et al., 2013). As noted in Chapter 4, community leadership and models of local government are not democratic in terms of 'outcome' legitimacy if they do not also contain the ability to have an actual impact on decision-making.

The debate concerning councillors has also paid insufficient attention to the institutional designs which might allow for connections between public discourse and locations of power and decision-making. Firstly, the growth of unitary authorities, the amalgamation or disappearance of many district authorities and the creation of new agencies such as police and crime commissioners have decreased the number and influence of councillors, leaving them increasingly with many roles, including representing what they can discern as local opinion within a wide range of communities, and with often indirect contact or channels of influence with a range of other bodies in the local governance environment. The emphasis on consensual politics which has permeated the debate also advanced utopian notions of depoliticisation, with councillors 'of the future [moving] to play a supportive rather than an unnecessarily antagonistic role' (Copestake, 2011: 50). Conflicts are, however, an integral part of politics at any scale, and the size of councillors' wards makes it more likely that the councillor will be required, of necessity, to play a more traditional role as representative. In this sense, without undertaking a more serious consideration of the implications for democratic practice, there has been too much of a haste to both underplay and sometimes dismiss the importance of representation, and the 'stage' of formal elective politics (Rummens, 2012).

Moreover, if councillors are to provide a 'linkage' between formal and informal settings, fostering deliberation and engagement, we not only have to consider the strength of their links to the wider formal and informal governance of the locality, but also their relationship with the important arenas of decision-making, both in the council and beyond. In the case of British local government, these are largely located in Whitehall. In short, councillors have little power or influence to operationalise the role, reimagined or not. Rummens (2012), like Hendriks (2006), calls for a consideration of how 'micro' deliberative sites (which backbench councillors have been encouraged to foster) relate to the 'macro' centres of power. Councillors may or may not encourage and provide a connection between local civil society and local authority decision-making, but, as Parkinson (2007: 26) notes,

> In a localist environment, one can think that a given deliberative process is a good one; and that the local bureaucrats who respond to it have all the willingness in the world; but they often lack the authority to make the macro-level changes that are often necessary to ensure that local initiatives make a difference.

There may be good reasons, in terms of context, then, why the role of the backbench councillor appears to be in limbo. Also, there are practical difficulties. Even advocates of the 'community champion' role recognise that it will require considerable skill, support and effort (Sorensen and Torfing, 2009). At best, councillors would have a tricky balancing act to perform: needing to be both open and neutral minded, while representing their constituents and also party, and having views of their own on the basis of which they stood for election. Following Hoppe (2011), they would be required to be facilitator, process manager, director of the show, counsellor to all parties, interpreter between all parties and empowerer of the weaker parties. Given the number of competing roles councillors have traditionally been required to bear, it seems an understatement that this might appear onerous, if indeed possible. Councillors would be required, unreasonably, to resolve clashes between local representative and participatory democracy, as well as to meet increasing demands from service users for more engagement and flexibility in local provision (Carr-West, 2013; Lepine and Sullivan, 2010). Councillors can provide a link between formal discursive arenas at local level and the messier local macro environment of 'life outside', but this role is fraught with tensions and is far more difficult to operationalise than has been assumed, particularly in a centralised polity. The argument here is that the more recent exhortations for councillors to change, when unpacked, have paid insufficient attention to some of these dilemmas and tensions, which remain inherent in democratic politics. Such considerations need to be at the forefront when considering how to revive local government and make it meaningful in practice.

Directly elected mayors

Behind the 'modernisation' of council decision-making and the strengthening of executive leadership, there has been an interest in central government to promote political leadership through the introduction of directly elected mayors (DEMs). In keeping with the more general subservience of local government to issues of perceived economic necessity, the leaders suited to the new governance landscape have been those deemed to be 'deal makers' in a world of networks, partnerships and complex, tangled social and economic problems. The value of having 'strong' leaders – charismatic individuals who could provide a ready answer to the question 'who is in charge?', and with the power to exercise 'transformational' leadership – became established as part of the discourse of economic growth (Heseltine, 2012).

In this environment, political leadership was deemed to be failing, outdated and in need of high-profile political leaders who could 'articulate the demands of their town or city' (Stoker, 2004: 137). City leaders in particular were seen to be increasingly important in driving economic growth, and 'place leadership' was necessary for promotion and to attract investment. For its advocates in New Labour, a mayoral system was also associated with the 'democratic renewal' agenda, providing a clearer focus of accountability, and the hope that charismatic individuals would stand for election and boost interest in local affairs (Hope and Wanduragala, 2010: 6).

However, for New Labour and subsequent governments, the overriding incentive has been more to 'cut through the lengthy processes of local democratic institutions by providing streamlined high-profile leadership' (Fenwick and Elcock, 2014: 581) and, particularly in their later incarnation as 'metro mayors', associated with devolution deals and CAs to provide central government with a convenient figurehead with whom to cut deals. The first DEM was elected in London in 2000, having been created by the Greater London Authority Act of 1999 following a referendum in 1998. The Local Government Act of 2000 allowed for all councils in England and Wales to adopt a DEM, initially following a referendum in favour. This did not apply in Scotland. Only eleven councils initially adopted DEMs, mostly owing to particular local circumstances. Of these, the post was subsequently abolished in three places: Stoke-on-Trent in 2008, Hartlepool in 2012 and Torbay in 2019, following referenda; other referenda, in Middlesborough (2013) and North Tyneside (2016), saw votes in favour of retaining a DEM (Fenwick and Elcock, 2014; Sandford, 2021). Two councils, Liverpool and Leicester, introduced DEMs via council resolution using the power given to them in 2007, and the government clearly hoped that this route would lead to their greater uptake following earlier lack of interest or negative referendum votes. However, in general, DEMs did not capture the imaginations of either councils or the public.

The Coalition government sought to revive and add impetus to the policy in the 2011 Localism Act by calling for referenda in England's ten largest cities, but only one, Bristol, voted in favour, while further referenda in Tower Hamlets (2010), Salford (2012) and Copeland (2014) led to the adoption of a DEM, leaving by 2022 a total of just fifteen local authorities with DEMs. In total, of fifty-four referenda between 2001 and 2016, only sixteen saw a vote in favour of a DEM. Further, turnouts for both referenda and mayoral elections were poor, indicating that the suggested impact on local democratic health had not materialised. Indeed, in Wales there proved to be no interest in the mayoral model at all, with only one referendum being held to adopt one, and all councils choosing the leader and Cabinet model. The Northern Ireland Assembly chose not to adopt it as an option for councils. Despite this lack of public support, since 2010 DEMs not only remained on the agenda in England, but rose in importance in policy agendas (Fenwick and Elcock, 2014). They were a component of successive governments' 'devolution' agendas, while the focus moved from single authority leadership to 'metro mayors' elected for CAs in city regions, as detailed in Chapter 3. Increasingly, and to the frustration of many councils seeking devolution deals, government policy was firstly not to impose elected mayors, but to require DEMs as part of any deal, on the grounds that 'it's right people have a single point of accountability: someone they elect, who takes the decisions and carries the can' (Wintour, 2015).

Under the provisions of the Cities and Local Government Devolution Act of 2016, constituent councils who did not agree to a DEM would be removed from the area of a CA. Mayors would thus be introduced very much on the terms of central government. In 2017, DEMs were elected for newly created CAs in the West Midlands, the West of England, Liverpool, Manchester, Cambridge with Peterborough, and Tees Valley, with a metro mayor being elected for the then Sheffield City Region CA (since renamed as the South Yorkshire CA) in 2018, and for North of Tyne CA in 2019. An election for the West Yorkshire CA took place in 2021, bringing the total number of DEMs in England up to twenty-four (Sandford, 2021). Public interest and electoral turnout, however, remained low, the highest being 36.5 per cent in West Yorkshire, the lowest being 21 per cent in Tees Valley. Metro mayors could potentially have responsibility for a 'menu' of functions, depending on the deal struck with the centre, thus having, on the face of it, considerable power. However, as seen in Chapter 3, these powers have been considerably constrained by financial and performance controls from central government.

After the departure of George Osborne from central government there was greater equivocation over whether or not to impose DEMs as a condition of further devolution deals and restructuring in general. In particular, the lack of enthusiasm from shire counties to form mayoral CAs was seen to be a major stumbling block in the rolling out of the CA model in these areas. Robert Jenrick, Communities and Housing Minister, indicated in July 2020 that mayors would be part of a reorganization, with 'greater powers and financial incentives to be given to local councils who embrace reform' (Elledge, 2020), pointing to a continuation of the contractual/conditional approach. There was clearly party political motivation at play here, with Conservatives calculating that they had more chance of winning the mayoralties in combined areas which otherwise had individual Labour councils (Smyth, 2020).

As seen in Chapter 3, the *Levelling Up* White Paper of February 2022 set out the Johnson government's intentions for incremental change and of continuing the policy of not enforcing a DEM model. However, the incentives associated with 'Level 3' devolution made it clear that DEMs were intended to be the direction of travel.

Again, the benefits of 'strong' leadership were expounded, and accountability was associated mainly with clarity of responsibility. The 'benefits to be found from having a prominent, accountable individual in an area' were extolled (HM Government, 2022: 333). Such strong leaders would provide coherence across 'sensible geographies' and provide a clear focus, of course, also for central government monitoring within the newly proposed Performance Framework. Thus the preferred model of devolution was 'one with a directly-elected leader covering a well defined economic geography with a clear and direct mandate, strong accountability and the convening power to make change happen' (HM Government, 2022: 336). This 're-boosting' of the mayoral programme was underlined by the inclusion in the White Paper of the intention to create a new mayoral CA by combining the City of York with the newly created North Yorkshire unitary (see Chapter 3). The White Paper also underlined a recommitment to 'strong' leadership in single councils despite the earlier ambiguity towards it during the Coalition years, stating that 'Where an area does not have a directly elected leader, devolution needs a clear decision-making structure. For a single large local authority, this means a leader and cabinet system' (HM Government, 2022: 137). However, there remained resistance, with areas indicating that they would opt for a more limited devolution deal rather than accept an elected mayor. This was the case with Hull and East Riding, as noted in Chapter 3, and with Devon, Plymouth and Torbay (Kenyon, 2022). In contrast, Derbyshire and Nottinghamshire, previously reluctant to adopt a joint mayor, by mid-2022 were willing to accept one for an East Midlands CA.

The democratic consequences

The equivocation over mayors reveals a lot about the status of local government in Britain and the state of local democracy. DEMs have hardly proven popular, but their use is determined by calculations of advantage by central government. Leaving that aside, the issue of whether DEMs could and should become more prominent is open to debate. Certainly, to be effective, DEMs would need more powers, autonomy and financial independence like some of their overseas counterparts. Their introduction in England, in the current context of weak local government, has reinforced the increasing centralism and provided a number of 'strong leaders' – a relatively small number with whom Whitehall can deal directly, and who are seen to be a 'cut above' local authorities (Roberts, 2020) – further marginalising mainstream local government. Party political considerations have played a large part; New Labour hoped that 'strong' individual mayors would be likely to be less troublesome than, potentially, some urban local authorities, while since 2010 the Conservatives have seen mayoral elections as a possible means for gaining an electoral hold in areas traditionally held by Labour, as indeed happened in Teeside.

The lack of opacity and democratic engagement in the construction of the associated deals, and the speed with which they were made reinforces this impression, as does the highly constrained legal and financial environment in which mayors have to operate. Moreover, alongside the creation of CAs and subregional bodies, it could be argued that mayors have added to the complexity of the system of local government, further clouding rather than enhancing accountability, with potentially problematic relationships with existing councillors and managers in the constituent councils and a direct relationship to the electorate which cuts across that of councillors. Roberts (2020) reported that council leaders generally had been unconvinced by the 'added value' of mayors, but had pragmatically accepted them, while also having seen mayors step into areas of policy like homelessness, which were council responsibilities, thus leading to a 'drawing upwards' of powers rather than devolution.

More seriously, the actions of subregional mayors are subject to overview and scrutiny committees, made up, in the case of CAs, by councillors co-opted from constituent councils, but it can also be argued that they further reduce the role of councillors, particularly 'backbenchers', now one step further removed from decision-making (Roberts, 2020). In this sense, the London DEM stands out as having some clarity that is missing in the other cases, as the mayor is accountable to the directly elected, twenty-five-member Greater London Assembly. However, the mayoral relationship with councillors in the London Borough councils is opaque, as the fourteen Assembly constituencies are made up of amalgamations of council areas plus eleven members who are elected as London-wide representatives. The mayor holds key strategic powers, preparing the Plan for London and promoting general well-being through influencing other bodies. There are also important executive powers including running Transport for London, and in police, crime and fire services. Again, there is complexity in the overlap and sharing of responsibilities with the London boroughs, with for example the mayor being responsible for setting a conurbation-wide waste management strategy and councils being responsible for the service itself.

Taking a more positive view, several writers have pointed to the success of mayors' facilitative leadership styles (Gains et al., 2007) and in forging a clear role as the out-facing representative of a city, like Liverpool, in need of a global profile (Headlam and Hepburn, 2017). Ayres et al. (2018) suggest that in future mayors may become adept at exploiting 'cracks and wedges' in the government's agenda, as noted in Chapter 3. Thus, despite central government's intentions, 'the genie may well be out of the bottle' (Roberts, 2020: 1010). Certainly, the Mayor of Manchester, Andy Burnham, during the COVID-19 pandemic showed how an astute politician with an elected mandate can use the position for impact, regardless of what 'hard power' they may actually possess.

Similarly, those dismissive of the 'strong leader' caricature have focussed on the new forms of relational local leadership required to secure public value goals amidst the 'shared power' demands of a complex governance environment, the global economy and diverse channels of political engagement. They stress that such conditions had made strategic, visionary leadership, which works across institutional and territorial boundaries at local scale, more important than ever (Beer and Clower, 2014; Liddle, 2010). Hambleton (2019), using the example of Bristol, identified a 'New Civic Leadership' based on collaboration, conducive to innovation, and a 'place based leadership' (Hambleton, 2016) which is grounded in the differing values, beliefs and norms, and the possibilities and limits, of places. Sweeting and Hambleton (2020) also use the Bristol example to note a leadership style which is more outgoing on the international stage, and that business interests in particular have a more positive attitude to this form of leadership. By practising 'interactive political leadership' (Sorensen and Torfing, 2019), such leadership models are seen to embrace inclusive styles conducive to enhancing democratic engagement, with elected leaders bridging the gap to new forms of citizen participation.

This shift in emphasis towards strategic, visionary leadership has thus been associated with the discourse around community leadership and metagovernance discussed earlier in the context of councillor roles. This is seen to require a set of 'soft' relational skills as a style befitting the twenty-first century (Mangan et al., 2016). However, in turn, taking into consideration the broader context within which local government sits, this discourse of 'Leaderism' (O'Reilly and Reed, 2010) can equally be seen as an evolution of the New Public Management of the 1980s as it morphed into a newer managerialist format in the 1990s in the New Labour years (Lawler, 2008; Newman, 2005), taking on as it evolved a more 'inclusive' format (Cochrane, 2007). This mangerialism puts more emphasis on cultural organisational controls, 'empowerment', 'vision', 'transformational' leadership and the harnessing of 'soft' leadership skills with entrepreneurial spirit and innovation. Political leadership here is interpreted as an all-encompassing format which allows for both 'soft' horizontal networking and 'strong' vertical accountability in the form of a clearly recognisable individual (Melo and Baiocchi, 2006). This version of leadership can, then, be interpreted as a set of practices, discourses and narratives designed to address contradictory tensions in managerialism – placing leaders at 'the nexus of control and delegation' by the construction of a common goal between leaders and led (O'Reilly and Reed, 2010).

In this light, this focus on leadership can be associated with a second or 'consolidating' phase of 'roll-out' neoliberalism, which seeks to combine economic growth with social cohesion (Geddes and Sullivan, 2011: 404). The 'participatory twist' in this discourse of leadership is supported by political rhetoric around inclusion and community engagement, underpinned by a consensual discourse, serving to present an imaginary, post-political 'harmony' within places (Guarneros-Meza and Geddes, 2010), and to incorporate or 'outflank' resistance via the 'internalising of disparate interests' (O'Reilly and Reed, 2010: 1095). Seen in the light of this broader context of advanced managerialism, then, the promotion of the mayor as a relational, empowering and facilitating figure is interpreted as being part and parcel of a governing strategy which seeks to 'control at a distance', cloaked in the language of local empowerment.

These techniques, however, as we point out further in Chapter 7, again do not completely shut down the democratic potential of mayors, even in the current environment, meaning that to some extent the jury is out. The extent to which the turn to leadership is conducive to healthy local government depends on the extent to which local agents are deemed to have space for degrees of autonomous action in the social, economic, legal, financial and cultural context in which they operate. Some have argued that, despite inhospitable conditions, it is worth persisting with the DEM idea, and that indeed DEMs provide a route towards a necessary leadership of place. Gains et al. (2005) noted that mayoral leadership showed tentative signs of leading to improved local government efficacy, and that while existing institutional path dependencies were preventing its widespread adoption, this evidence would lead to its increasing use, as a 'tipping point' would be reached and the model would become established as the new norm. This tipping point has never been reached, as we have noted, but in the meantime austerity and COVID-19 have occured, and measures of effectiveness have changed, preventing, it could be argued, the further development of the potentialities of the model. Similarly, Copus suggests that councils which had adopted a mayoral executive model had seen 'some success' (Copus, 2008: 598). Copus (2010, 2013) and Stoker (2004) both identify DEMs as an inherently positive model for local government, hampered by resistance which is deep-rooted in institutional practices. Copus in particular explains the lack of enthusiasm for the model as being rooted in the self-interested domination of party groups unwilling to embrace new forms of democratic engagement. In this light, the number of independent, non-party-affiliated candidates elected as mayors (seven out of twenty-two by 2012) is seen as a positive step towards embracing a new local political reality (Lodge, 2012: 29). Copus and Dadd (2014) argue that the new mayor of Leicester was able to establish 'a proper job' and a personal agenda in an indication of the potential of the role outside strict party constraints, and Copus (2013: 128) suggests that the DEM is a good idea 'whose time has not yet come'.

Others have in turn argued that it is 'Time to put the dream of elected Mayors to Bed' (Marsh, 2012: 607). It is difficult to point to evidence of a 'mayoral effect' as, as Marsh points out, the criteria for their performance has never been too clear, and the fact their introduction was based on an incoherent rationale with, for example, conflicting requirements to both meet central demands and enhance local accountability. Marsh (2012) suggests the mayoral system on offer in the 2012 referenda was vague, with mayoral powers and accountability mechanisms left undefined, and Roberts (2020) points to confusion as to whether their main purpose was as a new democratic form or a driver of economic growth. Pike (2017) notes that the 'hype' surrounding DEMs has been based on a lack of evidence and thus that 'the case for metro-mayors risks becoming an article of faith rather than of fact'. He cites a lack of evidence of causal relationships between types of governance and economic growth, the potential negative effects of concentration of political power, unproven assumptions about increased visibility, accountability and democratic renewal, and lack of evidence about the scale at which DEMs may be most effective. Also, as Sweeting et al. (2013), Sweeting and Hambleton (2017) and Haus and Klausen (2011) suggest, their impact or otherwise may be highly context-specific, with the particular favourable conditions for establishing the model in Bristol, for example, perhaps not being replicated elsewhere in the British context. This makes the 'importing' of international mayoral models to promote growth particularly problematic, and further underlines the significance of past leadership, the specifics of localities, and institutional and political legacies in explaining the uptake and success of the new agenda (Lemprière and Lowndes, 2019). Somewhat ironically, also, given the amount of academic and research interest which had been generated by the experience in Bristol, in 2022 a city-wide referendum voted to scrap the DEM model and return to the committee system from 2024.

Scepticism is also supported by the varying geographies which have been applied during the agenda through, firstly, DEMs, potentially for all councils, then for the major cities, and then for city regions and CAs. As Fenwick and Johnston (2020) point out, and as outlined in Chapter 3, these latter areas have been constructed by governments as they have gone along, rather than being identifiable political units, thus weakening the link between mayors and local places. This is not helped by the 'grey areas' caused by overlapping jurisdictions and responsibilities. By 2022, six mayoral CAs also contained DEMs in a constituent council. Roberts (2020) noted from her research that CA mayors identified themselves as leaders of place, but that they recognised that the CA areas they represented had not emerged yet as places even though their role was to promote or establish them as such, after the fact. 'Place leadership' here involved the attempt to attune existing institutions to the new place, bargaining, convening and building collective agency, while also providing a symbolic representation of the 'place' externally. Thus, while more relational and 'softer' models of leadership may alleviate some of the critiques concerning the dangers of 'strong' leadership, issues remain concerning the construction and meaning of the places they are to facilitate, which, as we have seen, have been created largely on the understanding that functional economic areas are, or can be made to be, suitable democratic units. In addition, the patchy take-up of DEMs in council areas, the ad hoc nature of the bidding process for CAs and the reluctance by successive governments to apply the mayoral model universally has led to an uneven distribution of areas with mayors and those without.

Conclusion

The extent to which changes in the internal structuring of local government restricts or enhances democracy is contingent on how democracy is defined and the weights and values attached to the variety of forms of democracy and democratic practices. On one measure, elected mayors and executives/Cabinet systems could in theory enhance transparency and accountability. However, the changes point towards a trend to ensure a more professionalised and elitist framework for decision-making as opposed to a system that is likely to empower citizens to be directly involved in understanding, let alone be involved in, the policy-making process. Most of the reform initiatives have never been popular with local government or the public but have been pushed through by central legislation rather than local opinion. There has been a substantive decline in the ratio of elected representatives to voters, so councillors must be further removed from being in touch with those they represent. Moreover, in relation to development of executive Cabinet government and directly elected mayors the majority of backbench councillors languishing in scrutiny committee roles have less influence. While the 'gaps' in which agents can work locally can never fully be closed, and indeed are worked on a daily basis by those who push at the constraints to seek benefits for their communities, any democratic potentialities offered are stymied by the context and method by which they have been introduced. Further, they have been not accompanied by suitable structures and conditions which allow for the associated promotion of other democratic 'goods', including participation and public engagement, which are necessary for a democratic culture. The top-down, government-inspired initiatives around councillor roles and mayors have been rhetorically hitched to democratic language, through appeals to visions of the 'metagoverning' councillor as community facilitator, or the more visible and accountable elected mayor. They have not emerged from a serious consideration of local government's place in a democratic polity, or how important it can be in addressing the difficulties and dilemmas currently facing liberal democracy.

6

Central control and local autonomy

The relationship between central and local government since the latter half of the twentieth century reveals a changing pattern in the character and techniques of central government control, and their intensification since the early 1980s. It is now hard to disagree with the view of Leach et al. (2018: 5) that 'It is indisputable that over the past 30 to 40 years there has been a profound shift in the balance of power between the central and local state. We are currently living in one of the most centralised states in Western Europe.' Even accepting that there are conceptual and practical difficulties in measuring local self- government or autonomy, this assertion has been borne out by studies over the years, with the United Kingdom, for example, being ranked as thirty-first out of thirty-nine countries in a comparative table of 'local self-rule' in 2014 (Ladner et al., 2016).

While recognising the undoubted shift noted by Leach et al., it is important also to stress a continuity in central control which is born out of local government's essentially weak position, and in particular its lack of constitutional protections. This is not to argue that local government has no agency; indeed we recognise that despite each 'turn of the screw' from central government, local governments have remained innovative and reflective of local distinctions. Rather it is that local government's position as a creature of statute has seen it increasingly constrained. Also, we need to set the pattern of central–local relations in the context of government's changing perception of what local government is for, what purpose it serves and its role in reconciling tensions within the polity. Loughlin (1996b: 59) sets the development of central–local relations in the context of adapting unwritten constitutional traditions to 'the exigencies of the modern administrative state'. This necessitated the development of an informal system based on facilitative Acts of Parliament and administrative supervision by central departments, sustained by a political consensus over the growing importance of local government in the delivery of national social welfare. Bulpitt (1983) identified, in this context, an accepted 'operating code' in which central government was responsible for matters of 'high politics', and in return accepted some degree of local autonomy over the 'low politics' of implementation. This, however, was an 'uneasy compromise' (Loughlin, 1996b: 60), and local government's ultimate weakness in the relationship was revealed when ideological differences over welfare and public services, and trust in local government to deliver them, broke down from the mid-1970s, and significantly during the Thatcher administrations.

Thus central–local relations 'and the variations in local government powers and responsibilities across time, have to be understood within the context of the changing politics of the welfare state' (Laffin, 2009: 35). It is important to recognise that over time considerable complexity has thus been added to the relationship, with local government, in a 'new world of governance', sharing the local sphere with a disparate array of private, voluntary and quasi-governmental actors. This has required governments to adopt 'new strategies to manage and coordinate policy with actors who are now outside the usual governmental chains of command' (Laffin, 2009: 22). This has undermined any assumed 'duality' where the 'local' in central–local relations refers solely to local government, and increasingly exposed the contradictory and non-linear impacts of government's actions in specific contexts (Lowndes, 1999). It also led some to argue that this complexity had left the centre weakened or 'hollowed out' and needing to conduct central–local relations more via partnership, interdependence, diplomacy and 'steering' at a distance (R. A. W. Rhodes, 1997).

Moreover, as seen in Chapter 3, the subnational arena has become populated by a range of bodies at a range of geographical scales. Such a system of 'multilevel governance' implies more negotiation between 'nested' tiers of territorial governance (Bache and Flinders, 2004). While this is less the case in a highly centralised polity like Britain, where central government retains key powers over its subregional creations, it adds to the diverse array of other actors in the 'central–local' relationship and additional sets of central–local linkages (Laffin, 2009). In addition, we have to again recognise that devolution to Scotland and Wales means that, along with Northern Ireland, the UK now effectively has four local government systems, adding further complexity and meaning that 'central–local' narratives have to be increasingly sensitive to context.

Thus we do not imply that central–local relations involve a straightforward and totally coherent imposition by a unified centre onto a homogeneous local. Firstly, we can recognise again the divergencies which have emerged in the relationships between local government and the devolved administrations in Scotland and Wales. In Scotland, for example, local government has 'signed up' to a broad set of performance outcomes set out in the National Performance Framework launched in 2007, and similarly in Wales the Improvement Framework was established in 2010. Although set by the devolved administrations, both put local government's responsibilities in the context of broad strategic outcomes with considerable scope for local adaptation. In Wales, this theme was further consolidated in the Well-being of Future Generations Act, which set out a legal duty for public bodies to contribute to seven long-term outcomes.

Indeed, more broadly, central government should not be seen as a homogeneous joined-up entity that has consistently delivered coherent policies and practices towards subnational governments. Responsibility for local government services has since the eighteenth century been distributed across a range of government departments, often with competing agendas, with the department responsible for local government 'overall' undergoing frequent changes over the years and essentially having a coordinating role. Over time the various central departments responsible for local government have 'struggled to define and defend a role for [themselves] in the face of powerful service departments' (Laffin, 2009: 28). Indeed, local government has now been demoted in the ministerial hierarchy, such that in 2020 it was left out of the title of the department responsible for it, finding itself in the portfolio of one person holding the position of Secretary of State for Levelling Up,

Housing and Communities *and* of Minister for Intergovernmental Relations. However, while central government's relationship with local government progressively became more complex and opaque, it remained essentially underpinned by a continuity rooted in the instrumental role of local government as a service provider and, fundamentally, its lack of constitutional protection. In this sense, any changes in the central–local relationship have been, as Leach et al. (2018) argue, incremental, emerging from the same underlying soil.

Up until the 1980s, central–local relations can be perceived, with hindsight, as 'relatively benign' (Leach et al., 2018: 59), essentially based on a partnership and conducted mainly via a consultative process in which local government affairs were governed within permissive legislation which allowed considerable discretion as to local delivery (Loughlin, 1996a). This broad picture stemmed from a general consensus that local government's role was key to the delivery of expanding welfare and environmental services and agreement that it was capable of doing so. It is possible to see local government here as an agent or steward of the centre (Chandler, 1988: 186), carrying out its wishes and trusted in that regard. This, however, was an 'uneasy compromise' (Loughlin, 1996b: 56), with local government's ultimate weakness in the relationship revealed when it began to break down in the 1970s, and particularly, as we have seen in Chapter 1, with the election of Mrs Thatcher in 1979. Henceforth, the nature of legislation changed from broad to precise, leading to a 'juridification' of central–local relations in which they were defined by a precise 'formal rule-determined relationship of superior and inferior' (Loughlin, 1996b: 59).

The following decades saw central control implemented through a range of tactics, including the increased use of performance monitoring and 'earned autonomy', as exemplified under New Labour and outlined in Chapter 1. This underlines the point that central–local relations cannot be captured only by the formal legislative and regulatory powers which central government holds, but are also conducted via a diverse range of governing 'technologies' including getting 'buy in' from local government and attempting to 'steer' partnerships and networks from the centre. This resonates with Michel Foucault's concept of governmentality, which 'recognizes that governments have to face up to the limits of their power' and work through the 'conduct of conduct' via 'modes of government [which] work through the freedoms and nurtured capacities of the governed' (Barnett, 2003: 31). A consequence of such approaches is that more of the relationship rests on establishing meanings, behaviours and accepted beliefs, all of which may leave scope for local agents to 'work the gaps' in these meanings, to open up spaces for contestation in the gaps between rhetoric and reality, and for opportunity for 'everyday' resistance.

Thus, not all forms of central control may be immediately apparent, in that they can be identified clearly in legislation or financial constraints. More subtle forms of control could be found, for example, as we have outlined in Chapter 1, in New Labour's Comprehensive Performance Assessment, with its judgements about the quality of political leadership and exhortations of particular dispositions towards change among councillors, as outlined in Chapter 5. Such technologies were downplayed by the Coalition and Conservative governments after 2010, but were still in clear view in the 'localism' agenda as applied to local government in England. Here, as we set out below, there is clear evidence of central control masked in the rhetoric of localism. At the same time, together with the 'Big Society' agenda generally, some have identified 'gaps and fissures' which could be exploited to develop genuinely local practices (Williams et al., 2014). The localism agenda, and in particular the neighbourhood planning initiative which it included, serve to bring the interplay of some of these varied technologies of governance to light, revealing both centralisation and, at the margins, localist potentials. However, central government continues to hold the key financial and legislative levers which set the context and parameters of local agency; if there was any need for a clarification of this point, the impact of austerity and financial restraint imposed by the Coalition government provide more than ample evidence.

Coalition and Conservative governments

By 2013, the Parliamentary Political and Constitutional Reform Committee was able to note that 'All parties appear to accept the need to reduce central burdens on local government' (House of Commons Communities and Local Government Committee, 2013: 9). The Coalition government had stated in its Programme for Government (HM Government, 2010b: 11) that

> it is time for a fundamental shift of power from Westminster to people. We will promote decentralisation and democratic engagement, and we will end the era of top-down government by giving new powers to local councils, communities, neighbourhoods and individuals.

Indeed, a Minister for Decentralisation was appointed as a signal of this intent. However, this commitment to decentralisation and 'localism' has to be seen in the light of realpolitik. The Coalition government required some measure of concessions to the junior partner, the Liberal Democrats, and 'localism' provided some helpful common ground. The Liberals had a long-standing commitment to 'community politics' and a more radical policy of decentralisation than either Labour or the Conservatives (Huhne, 2007). For the Conservatives, localism allowed David Cameron to distinguish his approach from what was portrayed as the top-down, overbearing, state-based and heavily bureaucratic approach of New Labour. This theme was taken up with some relish and outright hostility by the Secretary of State, Eric Pickles (Leach et al., 2018), who was nevertheless quick to identify local government itself as part of the problem and to intervene in specific areas, including telling councils how often they should empty the dustbins (Wilson and Game, 2011).

In practice this 'anti-state version of localism' had a particular ideological flavour (Stoker, 2011a) and was closely associated with Cameron's 'Big Society' initiative, which appealed to Conservative traditions of self-help, and to notions of groups of homogeneous, consensual local citizens (Clarke and Cochrane, 2013) rather than local government per se, to which there was something of a 'cavalier attitude' (Leach et al., 2018: 11). In practice, the more radical Liberal Democrat party views proved to be the 'dog that didn't bark' in this respect (Lowndes and Pratchett, 2012: 29). Policy proposals were thus engineered to provide the appearance of a government wishing to give more powers, freedom and democracy at the local level while at the same time ensuring even harsher restraints, largely through financial austerity, on local authorities. What localist agenda there was in parts of government was not shared across the major service-related departments, or the Treasury, which mainly acted at odds with it, such that 'the main barriers to the development of localism lay in central government itself' (Leach et al., 2018: 48). The 'Minister for Decentralisation' held little power other than reporting to the Prime Minister on progress, or lack of it, as central–local relations 'reached its nadir' (Leach et al., 2018: 3).

Initially the change in approach had been signalled by several measures which aimed to reduce bureaucratic burdens and regulation – to 'free up' local government. The Audit Commission was abolished, as were Regional Strategies and the Comprehensive Area Agreements. Councils were allowed more freedom with respect to internal structures, and to return to the committee system if they chose. There were fewer centrally set targets and less micromanagement from Whitehall. The headline strategy was established in the Localism Act of 2011 which gave local government what had long been considered the holy grail, a general power of competence, which allowed councils to do 'anything that individuals generally may do', freeing them from the constraints of *ultra vires*. However, no existing regulation was repealed, and local governments lacked the finance to operationalise the powers meaningfully. Moreover, the Act contained around 140 reserve powers for the Secretary of State (House of Commons Communities and Local Government Committee, 2013). It was unclear, in any case, what additional benefit the general power brought, as local authorities had had, since 2000, a general power of well-being which had been little used and tightly interpreted by the courts. The Act gave the Secretary of State the discretion to 'make orders to prevent local authorities from doing anything specified in the orders', a 'sting in the tail' which undermined the whole point of the general power (Leach et al., 2018: 45). Other new measures further restricted local discretion by giving more reserve powers to the Secretary of State on planning regulations and by the associated National Planning Framework. Referenda were required to be held for elected mayors in the twelve largest city councils and a council tax freeze imposed. Thus, as Leach et al. (2018) note, there was a lot missing in this brave new world of localism. There was nothing to address loss of local government powers in the key policy areas. In education, if anything, the powers of central government were, as shown in Chapter 4, strengthened.

The ambiguity in the localism agenda reflected its malleability and the differing interpretations to which it was open. Thus, while local authorities were sometimes the 'local' to be empowered, they were more likely to be seen as an obstruction as the direction of travel of 'empowerment' was to be downwards to a range of other 'locals' – self-organisng groups of local citizens. This was enacted without any clear principles as to how these entities, in turn, related to the local authority, or to how what were sometimes competing claims to democratic legitimacy and 'localness' could be resolved. There were other instances where the devolution of powers was to be aimed at empowering individuals, to act as a check on local councils through the increased use of local referendum proposals. In particular, council tax referenda were required to be held whenever a council proposed an 'excessive' increase – that is, above a threshold set by the Secretary of State.

The localism agenda, then, was 'oversold'. Liberal Democrat leader Nick Clegg, rather embarrassingly in hindsight, had said 'No government has ever passed a piece of legislation like the Localism Bill we are publishing this month. Because instead of taking more power for the Government, this Bill will give power away' (Clegg, 2010: 1). At best, however, there were mixed images of the local as targets and beneficiaries of the resulting Act, and the agenda was only superficially local in focus, doing little to reverse centralist trends. Overall, the impression was that local government would be left to 'sink or swim' (Lowndes and Pratchett, 2012: 37), free from some of the regulatory constraints and 'earned autonomy' of New Labour, but left adrift amidst a reduced service delivery role and increasing financial constraint. Moreover, as noted in Chapter 4, the ability to 'swim' became more unequally distributed as a result of austerity. In addition, a simultaneous programme of reform led from the Treasury was creating subregional CAs with little democratic mandate and tenuous connections to 'local' areas, although this programme was also bundled together, rhetorically, with the commitment to localism. This represented at best a 'conditional localism' (Hildreth, 2011), in being contractually tied to deals signed, agreed and policed by central government. This trend would be intensified from 2015 onwards.

Following the election in 2015, the Conservative government of David Cameron consigned the 'Big Society' idea to history, it having proven a 'difficult sell' in electoral terms, and with it went much of the explicit reference to localism at local government level or below. It was replaced with a combination of 'super austerity', 'devolution' and the 'smarter state' (Lowndes and Gardner, 2016: 361), which largely continued to be the case through the administrations of Theresa May and Boris Johnson. Lowndes and Gardner (2016: 367) identify the lack of a 'big idea' and the more laissez-faire approach to local government under the Coalition as equating to a message of 'make the cuts and let the structures look after themselves', quoting Eric Pickles (Oral Evidence, House of Commons Communities and Local Government Committee, 2013: 13) as saying

> [in this country] we are obsessed with governance and structure. The way we change things is by putting in a structure and governance. We try to put things in terms of balances and checks. It is not like that in the real world. Fundamentally, you should try to change the nature of the service and let structure and governance catch up with you.

Thus, despite the continued rhetorical use of localism in justifications for the agenda, structural reform was driven by austerity and images of economically functional areas, expressed in the 'devolution' agenda of George Osborne and associated state restructuring to promote economic growth, as detailed in Chapter 3. The extent to which local government was a consideration in this restructuring was seen in the relatively minor government interest in the voluntary amalgamations of councils during these years. While these primarily stemmed from individual councils struggling with the effects of austerity, they did not appear to emanate from any governmental plan or overall approach to local government, other than in successive secretaries of state indicating their broad support for unitary councils. We can see in this agenda a desire to restructure central–local relations incrementally, to facilitate clearer ministerial and Civil Service control, underpinned by a desire to deal with a small number of mayors and leaders rather than large numbers of councils. In turn, local leaders were 'turning like moths towards the bright light of devolution, and away from the "too hard" box of delivering day-to-day local services' (Lowndes and Gardner, 2016: 369). Ayres et al. (2018: 860) see in this evidence of Bulpitt's central autonomy model, where 'court politics', conducted among a 'small number of key individuals that form the decision-making political elite', becomes the dominant mode of statecraft.

Through the essentially contractual relationship in devolution deals, the government was also able to develop its own version of 'earned autonomy', via political patronage and rewards for those who met targets, accompanied also with the potential gift of future powers and resources from the centre (Lowndes and Gardner, 2016). Local governments were willing to submit to a contractual, earned autonomy-style arrangement by seeking to negotiate with central government based on a series of offers to deliver central targets in return for a series of 'asks' for more freedoms and powers. Such an offer was made by the LGA in 2010, and again in 2020. Reflecting on this on behalf of the councils involved, Jameson observed (in Lowndes and Gardner, 2016: 371) that 'If we are going to sell our soul, we are going to have to make sure we do it for a decent price.'

Importantly, these developments have to be seen in the light of continuing financial restraint after 2015, and the continued pressure to create a 'smarter', more efficient, state, which could do more with less. Local governments had already shown themselves more than capable of adopting new and more efficient forms of working, including digitalisation and innovative forms of service delivery and yet, as Lowndes and Gardner (2016) note, this was largely ignored by David Cameron when setting out his vision of the 'smarter state' in 2015. The promotion of subregional state restructuring, New Public Management-style initiatives and austerity at the same time amounted to a 'roll-out' strategy of neoliberalism, which combined the search for economic growth via scale-craft with the 'rolling out' of responsibility for services to co-producing citizens and the private sector (Lowndes and Gardner, 2016; Peck and Tickell, 2002). There is, then, a continuity through the period 1997–2020, and whatever tactics were deployed, the 'weak centre' or 'hollowed out' narrative of the 'new governance' does not stand up to scrutiny when applied to relations to local government during these years (Entwistle et al., 2016). Thus Fyans et al. (2019: 9) were able to report that 'A former minister told us: "Local and central government have been going in opposite directions and I can totally understand why – less contact, less respect, less belief in what they're doing."'

The comparative lack of interest with respect to overall local government structure, exemplified in the quote earlier from Eric Pickles, was tempered to some extent by the *Levelling Up* White Paper in 2022, which set out the new Framework for Devolution. This at least was some indication of an attempt to 'get a grip' on central–local government relations by setting out a more formal process and, in theory, adding clarity on the future government attitude towards local government. However, this was far from a reset; as we have seen, it actually indicated an intention to intensify and extend the deal-making, contractual relationship to new areas, with the aim of making it even more of a lynchpin of the relationship. The White Paper further indicated something of a return to New Labour's control via performance assessment, in the proposal to introduce a new accountability framework with 'clear roles and metrics for assessment … alongside strong scrutiny mechanisms' (HM Government, 2022: 139) and a new body to collate the necessary data. The metrics would be aligned to the twelve 'levelling up missions' identified in the White Paper rather than emerging from the 'bottom up'. Commitments to 'rewire' the machinery of central government to facilitate implementation and enhance central–local relations, including a new Cabinet committee and a proposal to appoint nine regional directors to improve central–local collaboration and act as a single point of contact, at least indicated a desire to address some long-standing issues. It is hard to envisage regional directors appointed by the government, however, as having anything other than the primary role of overseeing the implementation of the government's agenda. Overall, the White Paper can be viewed in the context of a post-Brexit recentralisation of powers, as the Johnson government in particular set about 'restoring the centre' in England (Morphet, 2021).

Taking advantage of the reduced constraints after leaving the EU, after 2016 a concerted effort was made to centralise power ever more at the centre of government, and to begin a process of taking back powers from the devolved assemblies of Scotland and Wales (Morphet, 2021). The process also saw an intensification of a trend which had been growing over the decades, with increased use of secondary legislation which did not require full parliamentary approval, and ministers being granted substantial delegated powers to effectively legislate without parliamentary scrutiny.

Localising planning – a microcosm of central–local relations post-2010?

The localism and 'Big Society' agendas, as noted above, claimed to 'give power away' and promoted initiatives aimed at facilitating greater public engagement in localities. The 'local' was imagined here as a homogeneous social entity counterposed to an overbearing central state (Clarke and Cochrane, 2013). The type of participation encouraged was primarily that of direct management of community assets, again utilising a range of differing geographical entities. 'Communities' could thus be interested parties who wanted to run a local pub that was under threat of closure, for example. Running concurrently with this was the neighbourhood planning initiative, introduced in the 2011 Localism Act. This saw the government 'surrounding the neighbourhood concept in a new set of ideological clothes' (Bailey and Pill, 2011: 939) and offering particular definitions of 'neighbourhood'. Secondly, it also promised actual material impacts and direct outcomes for the participants – neighbourhood plans would be statutory documents and could directly influence local planning decisions, and were connected into the broader system of planning, fitting into wider local development plans and strategic plans. In terms of central–local relations, neighbourhood planning represents an attempt to bypass local government and micromanage at a distance, utilising neighbourhoods, revealing tensions and pitfalls for central government in adopting such techniques.

The chosen primary sites for encouraging participation via neighbourhood planning were existing town or parish councils, automatically authorised as the plan-makers if they wished to draw one up. Where neither of these existed, bids could be received from local residents and community groups to form a neighbourhood forum. The neighbourhood was here then, self-defining, and the creation of such a forum is in itself an act of engagement. Participants in the creation of the neighbourhood development plans (NDPs) are self-selecting volunteers, who put themselves forward to 'represent' the community. They are representative in a 'descriptive' sense in so far as they are accepted as such by those living in the area covered by the forum (Davoudi and Cowie, 2013). However, the requirement is only for a minimum involvement of twenty-one people. In the town and parish councils, participation is via the initial election of councillors, and thereafter any form of consultation which the councils wish to undertake. In addition, before adoption each plan has to be examined by an independent professional to verify that it is in compliance with the broader planning and legal framework, and then must secure a majority in a local referendum. Several types of participatory practices, including differing definitions of representation, are at play here.

Interesting questions are raised as to how neighbourhood forums in particular are constituted, how they 'come into being' and construct themselves as a collective or polity. For the most part, the areas of neighbourhood forums have been uncontentious, or successfully negotiated. Interestingly, one inner London forum, Highgate, straddles the London borough councils of Camden and Haringey, providing an alternative institutional geography to the local governance of the area. However, there have been occasions when both the area to be defined as neighbourhood, and who it should be defined and represented by, has proven controversial. Thus, the London Borough of Hackney received rival bids covering Stamford Hill, from both a Stamford Hill Neighbourhood Forum and a North Hackney Neighbourhood Forum, and Hammersmith and Fulham LBC (2020) rejected an application on the basis that 'The forum membership is not considered to be drawn from different places in the neighbourhood area concerned and from different sectors of the community in that area.' One proposed forum in Hartlepool was blocked due to the small number of people proposing it and a lack of consultation.

Further, the neighbourhood planning process highlights issues concerning the relationship of participatory initiatives to wider macro-economic issues and the importance of the context in which they are set. By 2020, 2,612 areas had been designated and had either made or started the process. Of these, 865 had been adopted and only six had been rejected in a referendum; 94.3 per cent of approved plans had been led by a parish or town council (Parker et al., 2020: 12). Pycock (2020) noted that this meant that 14 million people had been 'involved' in the process. However, the predominance of parish or town council-led plans and the low number of forums which completed plans is testament to the labour-intensive, time-consuming nature of the process, and the statutory procedures to be negotiated, which posed 'huge challenges even for relatively well-resourced communities' (Gunn et al., 2015: 165). Many areas lack the individual and civic capacity to undertake such a task, and take-up rates slowed considerably after 2011. There was low take-up in urban areas; only 3 per cent of plans, for example, came from the north-east of England (Parker et al., 2020: 12). This resulted in an uneven geography of plan distribution in favour of more affluent areas, raising issues of social justice as asymmetries of power were reinforced (Davoudi and Cowie, 2013: 186). This directs us to a conundrum; those areas where increasing levels of engagement are most needed have been least able to generate it. Tribillon (2014) thus argues that neighbourhood planning in London has only served to highlight economic divisions and introduce a 'new parochialism', with the space to affect change highly constrained and limited to a select number of groups (Parker and Street, 2015: 794). Lay community planners found their ideas 're-scripted' by local planning authorities who advised and 'co-produced' the plans 'to ensure conformity to a bounded form of collaboration' (Parker et al., 2015: 519). Parker et al. (2017: 446) noted that 'Many groups have adopted conservative positions or are finding their NDPs are being limited by consultants, local authorities or examiners, often concerned with how the NDPs will fare in the contested environment of planning and development in neo-liberal times.'

The imbalance in plan creation between different areas underlines a key dilemma in central–local relations. On the one hand, central government can impose top-down solutions, as with neighbourhood planning, applying the same criteria to all areas in the name of consistency, but this fails to recognise the resources and conditions which are required in specific contexts. On the other hand, we would ideally see such democratic practices emerging from the bottom up, favouring a more 'enabling' framework, consequently meaning, again, that they are developed in some areas but not others. Bailey and Pill (2015: 301) note that 'those initiatives which are top-down, state led policy initiatives tend to result in the least empowerment, whereas the more bottom-up, self-help, state-enabled projects at least provide an opportunity to create the spaces where there is some potential for varying degrees of transformation'. Some areas clearly need support if they are to be presented with an enabling environment; however, there is a consequent danger that spaces created for participation are co-opted into state structures and lose their potential for extending democratic practices. Whether or not these balances can be negotiated successfully is highly context-specific (Bailey and Pill, 2015), but the neighbourhood planning agenda represented essentially a one-size-fits-all approach, displaying no meaningful recognition of these local particularities.

Again, however, others have found some solace and opportunity in the democratic potentials of neighbourhood planning despite its faults. Bradley (2015: 107), for example, detects the process as leading to contest and the formation of new collective identities, and 'might therefore be considered as offering the potential for a new democratic politics of localism'. Contestation and negotiation over boundaries, he feels, present a 'condition of possibility' to develop collective identities around 'shared definitions of grievances, antagonisms and feeling for place' (Bradley, 2015: 107). By prompting practices of negotiation with those who share proximity, he claims, connections have been raised concerning macro and global issues which 'touch down' in local areas, for example concerning property development and housing. Similarly, Wargent (2020: 4) argues that despite government exhortations and persuasion techniques, local actors have not been 'aligned' with housing delivery targets, indicating that 'interstitial spaces of hope' are emerging; outcomes can be uncertain and government initiatives are not totalising. Williams et al. (2014: 2811) see groups negotiating a role within the neighbourhood planning process which is neither 'outsider' resistance nor fully incorporated into its structures – they are able to occupy an 'interstitial' space and achieve progressive results.

Neighbourhood planning and its appeals to localism, community and neighbourhood thus reveals a mixture of direct and more 'hands off' practices by which the central government has attempted to reconfigure central–local relations – in this case by attempting to appeal to and establish a framework bypassing existing local government and 'empowering' communities and neighbourhoods in centrally proscribed legal constraints, together with, as noted already several times in previous chapters, ever tightening financial constraints. It again reminds us that central government controls can never be totalising, and that the local can indeed provide a wellspring of innovation, experimentation and hope for democratic renewal. However, overall, the agenda since 2010 in particular has also shown that the development of these potentials is set within the parameters of, and fundamentally restrained by, the overarching powers held by central government.

Intergovernmental relations – finance, austerity, COVID-19 and beyond?

Finance remains the 'elephant in the room' amidst the changing tactics and approaches which have characterised central–local relations over the decades, and the onslaught on local government finances most clearly illustrates the absence of any joined-up vision of its role. While some government departments pushed for greater autonomy, at least for larger principal, subregional and regional authorities, and other elements have even supported a more localised neighbourhood planning agenda, the Treasury has placed formidable barriers to local autonomy through its insistence on fiscal austerity. As seen in Chapter 3, austerity had a severe impact on local government, which bore the brunt of cuts to expenditure while also experiencing a rise in demand for its services and severe limitations on its ability to respond through its own sources of income.

The changing balance of council funding during 2010–19 presented defenders of local government with something of an irony. For decades, the increasing amount of local government expenditure provided by central government was lamented as an indication of loss of local discretion and as key to an inexorable path of centralisation. The system of funding of local government is one of the most centralised in the Organisation for Economic Co-operation and Development (OECD) (Gray and Barford, 2018). As shown in Chapter 1, this centralisation began in the nineteenth century. Critique of this trend has centred around the democratic need to tie the responsibility for services to the source of their funding, necessary for accountability and for clarifying in citizens' minds the differences in the duties of local and central governments. During the twentieth century, progressively higher proportions of local expenditure came via variously named block or specific grants from the centre. Control over the calculations behind the various assessments of need for funding, and of how far councils needed to be compensated for their weaker ability to raise local taxes (based, as they have remained, on property values), lay in the hands of central governments, who were able to manipulate them for political advantage. Local government finance thus increasingly became the major tool in central–local relations, highlighted by the Thatcher government's use of the complex funding system to 'punish' authorities deemed to be high spenders.

The increasing domination of central funding led to the recommendation by the Layfield Committee in 1976 for an increase in local financial independence, principally to be achieved by the introduction of a local income tax (Layfield, 1976). This and other mooted local taxes used in local government systems across the world – for example, local sales taxes – have been considered by various reviews over the years (Scott and Pitt, 2015) but these, let alone the underlying principle to allow local government greater powers to raise revenue, broadly failed to find favour with any government. In fact, the trend was in the opposite direction. Non-domestic rates were in effect 'nationalised' in 1989 in Scotland and in 1990 in England and Wales, to become the national non-domestic rate, or uniform business rate. It was now central government who set a national rate, which local governments collected, to be 'pooled' by central government and redistributed to councils according to a formula. As Wilson and Game (2011: 221) point out, this source of finance effectively became another form of government grant, and 'at a stroke ... local councils saw the proportion of their income they themselves controlled fall from over a half to barely a quarter'.

In England, the period 2010–19 saw what could be interpreted as a desirable move in the direction of local autonomy. A significant factor in the shift to financing spending more from local sources was intended to be the BRRS introduced in 2013/14, which enabled councils to retain 50 per cent of business rates revenue, with the other half going to central government. There was still some equalisation applied by central government as each council's 'retained' 50 per cent share was adjusted according to a set of tariffs and top-ups (Sandford, 2020c). In addition, cuts to grant funding meant that the share of local government revenue funding (excluding that going directly to schools) which came from local taxes increased significantly from 40 per cent in 2009/10 to 77 per cent in 2019 (Phillips, 2018: 44), with council tax receipts being the largest source of revenue, at 48 per cent, up from around 33 per cent in 2010 (Harris et al., 2019: 5). This was despite the fact that, between 2011 and 2022, councils were allowed to raise council tax by only 2 per cent without the need for a local referendum, and from 2016 an additional 1 per cent was earmarked for social care. In addition, many ring-fenced grants were replaced by a general Local Services Support Grant, giving councils more discretion over spending. Government policy was that all general central grant funding, principally provided via the Rates Support Grant (RSG), should disappear by 2020, and indeed '81 per cent of local authorities received no RSG at all in at least one year between 2016–17 and 2019–20' (Brien et al., 2020: 13). The financial settlement for 2020 saw a reversal of this trend in some cases, as austerity was eased and local government received a 6 per cent increase in spending power. The government intended to increase the locally retained proportion of business rates to 75 per cent by 2021/22, following the piloting of the policy in fifteen areas, with a long-term aim of moving to 100 per cent retention.

Alongside this long-term change of direction, a 'Fair Funding' review of relative needs and resources was announced to fundamentally revisit historic levels of central funding and recalculate it using different formulas. This proved to be controversial, and following a consultation document in December 2017, successive ministers announced delays in its introduction. The Johnson government, elected in 2019, was committed to a 'fundamental review' of business rates, with the express intent of reducing them and their 'burden on business'. By 2022 this had however failed to materialise, subsumed as it was by macro-economic difficulties and the changes of governments in the autumn. Overall, while central government grants were cut, councils had been restrained in their ability to raise council tax to match this loss and the growing demand on services.

The debate around 'Fair Funding' posed fundamental questions concerning the desirable level of local freedom with respect to the financing of important public services. Regardless of the amounts of expenditure, these questions concern the source of funding and the balance of local choice with central or universal standards – in short, the balance of diversity with equality. As Phillips (2018: 35) noted, local government finance has 'historically prioritised fiscal equalisation over fiscal incentives: central government grants were allocated to compensate for differences in local needs and tax bases'. The system during 2010–19 was intended to move away from equalisation and towards incentives, to give councils fiscal incentives to support economic development via inward investment and the improvement of non-domestic property. Phillips (2018: 45) notes that this method:

> increases the risk for divergences to open up between revenues and spending needs given that business rates revenues can evolve in a different way to spending needs over time. Alongside the ending of the more general annual equalisation of revenues and spending needs, this could make it more difficult to deliver a consistent standard of service across England for those services funded by councils' general revenues.

Also, controversially, 'Fair Funding' would most likely lead to a significant redistribution of funds away from those poorer areas most reliant on needs-based formula funding, potentially moving £320 million per year from councils in some of the poorest areas, while shire counties, mainly in the south-east, would gain £300 million (Butler, 2020). Moving to a higher proportion, if not perhaps all, of local income based on property valuations and business activity inevitably leaves areas with a low tax base in difficulty, and favours those with vibrant economies and higher property valuations; this could lead to a 'race to the bottom' as areas compete for inward investment by reducing business rates. In addition, it is unlikely that a move to more local funding would be adequate to meet demand for services. The IFS (2019: 12) estimated in 2019 that demand for adult social care would require an increase in the share of local tax revenues allocated to these services from 38 per cent to over 50 per cent, requiring sustained cuts to other service areas in addition to those already made after a decade of austerity. The danger in this, as they saw it, was that there would be pressure for social services to be removed from councils' responsibilities. Overall, as Ogden et al. (2022) point out, government formulas for funding for councils were by 2022 considerably out of date, and bore little resemblance to needs.

Changes to the funding regime have also been contradictory, despite the rhetoric of localism, in their impact on the balance of central and local control relations. In major respects there were increasing restrictions on local spending autonomy. In social care, the government was keen to drive up consistency and standards of services across all councils, most notably in adult social care, and the Secretary of State for Health and Social Care in March 2018 expressed the desire to address the 'unacceptable variation in quality and outcomes' in different parts of the country (Hunt, 2018). The Care Act (2014) introduced new national regulations concerning eligibility and assessment for funded services, and an increased proportion of government funding was ring-fenced and transferred from the NHS via the improved Better Care Fund.

The issue of equalisation and the funding of universal services thus raises key questions about local government's role and the scope of its service responsibilities. The 'postcode lottery' argument has been used for some time to contend against the wholesale devolution of funding to local areas. Some have seen the solution to be in the achievement, at the minimum, of the best achievable balance between local discretion and consistency of national standards. Greater clarity over responsibilities and a less opaque system of funding streams would at least enhance accountability. Stoker and Travers (2001), for example, set out a compromise between central and local funding based on agreement on outcomes rather than spending, recognising expectations about universal provision in services such as welfare, education, social care and policing, while allowing their delivery and funding to be negotiated between local and central government, with local government responsible for financing the remaining services. In contrast, Copus et al. (2017) feel that local autonomy trumps concern for national standards, and argue for freedom for local authorities to raise and retain a range of locally set taxes and fees as they see fit.

Debate concerning the balance between local and national sources of income, however, seems perpetually to open up fundamental questions concerning the extent to which local choice and diversity are compatible with wider concerns about social justice and equity. Some, such as Copus et al. (2017), argue that more local determination of finances would be *more* equitable, as it can be more closely tailored to the area's specific needs and choices over distribution of resources as determined by a locality. We argue, alternatively, that local choice should be set within a larger framework of rights, social justice and equity, meaning that elements of equalisation and the setting of universal standards of needs, tailored to specific cases, is necessary on ethical grounds. Within this, the 'balance' between local and central funding can never be clearly demarcated or set in stone, but must be the subject of collective political debate and changing values over time. It is, essentially, contentious. We recognise, however, again that the approach to local government finance has not been determined by serious debate over principles, but by the changing interests of central government, which has seen the case made for various balances of reforms to funding wax and wane according to changing calculations of political advantage and ideological preference.

Events following the 2019 election serve to underline this point. 'Fair Funding' is in principle to be welcomed, although of course our view of what it means will depend on our understanding of what is 'fair'. The government's interpretation of 'fair' funding, involving a redistribution of funds as noted above, was due to be implemented in April 2022, with the move to 75 per cent local retention of business rates being completed at the same time. In 2016 the government felt that the policy marked 'an important milestone in the devolution of power and resources from Whitehall and will help shape the role of local government for decades to come' (*Public Finance*, 2021). However, as noted above, it did cause some controversy and was delayed several times. That delay gave way to explicit rejection of the idea, with the Secretary of State for Levelling Up, Housing and Communities, Michael Gove, announcing to the House of Commons Housing, Communities and Local Government Committee in November 2021 that it would lead to 'a situation where those local authorities that have the most resilient council tax base and also the highest portion of business rates are, relatively speaking, in a stronger position, relatively speaking, with more in the South East' (*Public Finance*, 2021). This conversion to the acceptance of critiques of a proposal previously supported by Mr Gove can of course be explained by events and the changed political climate. Politicians can, and should, change their views according to changed circumstances, and these had been significant. The COVID-19 pandemic required a reset of thinking on local government finance, and it had deeper impacts in the poorest areas of the country. In addition, government provided various forms of business rate relief during the pandemic. It could be argued that the immediate aftermath of these events was not the time to proceed with any significant changes, until their full impact was known. However, it is clear that the key reason for the change of heart was due to the changing fortunes of the Conservative Party and the winning of 'red wall' seats in the 2019 election. The trend of 2010–19 would, if continued, cause further damage to those areas to which the government now wished to direct funds.

Thus, we recognise that central–local relations can indeed be complex, and that central government does not have the machinery, expertise nor even desire to control everything local governments do. Also, there is always scope for agency and innovation, and indeed this is a key reason why we continue to argue a case for local government. However, the central–local relationship appears to be ever more tightly determined by central government. Recent events make this clear. As noted in the Introduction, despite proving its essential value during the COVID-19 pandemic, local government during this period was treated almost as an afterthought, with government looking rather to the private sector and central agencies.

Moreover, the pandemic left local government with additional pressures and questions over its role. The role of care homes in the pandemic promoted renewed debate concerning the integration of social care with the NHS, thus threatening to 'nationalise' local government's largest remaining service. Financially, budgets before and during the pandemic in 2020 and 2021 saw local government receive more favourable settlements, along with other areas of the public sector, than during the high points of austerity. Also, as we identified in the Introduction, packages of additional funding were allocated to meet additional COVID-related pressures. However, an estimated £9.7 billion of additional cost pressures were identified In April 2021 as a result of COVID-19 (NAO, 2021b).

The promised long-term consideration of council funding was in 2022 once again sacrificed at the altar of political expediency, with delays and changes of mind leaving councils unsure about the future. The *Levelling Up* White Paper in 2022 appeared to accept the need to revisit it, suggesting that a review of formula-based funding was necessary, along with a plan for 'streamlining the funding landscape' and simplifying the 'patchwork quilt of fragmented funds' (HM Government, 2022: 127). These are ambitions which have been stated over the years by successive governments, all of which have failed to surmount the hurdles of political expediency. However, the White Paper did not propose any serious reform of local government funding, failing to address tax-raising powers aside from a proposal that an additional council tax levy could be charged on holiday homes, leaving the bulk of local spending short-term, fragmented, with limited integration with health expenditure and highly centralised (Carr-West, 2022). The funding regime remained unsuited to tackling inequalities between areas, with no update to estimated spending needs since 2013. As seen in Chapter 4, in the meantime cuts fell disproportionately on poorer areas, with, for example, in 2022 the most deprived tenth of councils' spending on adult social care estimated to be 15 per cent below their share of need (Ogden et al., 2022). There is every indication that local government finance, without fundamental changes, will continue to be prey to national party political expediency, and continue along the ad hoc, unstable path it has followed since at least the late nineteenth century.

Conclusion

Central government, of course, is not one unified whole, and cannot control all events; nor can it expunge all agency from local and devolved governments. Indeed, its actions may leave spaces to be exploited. Thus, as Morphet (2021) argues, local government, CAs and the devolved administrations of Scotland and Wales increased their support during the COVID-19 crisis, despite tightening centralisation. There has been an underlying continuity, or path dependency, however, in central–local relations which has stemmed from the fact that, constitutionally, power remains with central government. Using Jim Bulpitt's (1983) classic thesis on territorial politics in the UK, we can identify changes over time in the statecraft, or 'operating code' adopted by governments. They have intervened more in the 'low politics' of local government, and 'the means of that domination have changed over time and inevitably those means appear more oppressive in periods of austerity and renewal than in periods of expansion' (Laffin, 2009: 35). Overall, governance arrangements have become increasingly complex, opaque and increasingly weighted towards control by central government. The House of Commons Public Administration and Constitutional Affairs Committee (2022: 3) 'found that the dominant reason for continued over centralisation is a prevalent culture in Whitehall that is unwilling to let go of its existing levers of power'.

It is of course not possible to detach recent trends in service responsibilities of local government, as outlined in Chapter 4, from the financial context. The long-term trend, as noted in earlier chapters, has been a move in the direction of local government becoming an agent for the delivery of a set of services which have increasingly been prescribed by central government, while at the same time losing responsibilities to a range of other mainly unelected or indirectly elected bodies. The delivery of remaining services has been contracted out to a range of other providers, and central control of overall funding has become ever tighter. The government retains a general power, under Section 15 of the Local Government Act 1999, for the Secretary of State or an appointee to take over any local function, a power which was used four times in the ten years to 2020. However, 2021–22 saw an indication of an upward trend in such interventions, and a further three being ordered, with commissioners taking over council functions, within nine months (Hill, 2022c).

Thus, overall, the balance of funding from central or local sources is important but has to be seen in the context of how much legal power and discretion local government has to spend the money, whatever its source; as Stoker (2004: 179) notes, 'It would certainly be bizarre to insist that local government was more autonomous in the late 1980s than in the mid 1970s simply because it raised more of its own income in the late 1980s.' Also, as we have seen, central–local relations raise key questions over the desired extent of local diversity. It may be the case, as Davies (2008: 18) has argued, that the public demand is for equity and national standards, 'meaning that discretion is only necessary at the margins'. In response, we would argue that local government with more discretion over what it does and how it distributes its finances has a primarily ethical, democratic basis, one which can be fitted into a democratic system which accounts for concerns around universal principles and standards. We have some grounds for optimism in that, however tight the central government grip on local government has become, it cannot be so overwhelming as to stifle any local initiative, and the actions of many councils over the recent past gives us an indication of a potential direction of travel should that grip be loosened.

7
How have local authorities coped with change?

In Chapters 4 and 6 we identified the cumulative weakening of local government's direct service responsibilities, and an underlying increase in restraint based on legal and financial control by central government. We set out how a period of austerity since 2010 intensified these trends, with even moves to 'allow' local governments to raise more funds locally taking place in the context of severe overall financial restraint. The COVID-19 pandemic ironically further served to highlight local government's value while also leaving it weaker still. As Peter John (2014) has noted, commentators have predicted the end of local government for many decades, only to see it survive in revised form. In many ways now, however, local government finds itself in unchartered territory. In response to austerity, local governments have had little choice but to implement cuts, while engaging more in commercial activities and sometimes speculative property investment. Local government has thus been viewed as a vehicle of 'austerity localism', providing a buffer for centrally imposed cuts, and contributing to a 'financialisation' of public service delivery. As 'austerian realists' (Davies and Thompson, 2016), local government actors are seen here to be complicit in the embedding not only of further central control, but of a 'roll with it' neoliberalism which is infused with the rhetoric of localism but which ultimately 'dumps' its effects on the local communities.

In recent years, however, there has been a growing interest in the tactics employed by local councils to provide resilience, if not outright resistance, to this agenda, via a range of innovative responses to protect communities, to generate more progressive alternatives, to meet the challenge of climate change and, of necessity, to become more self-sufficient (Morphet and Clifford, 2021). Some observers have noted the day-to-day resistances of actors at the local level who, in a process of 'bricolage', creatively make do and mend in ways which may coalesce into a broader programme (Lowndes and McCaughie, 2013). Alternatively, some councils have acted more purposefully and have arguably been able to offer visions based on innovative and entrepreneurial activity for the public purpose, based on, for example, community wealth building (CLES, 2020b). In this chapter we will examine a range of these alternatives. If local government is still able to exercise meaningful leeway, even in the most hostile of climates, then what does this tell us about the inherent qualities of local government and why it persists? On the other hand, are these activities simply tolerated by central government, which can, should it wish, legislate to prevent them, showing that ultimately central authority indeed continues to 'trump' local initiative? Moreover, despite their efforts, local governments have become increasingly constrained by macro-economic trends of globalisation, neoliberal restructuring of public services and growing business/private sector influence in local affairs. How much do such factors limit local government and essentially co-opt it into their implications for public services and economic policy?

The issue of autonomy

To begin, we need to make a brief return to the relationship between central and local government discussed in Chapter 6. While the long-term trend, we argue, has been in the direction of reduced legal and financial autonomy for local government, it is not the case that there will always be a straightforward and wholly coherent 'imposition' of a clear agenda by a unified centre onto a homogeneous local government. Central–local relations have become increasingly formalised; as noted, the 'bottom line' is that central government holds the financial and legislative cards. While it is true that the scope for 'formal' discretion may have diminished, within these constraints we have to look at the practices of local governments to see what actual leeway they have, and then in turn assess how significant this seems to be. This requires a widening of our scope of analysis. It is possible to have a strongly constitutionally protected local government which is weak, practically, in influencing the well-being of its citizens, and vice versa. While outright resistance to central government has been rare and, as we have seen, ended in defeat for the local authorities concerned, government policies have repeatedly been reinterpreted in creative and diverse ways by local governments, sometimes frustrating government intentions (Stewart, 2000). Many councils resisted CCT, for example, using contract specifications to favour in-house provision (Doogan, 1999). Similarly, 'signs of life' and local interpretation continued through New Labour's initiatives around community leadership and partnerships (Sullivan, 2004). As Pike and Tomaney (2009: 29) state, 'local and regional actors are not passive, nor do they merely respond to the initiatives of the centre. Such actors attempt to develop and pursue strategies shaped by history, and their national political economic context.'

We have, then, to consider the issues of local government autonomy more closely; the juridical and financial framework of local government does not tell the whole story (Stoker, 2004: 249). Local government, particularly in Britain, has been viewed through the lenses of 'autonomy' or 'freedom' from constraints, but in each case these are relational rather than discrete commodities and as such should not be seen in straightforwardly binary, hierarchical and zero-sum terms. Local autonomy is open to variation over issues and time, within the same constitutional system (Pratchett, 2004: 367). In turn, neither should we conflate local autonomy and local democracy. A local government which is constitutionally more autonomous from the centre is not necessarily more democratic in its practices (Pratchett, 2004: 365).

Local government is always, therefore, more or less independent, taking into consideration a range of factors beyond the formal. Using the typology developed by Gurr and King (1987), local government may have high Type II authority, meaning that it is able to pursue its interests without constitutional limitation or central government pressures, but low Type I autonomy, which requires freedom from its social and economic environment, including business and commercial interests, political organisations and social movements which can shape or constrain it. Pratchett (2004) draws on Wolman and Goldsmith (1990) to point out how local government may have 'freedom from' central government constraint, but little 'freedom to' impact on its area. In this sense autonomy is related to effectiveness, the extent to which local government *matters*, and the 'residual ability of local authorities, when all extraneous economic and political variables are taken into account, to affect the well-being of their localities' (Pratchett, 2004: 366).

Similarly, those who have focussed on the positive potential of local government as community leader amidst 'local governance' have stressed more informal behaviour, and local government's ability to mobilise resources to achieve outcomes through partnership working and collaborative networks, concentrating on the rules, norms and conventions which shape and influence collective action. Here, the important question is not how autonomous local government is, but what it can actually achieve, whether it has the right combination of resources to enable it to 'lever' action from others and to steer local system capacity towards social goods. At the base of this are revised notions of autonomy and power, away from the binary 'power to/power over' towards 'power with' or social production, derived from blending capabilities and resources from a range of actors (Mossberger and Stoker, 2001; Stoker, 1998). Following such arguments, even without 'hard' formal power, and despite loss of service delivery responsibilities, councils could exercise 'soft power' through influence, diplomacy, facilitation, problem-identification, goal- and vision-setting, to develop community leadership roles and assume the metagovernance, strategic leadership and coordinating oversight of the plethora of agencies, partnerships and networks in a locality. We have argued that this version of local government would leave it devoid of 'hard' power, too weak to offer sufficient leverage to establish effective leadership. However, such views do make the point that a snapshot of the formal picture may not necessarily tell us the whole story.

So, setting aside formal central–local relations, how much autonomy does local government have? One key focus of attention here must be the leeway local government may have within the constraints of global macro-economic forces, and its place in the capitalist state architecture, and in particular its 'freedom' from business interests. Broadly Marxist analyses have located local government in the wider context of capitalist society as a whole, and in particular the state's management of recurring crises (Goodwin et al., 1993). However, even such early analyses of the 'local state' varied in their interpretation of how much autonomy local councils retained. Cynthia Cockburn (1977) portrayed a scenario of the 'state writ small', where local government's role was that of securing conditions favourable to capitalist accumulation. For Cockburn, however, there was some scope for a class-based politics of resistance and room for manoeuvre based around conflicts and tensions related to the delivery of these services. Direct experience at a local level left the state more vulnerable, while conflict over state outputs was most likely to be focussed at the community level, and this could lead to the development of a distinct social and political consciousness (see also Corrigan, 1979).

Subsequent debate focussed on the extent and nature of this distinctiveness and the possibility of autonomy for local state actors and institutions. Structural marxists emphasise the role of the state in reconciling competing interests and fractures, seeing a role for some autonomy for local state institutions around issues other than class. Critics of Cockburn, notably Saunders (1982), built on previous work by O'Connor (1973) in promoting the 'dual state theory', dividing state activity into production and consumption fields, with local government being responsible for the consumption elements, mainly welfare services. Importantly here, these local state services, by their nature, were held to offer the opportunity for a distinctive, more plural and contestable politics. Dunleavy (1980) similarly characterised 'urban politics' as the politics of collective consumption, the site in which the inevitable conflicts surrounding issues such as housing were mediated.

Increasingly from the 1980s onwards, research began to draw more attention to contingency and the specific local impacts, in particular, of neoliberal forms of capitalism. Such 'middle range propositions' drew on uneven development and the specific local and political characteristics forged in places by the differing geographies of capital accumulation. Specific patterns of production, politics and social formation served to focus attention on 'locality effects' (Goodwin et al.,1993; Massey 1995). Here the 'local state' was underpinned by a set of unique social, economic, cultural and historical developments, which would 'bend' or refract state policies at local level. Local government was 'simultaneously agent and obstacle for the national state' (Goodwin, 1989: 153), both a focus of and for local resistance (as a locally representative body) and a mechanism to manage, dilute and fragment it (as a part of a bureaucratic, professionalised state) (Dunleavy, 1984).

The consequence of such approaches is to refocus attention on the scope for place-based specificities and divergences of approach. In addition, notions of the unified state have been deconstructed by broadly poststructural understandings which highlight 'the fragmented system and contradictory purposes that gather under its name' (J. Martin, 2002: 53), and identify the state as 'a more or less fragmented assembly of agencies and actors with no substantive unity', which is best 'understood as problematic, messy and internally antagonistic' (Orr, 2009: 44). This seems to be revealed in practice by the growing tangle of agencies, partnerships and private providers which have come to populate the local arena since the 1980s. The state is here viewed as 'a diverse ensemble of institutions and agencies' (J. Martin, 2002: 52), increasingly not congruent with local government, and as leaving 'gaps and spaces' which can be exploited by agents for progressive ends. Such thinking had to some extent already permeated into local government in the late 1960s via the community development movement, which recognised the scope for working 'In and Against the State' (Craig, 1989), and via the radical left, once dismissive of local governments as paternalistic, which began to see them as prizes worth gaining in pursuit of prefigurative, progressive agendas. The local socialist, 'New Urban Left' (NUL) councils in the 1980s reflected this mindset, with the approach in each area a reflection of the social, economic and cultural specifics of their place.

In turn, however, the 'fate' of the NUL councils is salutary. Firstly, the government was able to exercise its legislative and financial muscle, albeit over time and following resistance, to bring them into line, and indeed to legislate one of them, the GLC, out of existence. Moreover, by the late 1980s those remaining had 'fallen into line' with the economic consensus, favouring market-led growth and regeneration through the attraction of increasingly mobile capital (Seyd, 1990). This 'urban entrepreneurialism'

(Harvey, 1989), focussing on competitive bidding for pots of central government regeneration funding, place-marketing and the building of coalitions with private sector investors, was indicative of a 'new realism' and 'a full-scale retreat from many of the defiant positions they had taken up during the early 1980s' – an acknowledgment of 'a marked shift in the perception of what was actually possible in terms of the parameters and constraints on local strategy' (Quilley, 2000: 611). The new realism involved councils accepting that their social welfare role depended on economic growth, arising from what Cochrane (2007: 140) notes was an end to the 'clear division between the politics of economic policy and the politics of social welfare'. New realism required them to be more proactive in growth promotion, but within a framework of building a globally competitive economy through place-based competition.

Councils have thus appeared to be fundamentally restrained by economic interests, increasingly those of global capital. Hill (2000) and Chandler (2007) show that business elites were closely tied to local, civic affairs in the nineteenth century, but throughout most of the twentieth century they had been largely uninterested, content for councils to administer welfare services in line with a broad consensus. Since the 1980s, however, councils have increasingly been seen as players in growth-led partnerships in which business elites were key participants, if not leaders, and business interests have been encouraged to exercise increasing influence in local government affairs, initially in the field of urban regeneration, but also more widely. UDCs, business-led entities, were introduced by the first Thatcher administration as the first of a series of initiatives requiring business involvement in such partnerships, which placed local authorities in a more minor position. Local authorities progressively became involved in place-based competitive bidding for government grants, notably in the City Challenge initiative (1991) and the Single Regeneration Fund (1995–2001).

Evolving out of these more partnership-based initiatives and further embedding the approach (Fuller and Geddes, 2008: 265), New Labour placed more emphasis on broader community engagement and social exclusion. The 'new conventional wisdom' of regeneration was now firmly established, holding that economic competitiveness and social cohesion were linked, leading to a form of 'conservative liberalism' (Cochrane, 2007: 127). A renewed focus on social exclusion under New Labour was thus increasingly tied to economic growth, and local government provision of community and welfare services could be interpreted as 'socialisation' interventions (Fuller and Geddes, 2008: 256), or as 'social neoliberalism' (Guarneros-Meza and Geddes, 2010: 116). Thus, Raco (2005: 324) noted that 'Development agendas are, it is argued, increasingly dominated by the principles of market-driven reforms, social inequality, and a drive towards enhancing the economic competitiveness of the supply side of the economy'. Davies (2002: 317) similarly observed 'the emergence of a political culture among local government elites in the UK which conceives of business engagement in urban regeneration as a positive development. There has thus been a diffusion of neoliberal attitudes to the relationship between state and market.' As we have seen, the Coalition government continued to integrate business interests into local decision-making via the LEPs, and governments since 2010 have stressed subregional economic growth via incentives coordinated through devolution deals and CAs. Further, as noted in Chapter 4, austerity has driven local authorities into arrangements with national and global financiers (Beswick and Penny, 2018).

Thus in considerations of the autonomy of local government, the effects of neoliberal state reformation have become a central narrative. Since the early 1980s, local government has been both subject of and vehicle for the neoliberal trajectory in all its varieties, involving marketisation and urban entrepreneurialism, as a result of 'roll back' neoliberalism, which sought to shrink the size of the state and divest it of public services. Further 'roll-out' neoliberalism required the management and attempted alleviation of the consequences of this agenda (Fuller and Geddes, 2008) with, increasingly, subnational scales restructured to manage 'the interface between the local economy and global flows, between the potentially conflicting demands of local sustainability and local well-being and those of international competitiveness, and between the challenges of social exclusion ... and continuing demands for liberalization, deregulation, [and] privatisation' (Jessop, 2002:466, in Guarneros-Meza and Geddes, 2010: 116). Such neoliberal local state restructuring, it has been argued, has found particularly fertile ground in Britain (Guarneros-Meza and Geddes, 2010: 119). Restructuring, boundary changes and new regional and subregional institution scales can here, then, be interpreted as geographical/spatial strategies seeking elusive 'fixes' to the perpetual contradictions of capitalism, with each in turn trying to resolve the failure of previous interventions (Jones and Ward, 2002).

Further aspects of 'roll-out' neoliberalism have seen local government involved in using practices of active citizen engagement, participation, self-responsibility and co-production as technologies of governing, the subsequent 'normalisation' of which Keil (2009) calls 'roll with it' neoliberalism. Geddes (2006: 93), for example, in reviewing partnerships under New Labour locates them firmly within the context of neoliberal political economy and rescaling of government, with the 'core institutions of the capitalist state' maintaining tight control over any challenge to neoliberal hegemony. Even when business interests have shown little interest in taking part in these rescaled local governance arrangements, the internalisation of the 'rules of the game' by local state actors and residents has ensured the dominance of their interests. Thus Geddes identified a reluctance to impose any demands on capital in achieving local strategies which were not in its interests, while capital benefited from 'supply-side approaches to public service provision [which] imply an inherent bias towards the needs of capital rather than the needs of locations abandoned (or re-exploited) by capital' (Geddes, 2006: 92).

We must accept that local government is indeed located not just in a network of central–local relations, but also in a wider network of economic and social relationships, and has always been constrained, not just by central controls but also by economic interdependencies, and shaped by the prevailing economic conditions (Skelcher, 2017). Following this argument, other alternative models would require systematic change if they were to be sustained. But as we have noted, gaps and spaces will always be available, and the particularities of place cannot be completely smoothed out. Macroeconomic processes play out on a more or less uneven and bumpy terrain. The issue is, how much does this allow for meaningful local alternatives? Despite everything, can local government still innovate and provide some locally specific responses to external challenges? If so, how might these be built on and facilitated even further in the context in which local government sits?

Neoliberalism and local agency

Taking a more optimistic view of the possibilities for local action requires us to take a closer look at the dominant narrative in these debates over the past four decades: neoliberalism. With its associated technologies of governance, it has been the subject of considerable critical debate (Blanco et al., 2014). 'Actually existing' or 'variegated neo-liberalism' (Brenner et al., 2010) can be interpreted, in contrast to some of the views set out above, as a contested and contradictory process (Larner, 2003), always incomplete, highly contingent and re-articulated at different scales and localities. Neoliberal state programmes linking social exclusion with competitive growth have, for example, potentially unstable and contradictory appeals to both collectivism and individualism (Guarneros-Meza and Geddes, 2010: 115). These potential 'gaps' and associated new forms and techniques of governing have formed the basis of critiques drawing on Foucauldian perspectives, focussing attention on technologies of power and the micro-processes of practice, and finding resistance and continued renegotiation at the front line of service delivery and in the interaction between officials, professionals and intermediaries. Here, local histories, assigned meanings and understandings provide the ground on which neoliberalism is reinterpreted and played out. Newman (2014a) points out that local government is one stage on which the contradictions and ambiguities of neoliberal technologies of government are contested and mediated in the daily practices of councillors, officers and citizens; local government acts to mediate and translate neoliberal projects in line with 'local needs, goals and values' (Newman, 2014a: 3295). Further, an 'assemblage perspective' (Fuller, 2012) sees local formations articulated in distinctive ways, as dominant and residual local practices interact. Local governments here are both objects and sponsors of neoliberalism (Newman, 2014a); they are mediating actors, sites of political contestation, giving potentialities for distinctive local political formations and resistance, and for acting as 'dual intermediaries' between state and civil society.

Local practices and agency are therefore brought out of the shadows here (Griggs and Roberts, 2012: 202). With respect to the everyday practices of local government, as with any organisation, it is not possible to envisage actors working without agency. This was highlighted by Lowndes and McCaughie (2013), for example, who pointed to the contextual and institutional traditions which are found in local governments, forged in practice, which are distinctive and path-dependent. From their research they identified people delivering local services displaying an impressive resilience. The agency here is evidenced through daily creativity, which may go under the radar and which is 'not transformation, but not inertia either' (Lowndes and McCaughie, 2013: 546). The key question, then, is how much this inevitable local 'leeway' adds up to, how significant it is and what its potential might be. Resistance by local agents to central policies is potentially everywhere, but it is unclear to what extent a local council can facilitate, influence or direct these practices in any consistent way. These practices, in the day-to-day work of local government workers at all levels and of councillors, may perhaps under certain conditions build up relatively consistent and distinctive patterns which mean that local government, as a distinctly privileged form of local governance, matters, and that it could provide the potential for specific local political formations – which otherwise may not 'scale up' but remain disparate, fragmented and short-lived – to develop.

Innovation and entrepreneurial activity

There is some evidence that, indeed, despite the most hostile of environments, local governments have continued to find space for distinctive local action. This is the result of the very impossibility of 'total' control suggested above, but it also arises from the enduring salience of locality effects emanating from differing political, social, economic and cultural backgrounds, filtered through varied institutional histories (Pike et al., 2015). Thus, for example, the UDCs, arguably the most business-dominated urban regeneration vehicles outlined above, also displayed locality effects and local embeddedness, and generated local political contestation in a way which 'suggests caution against conceptualizing their actions as either instrumentalist and/or as seeking only to propagate forms of economic boosterism' (Thomas and Imrie, 1997: 62). Atkinson and Wilks-Heeg (2000) argue that despite the reforms of the 1980s and 1990s, local governments continued to exercise 'creative autonomy' to 'short circuit' the agenda. Further, as Quilley (2000: 601) argues, although there were contradictory effects left by the legacy of the NUL, with hindsight, 'the municipal left can be credited with redefining the role of local authorities in relation to the economy, creating a space for proactive local and regional economic strategies'. New Labour's partnerships, while underpinned by the narrative of the entrepreneurial city, also contained potential for dissent and community empowerment (Durose and Lowndes, 2010), while Coaffee and Headlam (2007) noted a 'pragmatic localism' in the local adaptations to central initiatives. In addition, as we have noted, the subregional agenda and austerity pursued after 2010, while heavily constraining, has seen councils continuing to be innovative. Local authorities have by and large remained at the forefront of LEPs, although they were intended to be business-led, and the partnerships continue to be subject to the control of central government in relation to funding and priorities, replicating long-standing central–local relationships (Broadhurst, 2018).

Following this line of thought, recent years have provided perhaps the sternest test yet of this more 'optimistic' take. As we have noted, local government has since 2010 been the subject of an intensification of central controls, particularly of its finances. And yet some have identified a corresponding period of local innovation, sometimes of necessity, in response to austerity, which has been driving managerial innovation. Bello et al. (2018) argue that while initially cost-driven, this can have longer term beneficial organisational effects. Here, austerity is argued to be a driver of social innovation, creativity and public value creation (Carr, 2015), but is only one part of a wider picture of increasingly complex social and environmental demands which 'require more than incremental change' (OECD, 2017) and changes to 'traditional' means of delivery towards a new paradigm or 'operating model' (Lloyd and Randle, 2019).

Such new models emphasise the need to tap into citizen knowledge for innovation and to tailor hard choices in relation to resource allocation. In this view local councils have been able to secure efficiencies, but have also taken on an enhanced 'enabling' role to become 'orchestrators' of co-production with civil society and service users, with councils acting as 'matchmakers' or 'incubators' of solutions (Mulgan, 2012). Local state actors here are seen to exercise more agency in a new, 'relational' form of governance, in contrast to a bureaucratic, 'traditional' top-down one (Liddle, 2016), as they are 'freed' to facilitate and leverage public value (Klein et al., 2010) and create the conditions for citizens to participate as co-producers. Such innovative practice is said to involve use of 'soft power' and collaboration with a range of actors across formal and informal settings (Liddle and McElwee, 2019).

Illustrative of such views is the fact that a collection of studies from the Local Government Information Unit, *The Future Town Hall* (LGiU, 2013), contained only one piece, from a total of thirty-nine written by a range of practitioners and commentators, envisioning a future for local government consistent with what at the time was a widely predicted 'doomsday' scenario. The majority foresaw a move consistent with the 'conductor-orchestrator' role. Certainly several councils, in reacting to austerity, have aspired to these models – for example, the 'John Lewis Council' model adopted by Lambeth LBC and based on the promotion of community, mutual and social enterprises.

This capacity for innovation and creativity has led some to highlight its continuation, if not intensification, during the COVID-19 pandemic, where local government has shown itself capable of adapting quickly to new ways of working, being the agency with the local knowledge and responsiveness necessary. Cretu (2020) noted 'new operating models' being further developed during the pandemic, including greater flexibility, more delegation to frontline staff, increased digitalisation, more collaboration, and support and coordination for a range of local organisations. COVID-19 had been, in this sense, a catalyst for change. In a similar vein, Munro and Burbidge (2020: 7) have encouraged local government to 'seize the moment' and build on relationships established with community groups and others during the pandemic to 'rethink the way public services operate'. Others have focussed on the role of community groups and mutual aid, ranging from formal to informal groups in localities, to argue for an enhanced space for civil society, community and local engagement in services provision and delivery (Tiratelli and Kaye, 2020), or for revisiting the importance of neighbourhood and proximity (Wargent and Talen, 2021). In conjunction with this has been a seemingly paradoxical increase in participation during the pandemic, not only through greater direct engagement of local groups, but through the efforts of councils to enhance direct communication with citizens.

However, in response, it could be argued that such efforts are mostly managerial in nature, relating to issues of service delivery, and broadly in line with a government agenda which favours outsourcing and 'choice' being extended to individual users and civil society (although at odds with the focus on the private sector during the pandemic). Also, throughout, local governments' leverage has rested to a large extent on retaining a core of – albeit diminished – service responsibilities, and legal and financial resources. It also resonates with government rhetoric around localism, and with the most recent incarnation of managerialism that stresses 'empowerment' of users and a 'loose-tight' strategy of devolving responsibility while retaining control and orchestrating the direction of travel. Moreover, local governments' innovative responses to COVID-19 are overshadowed by the more significant ways in which it was bypassed by the government during the pandemic in the key area of public health, and by the centralised and privatised nature of the response generally.

Other optimistic interpretations of the space for local agency, though, take a broader institutional view, identifying possibilities, potentialities and defences for local government more widely. Key to these have been alternative interpretations of commercialisation which see it as having more than neoliberal connotations. Firstly, there has been a trend towards councils taking back in-house, or 'insourcing', previously contracted out services, not only because it has proven to be the more efficient option, but also to facilitate greater strategic coordination across services – such that, it has been argued, 'it seems like contracting's heroic age is over' (Walker and Tizard, 2018: 7). This has taken place amidst a wider 'remunicipalisation' of services internationally (Cumbers and Becker, 2018). The high-profile collapse in 2018 of Carillion, a large facilities management company with around 450 public sector contracts, left thirty contracts with local councils unfulfilled and added impetus to this trend; Derby City Council saved more than £1 million by bringing highways maintenance back in-house after the company's demise (Merrick, 2020). Around the same time, the Local Government and Social Care Ombudsman, in evidence to the House of Commons Public Administration and Constitutional Affairs Committee, stated that accountability for services was often lost when they were outsourced. The New Local Government Network (NLGN) Leadership Index of 2018 found that 39 per cent of chief executives said their councils intended to outsource less (NLGN, 2018), while a survey by APSE (2019a) found that 73 per cent of local government senior officers said they were considering insourcing services. For example, in 2018 Stoke-on-Trent City Council brought housing repair services back in-house, ending a contract with the Keir Group. Notably, the London Borough of Barnet, which had previously promoted an 'Easy Council' model based on maximum outsourcing, decided in 2019 to bring five services back in-house, stating that this was less about saving money than gaining more control over strategic services (Rudgewick, 2020). Research carried out by APSE (2019a) found that 78 per cent of local authorities believed that insourcing gave them more flexibility, two-thirds that it also saved money and more than half that it had improved the quality of the service while simplifying its management. The research pointed clearly to drivers which went beyond a desire to make savings, including improving service quality and flexibility, having greater control over allocating resources and being able to support the local economy via local procurement of goods and services (Sandford, 2019).

Beyond insourcing, councils have increasingly engaged in more proactive commercialisation and entrepreneurial activity. This has, as noted in Chapter 4, not been without controversy, particularly in cases of investment in property outside of a council's own area, and large-scale housing redevelopment projects. Proposed schemes like the one in Haringey, described in Chapter 4, have raised particularly acute critiques which have viewed them as 'state led privatisation' (Raco, 2013). The council did, however, after considerable public pressure and a change of leadership, decide not to go ahead with the plan in 2018. Yet not all the entrepreneurial activity can so easily be labelled as straightforwardly commercial, and much activity of this kind is not the financialisation or speculation identified by Beswick and Penny (2018). As Morphet and Clifford (2021: 143) note, 'some of the inventive and innovatory activity of the local state can have progressive potential', and can be seen in the light of councils making, of necessity, difficult choices, but also of protecting services and as far as possible seeking positive social impacts (Christophers, 2019).

Certainly, there has been no shortage of innovative practices adopted by local authorities, aimed at creating social benefit. Sandford (2019) reports on the spectrum of alternative models of service delivery which had been adopted by local authorities in increasing numbers. This had been facilitated by legal changes to council powers in Sections 1–7 of the Localism Act, including the general power of competence, which allowed councils to act as a company, and undertake more widely commercial trading and provision of services. Adoption of international accounting standards in the UK brought private and public sector accounting practices into line, leading to a convergence in capital accounting and making it easier for public and private sectors to work together. Local authorities could now assess investments in conjunction with a range of assets, meaning that they could now consider wider social benefits or savings which might accrue from an investment (Morphet, 2016).

A range of trading vehicles have been facilitated by these and already existing powers, including those granted by the Local Government Act 2003. These include local authority trading companies (LATCs), established under Section 4 of the 2011 Localism Act, profits from which can be reinvested in other council services. In 2011, only 15 per cent of local authorities operated a trading company; by 2018, this had risen to 59.2 per cent, and an estimated 743 companies (Sasse et al., 2020: 17). A survey of local authority chief executives and senior officers, conducted by the *Local Government Chronicle* in January 2019, showed 66 per cent of respondents expected their council's commercial revenue to rise by up to 25 per cent in the following three years (Sandford, 2019). Carr (2015) reported that eight out of ten councils said they would have had to cut services and/or raise taxes without these activities. Nottingham City Council, for example, operated trade waste collection services for a number of local businesses and for neighbouring councils such as Rushcliffe and Derby City Council. Norse Group, a holding company owned by Norfolk County Council (Sandford, 2019) providing a range of services including refuse collection, grounds maintenance and pest control to councils across the country, was by 2019 the largest LATC, with an annual turnover in excess of £250 million. Other vehicles used in commercialisation strategies included joint ventures – such as Staffordshire Highways, set up by the county council and the private contractor Amey (Sasse et al., 2020) – in configurations giving varying degrees of council ownership (Sandford, 2019). Despite the 'hit' which commercial activity took during the COVID-19 pandemic, it is notable that insourcing and the establishment of a variety of commercial and trading vehicles continued; Bournemouth, Christchurch and Poole established a 'Placemaking' regeneration company in 2021 (Sharman, 2021), and East Sussex decided to end its relationship with private group NORSE and bring the services back into a council-owned arm's-length company (Hanson, 2021).

There may also be such 'signs of life' in service responsibilities. In education, for example, the drive for academies led in turn to a re-emerging role for councils as a 'middle tier', increasingly 'midwifing' and acting as convenors and coordinators of school improvement initiatives, making use of their existing pools of experience and knowledge (Crawford et al., 2022). The extent of this activity depended on how the councils themselves perceived their role, but many began to establish new forms of collaboration to address the dangers of fragmentation, developing a 'multidimensional middle' involving regional agencies, MATs, local authority and sub-local authority arrangements. While this in no way could be said to restore the once prominent position local government held in education, it does again show the continued persistence of local initiative, the key role of local knowledge, the need for collective responsibility for a key service and the persistent inventiveness of local government in the most hostile of environments.

Indeed, innovation has also extended beyond the delivery of services. Local government has over the years utilised a range of democratic innovations, 'institutions that have been specifically designed to increase and deepen citizen participation in the political decision-making process' (G. Smith, 2010: 1). These involve a spectrum of initiatives, ranging from the 'localisation' of larger councils into smaller, devolved units to which a variety of decision-making powers are delegated, to the use of more deliberative mechanisms like citizens' juries, for example by Leeds City Council, and participatory budgeting by Durham County Council, Tower Hamlets LBC and Midlothian Council. Certainly, the decentralising initiatives which were experimented with in the 1980s have seen a revival, admittedly at a time when the councils concerned themselves have less power to delegate. North Ayrshire Council, for example, amidst a range of community empowerment initiatives, established six locality planning partnerships. Often such initiatives are part and parcel of a wider strategic approach to service delivery, community asset transfer and engagement, as in, for example, Wigan MBC's Wigan Deal. As noted earlier, it has been argued that the experience of COVID-19 has led to councils building on and expanding such initiatives. Barking and Dagenham LBC, for example, extended its BD-CAN strategy to BD-CAN Plus to incorporate greater, more flexible engagement, facilitation of 'bottom up civil society action' and integration of service delivery (Lawson, 2020: 1), and Newham LBC introduced a standing citizens assembly in May 2021 in response to inequalities which had been further exposed by the pandemic (Oglethorpe, 2021). Also, in Chapter 6 we highlighted the 'localist' agenda after 2010 and in particular the weaknesses of the neighbourhood planning initiative with respect to enhancing participation, but noted also the view that in neighbourhood planning there was at least the potential for nurturing democratic engagement.

New municipalism?

Some councils have also set such initiatives into a broader strategy, raising revenues and intervening in local markets in a variety of ways. Research published by APSE (2019a) identified that councils were 'generating income for the public purpose', intervening in local markets, addressing market failure and 'driving forward community wealth building by using their purchasing power and assets to recycle economic benefit locally and build the capacity of small and medium enterprises to meet community needs' (APSE, 2019a: 6). More use of local suppliers was opening up opportunities for small and medium-sized businesses, helping to retain the 'local pound' and to 'tackle the "Klondike" economy whereby national companies "export" profits out of the area' (APSE, 2019a: 6). Procurement was increasingly being used to secure social benefits – for example, living wage clauses were being incorporated into contracts – using the Public Services (Social Value) Act 2012, which permitted local authorities to use procurement to deliver wider public goals.

Such 'intrapreneurial' activity (Phelps and Miao, 2020) saw councils being more proactive and strategic in their approach, and 'scaling up' their activities to align them with a broader vision for their areas. Enterprising Warrington, for example, was launched in 2017 as a commercial strategy to bring together trading activity across the council and align it with the council's values, and included developing a Local Authority Mortgage Scheme, which had by 2017 given more than 200 loans worth over £5.5 million, and was undertaking a £120 million redevelopment of the town centre (LGA, 2017). Councils also began to issue bonds, through the Municipal Bonds Agency, established in 2015, to raise finance; for example, the Agency gave a £250 million loan to Leicestershire County Council in 2020, and Sutton LBC issued its own £250 million bond in 2020. Collectively, this presents a picture of municipal entrepreneurial activity which is arguably 'redolent of nineteenth century municipal traditions' (Lowndes and Gardner, 2016: 370).

One area where councils have been particularly proactive is housing, through the creation of wholly owned housing companies, building for either sale or rent. Homes owned via a company lay outside of Housing Revenue Account or Right to Buy provisions, making this a more flexible approach for local authorities than providing housing directly. Morphet (2019) notes that councils sought to address a growing housing crisis, driven by frustration at slow building rates by private developers, and by changes to funding which required them to look at 'ways to support their income to deliver services and provide a sound financial basis for the future that are not reliant on government policies'. Thus 'councils [were] beginning to regard their approach as patient investors'. They re-entered into house building as a means of supporting local economies, improving skills and supporting local suppliers. In a report for the Royal Town Planning Institute, Morphet and Clifford (2017) reported that council house building was at its highest level in almost thirty years. Their survey of eighty-three English councils found that at least 9,000 homes had been directly created by local authorities in 2017/18, with 43 per cent classed as 'affordable' and 23 per cent for 'social' rent. Projecting these figures over the entire UK suggested that more than 13,000 new homes were delivered by councils in 2018/19, the highest amount since 1990, when 14,020 homes were built. Councils were providing these homes in increasingly inventive and diverse ways. By 2019, 78 per cent of authorities reported having a local housing company, and 57 per cent had joint vehicles for housing development (Morphet and Clifford, 2021).

Evidence of more strategic, broader alternatives being adopted by councils is provided by local government's role as a key player in addressing the climate emergency, with many councils pursuing 'transition economies' with an integrated set of policies across transport, energy, planning, housing, building control and environmental responsibilities. By 2020, 230 councils had declared a climate emergency, supporting energy transitions and sustainability with a range of innovative approaches. Woking Borough Council, for example, created an energy services company, Thamesway Energy, to build and operate a combined heat and power energy station in the town centre. Public Power Solutions, a wholly owned subsidiary of Swindon Borough Council, was in 2022 the only wholly public sector-owned renewable energy developer (Fyans et al., 2022). Councils increasingly used planning powers to build 'net zero' goals into statutory local plans, and building control powers to secure enhanced energy efficiency requirements. In 2020, West Berkshire District Council launched the first local government 'green bonds' to fund solar panel installations on council buildings

(Fyans et al., 2022). Other initiatives included the retrofitting and insulation of housing, and initiatives in transport including the introduction of clean air zones (for example in York) and low emission strategies for council vehicles and buses. Councils thus made progress without the support of a coherent overall policy framework from central government setting out clearly local government's role in the transition to net zero, with Bristol City Council, for example, developing a One Climate strategy with eighteen partners aiming to make the council carbon neutral by 2025, and the city by 2030 (APSE, 2021).

Arguably, then, councils 'reclaimed' entrepreneurialism to generate public value (Bello et al., 2018; Shearmur and Poirier, 2017). Going further, there have been claims based on the approaches of some councils, notably in Preston and Lambeth, that a 'new municipalism' emerged, which some argue offers a more radical path for local government, associated with a twenty-first-century version of municipal socialism. Internationally, such 'progressive municipalism' has been advanced by the 'Fearless Cities' movement, taking its lead from the radical left's electoral success in Barcelona and influenced by examples in the United States in Cleveland, Jackson and elsewhere. The movement has sought to promote 'alternative economies' and ownership and service delivery models which offer new democratic potentials (Russell, 2019). This was influenced by the growth of interest in 'civic capitalism' (Hay and Payne, 2015) and 'inclusive growth', which became 'a new mantra in local economic development' (Lee, 2019: 424).

Labelled the 'Preston model', as political and media attention was attracted by the council in that city, the British municipal variety involved legal compliance with austerity while using possibilities available to offer resistance and alternatives. Creative and 'entrepreneurial' activity here came in the form of 'community wealth building' and associated alternative economic models based on local inclusive growth and democratic ownership (McInroy, 2018; O'Neill and Howard, 2018). This developed originally in Cleveland, USA as a response to the 'place blindness' of global capital, offering 'a people-centred approach to local economic development that aims to reorganise local economies so that wealth is not extracted but redirected back into communities' (CLES, 2020b: 6). The aim is to support local economies and social infrastructure by using the purchasing power and influence of 'anchor institutions' – public sector organisations in an area which undertake to procure and commission more of their goods and services from local sources. Manchester City Council, for example, spent 51 per cent of its procurement in local supply chains in 2008, but by 2018 this had risen to 70 per cent (CLES, 2020a). In addition, support is given to broadening ownership models through social enterprises and cooperatives (Guinan and O'Neill, 2019), offering the potential to 'lay the groundwork for pluralist models of business to thrive' and a pathway towards 'economic democracy' (McKinley et al., 2020). Emphasis is put upon supporting the 'foundational economy': the essential goods and services which are collectively consumed and which provide 'the infrastructure of everyday life' (Earle et al., 2018: 39). In Preston, by 2019 this approach led, according to the council, to £75 million of spending being 'repatriated' to local suppliers – the equivalent of 1,600 extra jobs (Shafique et al., 2019). Other associated initiatives saw the council starting to move away from speculative investments via its pension fund, for example using it to fund local student accommodation and using Conlon Construction, a family business that used local contractors, to undertake a multimillion pound upgrade of a covered market.

The harsh reality

Several notes of caution are necessary, however, to temper this optimism. Preston, while pursuing this agenda, has also had to make cuts due to austerity, bringing an estimated drop in the council's annual central government funding from £30 million in 2012 to £20 million in 2022 (Faulkener, 2022). In addition, the council is a second tier district authority, and so did not have to face the additional pressures of increased demand in social services. It can also be noted that in-house provision in adult social care, the biggest and perhaps most politically sensitive service, has remained flat across councils in England, Scotland and Wales since 2010, at just under a quarter of total spending. This service, then, did not see the 'insourcing' growth seen elsewhere. There were only ten examples by 2022 of councils outsourcing children's social services to arm's-length companies, with at best mixed success (Turner, 2020). We have already noted the controversial nature of some entrepreneurial activities, but such initiatives have also often proven fragile. By 2022 it was clear that there had been both successes and failures (Lorimer, 2022), sometimes due to poor governance and oversight arrangements, but also in the light of local government's weakness in the midst of financial and macro-economic pressures. Thus the energy companies established by Nottingham and Bristol Councils failed; Together Energy, in which Warrington MBC had bought a 50 per cent share in 2019, had to cease trading in January 2020 due to rising international gas prices. A housing company, Foundation Homes, set up by Liverpool City Council in 2018, was wound down in 2022 after incurring estimated losses of £700,000, while Nottingham City Homes, a subsidiary of Nottingham City Council which managed its housing stock, was found in 2022 to have mis-spent £17.1 million of housing account funding. Preston, Wirral and Liverpool Councils announced in 2021 the joint establishment of a North West Mutual Community Bank which would 'strive to address regional inequalities and provide services and support to a diverse range of business and community ventures in the region' (Farnworth, 2021). However, by mid-2022, Wirral and Liverpool had both failed to commit resources to the project due to financial pressures.

Further, it can be argued that community wealth building and promotion of social enterprise are practices which the central government found at least tolerable, fitting as they do a 'localist' rhetoric and even sharing some genealogy with the 'Big Society' initiative. Certainly, central government seemed content to live with this 'community-orientated' approach, and happy to let councils get on with it. Again, when considered in conjunction with cuts, this could be seen as passing on, or 'dumping', the effects of austerity onto community groups. The emphasis on local purchasing, again, raised no eyebrows in central government, which itself engaged with the rhetoric of inclusive economy and community wealth building; indeed it overlapped with the purported 'levelling up' agenda of the Johnson government for 'left behind' towns. The focus on generation of local economic activity also rested well with the intention, until the change of direction announced in 2021, for local government to become more dependent on the generation of its own resources by increasing business activity, and the broad view of local authorities primarily as sources of economic growth.

Similarly, we cannot ignore the overall impact of the economic context when considering commercialisation activities. Taylor et al. (2021) show that in the UK local governments with higher dependency on government grants were more likely to have formed trading companies, and that these were more prevalent in deprived areas. Skelcher (2017: 928), in comparing the municipalist responses of Birmingham City Council in the nineteenth century and post-2010, found that in both cases the choices made were the result of material impacts of their surroundings and that 'it is the political economy within which a local authority is located that creates the conditions within which that choice becomes an imperative on the municipal leadership'. Thus, he argues that it was austerity which drove the council's 'corporatisation' strategy of creating trading units and joint ventures, which became 'the accepted method of managing the tension between reduced budgets and the Council's obligations to its citizens' (Skelcher, 2017: 941).

With respect to 'democratic innovations' we cannot entirely dismiss the emergent democratic practices or potentials which have been stimulated by local government initiatives. However, research has increasingly shown that context is crucial to success. Democratic innovations face contextual and institutional challenges (Bua and Escobar, 2018), need the right soil in which to flourish and are fragile unless nurtured in the right setting. Lowndes et al. (2006) have shown how local governments can positively contribute to a democratic ethos in their areas with practical engagement techniques, but also by shaping the 'rules in use' – the norms and expectations of democracy locally. However, it is clear from the history we have outlined that the 'rules in use', while subject to some local influence, are predominantly shaped by central government and macro-economic forces. Also, again, such efforts have been broadly in line with government rhetoric around localism, easily fitting into, for example, New Labour's agenda on community and social exclusion, and the Cameron government's 'Big Society'. Overall, both went hand in hand with fewer hard powers and ability to actually deliver what might be revealed by more democratic engagement as local wants and needs. Research on participatory and particularly deliberative democracy has increasingly emphasised the need for localised initiatives to be linked to a wider democratic institutional framework. Thinking around more participative and deliberative democracy has thus taken a 'recombinant' or 'systemic' turn (Curato et al., 2017; Owen and Smith, 2015) stressing the need for its institutionalisation and connection into representative forms to enhance the overall quality of a democratic system. What is required is a multiplication of the institutions which foster identification with democratic values, to create what Escobar (2017: 416) calls a 'vibrant democratic ecology'. As we have shown, due to its lack of 'weight' in the polity, local government and any democratic experimentation which it initiates increasingly lacks these connections, although there is undoubted potential in the local arena forming the basis for such an aspiration.

This is not to deny the value of what councils have been doing, but to point out that there are serious questions to ask about how sustainable it is and whether new models can 'take hold', or at least be given the chance to do so. Returning to a basic point, as a creature of statute, there are necessarily limits on the extent to which local government can pursue radical or progressive alternatives, particularly those which go against the prevailing dominant economic context. For this reason, some advocates of the 'new municipalism', taking what can be described as an 'anti-state' view for example, have at best an ambivalent attitude towards local government, seeing it firmly as a 'local state' organ and doubting its ability to deliver anything other than superficial amelioration of the worst excesses of austerity, placing radical potentials firmly in the realm of civil society (Russell, 2019). Such views foreground local agency, but this is to be found outside of the local government, in self-organising groups (Talen, 2014) which have prefigurative, radical possibilities and the potential to 'scale up'. Here, local government is a flawed and somewhat damaged vehicle, hampered by weak powers, financial scarcity and a lack of capabilities to address the issues and constraints generated by the global political economy (Blanco et al., 2019). It is subsequently dismissed as at worst repressive, tainted by compliance with austerian realism or simply by virtue of it being a state institution, incapable of offering any alternative. The only reason for engaging with local government here, would be to access what powers it has, in order to give them away (Russell, 2019). However, we feel local government cannot necessarily be assumed to have no radical potential, as a 'captive' of the central state and the global economy. This 'anti-state' perspective dismisses too easily the need for local political expression and protest to be given some institutional form in order to go 'beyond the fragments'. It also takes too much of a unitary view of the state, assuming that it inevitably engages in a form of 'top-down' rule (Cooper, 2016: 414).

Councils, then, have shown considerable innovative capacity and have striven, for the most part, to ameliorate the effects of austerity on their communities. This does not deny that the cumulative effect of central controls and transient global capital has weakened local government's relative autonomy over the past four decades, nor that any attempts to promote alternative approaches with local initiatives and mount 'serious challenges' (Fuller and Geddes, 2008: 277) face considerable difficulties. Rather it is to recognise that, despite this, there seems to be inherent in local governments some qualities of care for the places in which they are rooted. This seems to persist even in councils which are more or less the 'artificial' creation of reorganisations; the 'local' appears to provide inspiring ground for experimentation which can flourish in the most inhospitable of climates (Cooper, 2016).

This points to a 'middle way' to, in Cooper's (2016) words, 'retrieve the state' and recognise its complexity and plurality, with local government having at least the potential to prefiguratively offer alternatives. Barnett et al. (2022), for example, point to transformative capacities still residing at an organisational level with local councils, identifying a 'municipal entrepreneurship for the public purpose', an emergent discourse which offers a counterbalance to both 'anti-state' views and those which focus on the fragments of resistance by individual local actors. Similarly, Thompson et al. (2020: 1178) find, in the Liverpool City Region, local government initiatives which serve to re-embed economic growth in localities, a form of 'entrepreneurial municipalism' which 'reinvents entrepreneurialism as a progressive municipal idea for the 21st Century'. Local activity of this kind is able, at least, to offer challenges to other narratives of economic growth and social relations (Lauermann, 2016). Whether or not such initiatives can 'take hold' or persist is then the question, and in this chapter we have highlighted many of the reasons why this may not or cannot happen.

Conclusion – the dogs that do not bark in the night?

Painting the picture starkly, local government has, progressively since the mid-1980s, had to adopt a generally compliant and highly constrained stance in response to both government policy and the macro-economic context. Since the last round of rebellious behaviour by the NUL councils was defeated, the legal and financial constraints have been tightened such that a 'dented shield' approach has been adopted with respect to financial constraint. Councillors or officers defying legislation can be surcharged for any unlawful expenditure, thus bankrupting them and removing them from office. Later legislation has built on this platform and, as shown in earlier chapters, has also allowed ministers to unilaterally decide to abolish any council without serious debate, and raising little or no nationwide media or public interest. Such legislation is only made possible in a climate in which there is a lack of interest, let alone wholesale support, within the civic culture for local government. Despite – or because of – the many changes in local government boundaries and the erosion of attachment that this involves, there has been a steady decline in voting in local elections despite greater numbers of contested seats. Structures of local government have ceased to give local government a strong connection with the places in which we live, with many small towns and suburbs of cities being merged into larger authorities with which they do not have strong connections. Moreover, the reporting of local government elections in the national media, both printed and through television and radio, portrays them largely as referenda on the progress of the national political parties and their likelihood of success in national elections.

Local governments have survived, albeit in a very attenuated form compared to the twentieth, let alone the nineteenth century. However, the shaping of the system in which they operate lies not with local governments themselves but in the core executive. In the last fifty years there has been just one occasion when there has been a popular and decisive rebellion against legislation which sought to seriously curtail local authority action – over the introduction of the poll tax in 1990. Significantly, local governments could not openly support the public rebellions, despite being widely opposed to the poll tax, as they were also obliged to enforce the law and to prosecute those who would not pay the tax.

Local government does not, however, necessarily have be so subordinate to national governments. Governing elites within major political parties and the Civil Service, as well the national media and global business interests that drive policy formation, could, as in the United States or France, continue to value local governments as institutions that should have a strong measure of discretion. Given that we can still identify local spaces of innovation in local government after all that has happened to it over recent decades and the current position it finds itself in, as detailed in this book, we can only point to the huge potential capacity for local, democratically informed decision-making to deliver better care for places and communities if it were released from the shadows of the central constraint under which it now resides. However, fulfilment of this potential depends not on the resourcefulness found in localities; what local government is and does has been increasingly determined by how far local government is an expedient requirement to national governments. In Chapter 8 we therefore consider how local government is viewed in Whitehall and Westminster and Edinburgh, if not so much in Cardiff and Northern Ireland. These elements of the policy-making strata greatly determine how local government is shaped and also how it is expected to operate as an element within the British constitution, supported implicitly and subject to little comment, particularly in England, by much of the media and major private sector agencies which inform public policy. We examine the origins of this expediency in terms of the attitudes and views towards local government held by those with the ability, as things stand, to secure its viable future. In doing so, after drawing attention to some grounds for optimism above, we seek to re-emphasise the scale of the task.

8

Local government as expedient agencies of central government

A prominent backbench MP who had been active in local government before their election to Parliament remarked to the writer that once 'in Parliament, local government looked very different from there'. Legislators, and particularly those in government, the Civil Service and their personal advisors, clearly do not often turn their minds to the more localised and unheralded niceties of local government, but see themselves as operating on a national stage. In this context, for many in political and economic elites, and moreover for many academics, globalisation and the capacity to travel the world, both virtually and in reality, may develop a mindset that localism and locality has little meaning or relevance to their policy *weltanschaung*. In as much as technological change gives access to a global society, the concept of 'local' in a geographical sense could be portrayed as having little meaning. This view is widely debated in the sociological literature and, as we have noted earlier, the meaning of 'community' is widely contested (Brent, 2009; Mayo, 2000; Skerratt and Steiner, 2013; Stacey, 1969).

Within the framework of central control a diffuse but potentially pervasive institutional reason for the decline of local government may be the effect that globalisation has on the mindset of legislators. Mass transit communications, growth of global businesses, the use of mass communication of news and views through the internet ensure, some argue, that local customs and values are in serious decline and that individuals, wherever they live, may have freedom to choose for themselves the cultural and aspirational societies in which they live, rather than being bound by physical geographical restraints. For many legislators and senior bureaucrats, the notion of loyalty to place, community and settlement within a specific geographical area may well appear to be inimical to demands of a global economy. While it is difficult to substantiate how far the belief in community is not seriously embedded in the mindsets of elite politicians and bureaucrats, changes in the pattern and powers of local institutions show little interest in a concern to devolve power to a community level. As shown in the preceding chapters, there were initiatives in the 1970s and 1980s, and later under New Labour and Coalition governments, to decentralise decision-making, and these policies, along with local socialism and attempts at decentralisation to localities, withered on the vine as a consequence of austerity, to be replaced by more streamlining, cost saving and attempts to balance their budgets by undertaking revenue accumulation through entrepreneurial activity.

What does seem more certain is the instrumental use of local government, especially from a bureaucratic perspective, in the incremental restructuring of the system from community governance to subregional governance, as shown in Chapter 3. The process of moving to a smaller number of larger unitary local authorities is highly favoured at the elite level as they can be subject to comprehensive overview by the central bureaucracy and ideally controlled by individuals who can, behind the scenes, be closely networked into the central government (Chandler, 2007: 202–203). This we have illustrated in the many initiatives post-1945 to reshape local government into fewer, more populous unitary or subregional authorities. Chisholm and Leach (2008: 144) report that in relation to the ad hoc restructuring from 2006 of local government areas by the Labour governments, a senior official in the Department of Communities and Local Government 'extolled the administrative benefit to the Department of dealing with unitary councils instead (of) with counties and districts in two tier areas'. Among the policy-making elites in Britain, their use of the European Union principle of 'subsidiarity' stopped at the level of national rather than local government, with at best decentralisation of some government business to regional offices and agencies being the minimum concession given to meet EU requirements (Morphet, 2022). Among both the Conservative and Labour elites, in debates on the role of local government in the European Union there appears to be almost no interest in the concept of 'subsidiarity'. In a rare House of Commons debate on this issue in the confines of the European Committee B, the concept of subsidiarity was discussed between Rees-Mogg and David Lidington, then Minister for Europe, solely in terms of national and European relations (Hansard, HoC, Series 6, 7 December 2015, Vol. 590, European Committee B, Cols 1–16).

The need for some form of devolved governance

Despite, or on occasion because of, the relative lack of interest in community matters, core executives of both public and private institutions have several possible interconnecting reasons why they should nevertheless still value forms of elected local governance. Firstly, senior executives managing policy for a large multinational business, let alone a national or regional government, cannot be so overloaded with information and problems that it becomes impossible for them to function as a determinant of their corporate policy objectives. Through an element of delegation of power to local units, it is possible to relate the laws and general policies made by the central polity to differences in each region and community occasioned by geography, social and political culture and economics. In many organisations this is achieved by setting out the aims and objectives for subordinate elements of the organisation and establishing systems to monitor whether the dependant units keep within their assigned objectives. It would also be expected that within these objectives the layers of subordinate policymakers would have a measure of discretion as to how to effectively manage their tasks, but only as junior members in the political and bureaucratic hierarchy who would be expected to be loyal to their superiors. In the case of local government, however, theories of management based principally on efficiency in private organisations may not be transferable, as the subcentral policymakers are elected and have some accountability, not only to their masters in central government but to those who elected them to office.

In a national liberal democratic polity, some elected agencies of devolved governance are, however, able to have some discretion in how they may implement national policies, as we have seen in previous chapters, and may have some value within a representative liberal democracy. The retention of a vestige of locally democratic governance in Britain has, in part, an institutional basis given that local and regional government in the nation emerged, in many cases, prior to and independently of a highly centralised bureaucracy, and has over time been insidiously incorporated into the national political framework. The process of incorporation of local and community governance into the bureaucratic straightjacket of centralisation could lead to the emergence of political problems of managing potential hostility to such a turn of events. There can, as noted above, be a strong reaction against the loss of local liberties, especially where there is a strong civic culture favouring some form of liberal democracy. Central governments which themselves rest their authority on their pretensions to be liberal democratic cannot easily deny the claims of communities and regions to retain their former capacity for a measure of self-governance.

In the United Kingdom the demand for regional governance has been a major characteristic, and remains a live issue with demands for Scottish and Welsh independence and the troubled status of Northern Ireland. In England there has been much less tension between regional aspirations for independence from the centre, but in the nineteenth century demands for geographically based political equity was a prelude to the pressures to ensure an equitable franchise for the national Parliament. Such tensions are also being awakened by the economic disparities between London and the south-west and many northern counties and cities. The dangers of establishing large regional government structures in England were arguably recognised in the Conservative government's lack of support for the establishment of a Yorkshire-wide authority. It would be foolhardy for any government to peremptorily close down any semblance of democracy at the local level, given the status and history of local government and the probability of serious popular opposition in its defence. Despite a seeming lack of interest, the public still support the generally 'nice' idea of having local government.

Local authorities as popularly elected institutions may also have a further use for central government as a means of independently resolving policy problems facing the core executives, or failing that serving as a scapegoat for centrally imposed ills. Local authorities may have the capacity, as noted by Stoker (2002), to find answers to social and economic problems that had not been grasped by the central bureaucracy. This trend has been broadened by serious cuts in local government finance since 2010 that have compelled local authorities to find novel ways of managing their responsibilities, as we have shown. These include privatising delivery of many of their services such as refuse collection to the private sector, or many other methods which we set out in the previous chapter – or, as is the case with some library services for example, handing control of these facilities to voluntary organisations.

This strategy has been demonstrated by the tendency of Conservative MPs to justify the cuts in local government grants by statements suggesting they can carry out their tasks despite a lean financial framework just as, or even more, effectively, than when cash rich. David Cameron, addressing an LGA meeting in June 2008, ended with the statement that 'local government has been better frankly than central government at being efficient and providing good value for money' (Cameron, 2011). Subsequently his Coalition government argued that as they had decentralised more choices on service provision to local government, particularly through the removal of the *ultra vires* rule, the better authorities had greater power to resolve any financial shortfall by attracting greater economic development into their communities and hence increasing their ability to raise further revenue from local property taxation and the business rate (Hansard, HoC, Series 6, 18 December 2014, Vol. 589, Cols 1590–1606). This position is also fortified by statements from Conservative MPs, presumably well schooled by party whips, that despite cuts in service funding, satisfaction concerning the activities of local authorities in their constituencies had increased. Typical is the following House of Commons intervention in a debate following the annual statement on the financial settlement to local government:

> Mark Pawsey (Con: Rugby) The Minister will be aware that the Conservative-controlled borough council has gone further in the current year, by giving council tax payers a rebate of three per cent. However, given the increasing satisfaction with local government as

shown in surveys, does the Minister agree that councils have risen to the challenge to be very effective at doing more with less? (Hansard, HoC, Series 6, 18 December 2014, Vol. 589, Col. 1597).

It has to be accepted that the honourable Conservative is probably correct in relation to his constituency. It could be argued that a real cut in council tax increases local satisfaction with local governments in affluent areas. However, there remains the challenging implication that, for the majority of citizens, decline in local government services has not seriously affected their well-being. Of course, if local governments fail to manage or offload their responsibilities and subsequently fail either completely, like Northampton County Council, or are instrumental in creating a disaster, as in the case of the London Borough of Kensington and Chelsea in respect to the Grenfell Tower fire, central government can, at some remove from the damage austerity occasions, make a scapegoat of the offending local authority.

Reining in local government

In many liberal democracies in Western Europe and North America, legislators and senior civil servants respond to what could be seen as a variety of assumptions and commitments that influence what these actors regard as the appropriate interpretation of the institutional structuring within the political system in which they operate (Lowndes and Roberts, 2013). These values are often enshrined in a nation's constitution and in the legacy and practices developed with the creation of the nation. Such a perspective is often less clear in Britain than neighbouring countries given the lack of a written constitution. The absence of any embedded constitutional role enshrined in law has had a serious impact on local government, as is demonstrated in the constant restructuring of local government in terms of geographical units, powers, internal structures and funding since the 1950s. While institutions of local government survive, since the 1970s they have been, as individual units, frequently restructured and moulded to changing geographical areas. Consequently, they appear to be losing much of any claim to exert the trappings of government, to become instead administrative entities undertaking the need for the core executive in Cabinet and Whitehall to ensure the implementation of central policies. There have been several recent critiques of what may be termed the hollowing out and diminution of local government powers since 2000 (Chisholm, 2000; Copus et al., 2013; Newman, 2014b).

It would be unnecessary to reiterate the volume of cuts in local services, reduction in funding, enforced privatisation of service implementation and structural changes that have diminished local discretion, let alone the consequences of the 1984 Rates Act. Although local government is far from dead as an institution, it has become a much less significant element in determining policy for communities, and may be better termed as predominantly part of the machinery for the central governance of localities. Thus if we apply Rhodes's power-dependence formula (1981, 1999b) concerning the balance of power between centre and periphery we can see that by 2022 almost all the cards concerning resources of finance and control are falling increasingly in favour of central control. Many former resources, in terms of power once in the control of local governments, have been privatised or lost to other agencies. The constitutional status of local government has firmly and widely been placed in the hands of the Westminster government, the capacity of local authorities to raise their own financial resources outside limits set by central government has been largely reduced, political resources of access to government have been undermined, and professional resources, as in the example of policy concerning the COVID-19 pandemic, have shifted from local experts, in this case particularly local public health officers, to teams of experts assembled to advise government ministers.

There is, nevertheless, some stability in one crucial aspect concerning the institutional role of local government in the British constitution. The insistence that Parliament alone is sovereign has been reinforced in post-1945 official reports and it is most clearly stated in the Widdicombe Inquiry conclusion that:

> Although local government has origins pre-dating the sovereignty of Parliament, all current local authorities are the statutory creations of Parliament and have no independent status or right to exist.

> The whole system of local government could lawfully be abolished by Act of Parliament. (Widdicombe, 1986: 3:3: 45)

Such a belief appears to be widely ingrained in central government policy-making and underwrites central government's capacity to have little or no compunction to initiate major changes in the structure of local government or management of local government which would seriously enhance its position in the polity. Given this strong institutionalised attitude that national governments have dominance over local government, it is therefore the attitude and motives within the core policy-making circles of British government that largely determine the structuring and powers of localities. The absence of a written constitution with embedded legislation that requires a substantive process of referenda to change is also a cause of the complex path taken by the United Kingdom to remain as a nation, given the strength of nationalist feeling in Scotland and to a lesser extent Wales, and the division of loyalties in Northern Ireland. Moreover, in England in particular, compared with many liberal democracies, a concentration of the media in the hands of a few wealthy families and the decline of the local press has eroded attention to local issues.

Broadly we can conclude that in Britain the lack of an embedded constitution that ensures some protection from restructuring the power and values of local government has allowed the centre to insidiously mould the system of subnational governance into one that serves the needs of the centre, to the detriment of active democracy at local level. Local government has increasingly been shaped to serve the interests of central governments rather than local interests.

While local government may be shaped by the views of those in power in central government, divisions in ideology between the major parties contending for power ensures that expedience has created different, and often contradictory, paths in central–local relations. Attitudes and values are far from being uniformly held among those who shape policy, and are operationalised through differing ideological and personal values. The leaderships of the Conservative and the Labour parties, and also of the Civil Service, may be widely imbued with an expediential view of the role of local government, but how this attitude is operationalised in practice may differ from party to party and from individual to individual dependent on their beliefs and emotions. Similarly, the consequences of differing attitudes to globalisation or institutions can vary widely depending on ideological and self-interested beliefs. It is a problematic task to define and differentiate human motives, but it is also impossible to reach a satisfactory explanation of how public policy is formed and sustained without attempting to clear through the jungle of overlapping and often contradictory concerns and interests that underlie political motivation. The motives that determine policy decisions have been classified by Chandler (2017) as a combination in varying degrees of ethical, ideological and self-interested principles. There is of course overlap between these motives. Ethical beliefs may inform ideological interests but may not be pursued within a working ideology. Frequently ideologies are intertwined with self-interest, may often lack ethical justification, and may be accepted, sometimes unconsciously, without any reference to rationality.

The self-interested perspective

We cannot quantify the extent to which the direction in policy towards local government was motivated by self-interest among senior politicians by their view from the heights of national government and policy-making. It is almost impossible to delineate self-interest from other motivations, particularly ideology and individuals' perception of the wider public interest. In the context of New Right economics and ethics, for example, it is difficult to clearly disentangle the motive of self-interest. We have shown, also, in previous chapters how rhetorical use of the language of the local and community by governments has actually masked a range of alternative motivations, and these can be ascertained with evidence but we also have to rely to an extent on assumptions about 'real' intention. While much political posturing is based on ideological grounds, it is also the case that concern over policy issues can become interlinked with matters of personal self-interest, based around ambition and conflict, to rise to the top of the political hierarchy or to gain a post from which politicians and bureaucrats may, by fair means or foul, extract greater wealth and prestige. In this context, however, for those elected to Parliament or seeking to reach the highest levels of the bureaucracies of central governance, local government does not provide the most alluring pathway to promotion. Winston Churchill, for example, turned down the offer of President of the Local Government Board on the grounds that

> There is no place in the government more laborious, more anxious, more thankless, more choked with petty and even squalid detail, more full of hopeless and impossible difficulties: and I would say deliberately that so far as the pace and comfort of my life are concerned, I would rather continue to serve under Lord Elgin in the Colonial Office. (Churchill to Asquith 14th March 1908, Churchill Papers, House of Commons Library)

In the Labour Party some policy advocates, such as Nye Bevan in South Wales (Foot, 1962: 84–85), had experience as councillors in small urban districts and county councils which left them with a principled aversion to small-scale politics. For many other Labour MPs and ministers, including Attlee, local authorities if given their head could, as in the saga of Poplarism, be a serious source of disunity in the socialist movement and dangerously alienate moderate voters wedded to the rule of law (Branson, 1979). Many MPs and not a few senior civil servants are largely indifferent to the issues surrounding local government and few party leaders have demonstrated a serious enthusiasm for change in the institution, or recognise the democratic possibilities inherent in participative local governance. The 'local' of interest to them is their constituency. Although a considerable number of MPs have reached Westminster through service in local government, a return to this arena would be seen as a demotion, and there are few occasions where former MPs appear to look for a return to their community roots, although it could be argued that the growth of regional executive mayors may attract some MPs back into the localist sector and indeed some Mayors are establishing a national prominence – notably Andy Burnham. This route to the top was successfully negotiated by Boris Johnson. Similarly, the growing band of local authority chief executives who join the Civil Service would view this as a route to higher office.

The ideological perspectives

While there is little evidence within ruling elites of principled, well thought out ethical standpoints on the role of local government in British society, it is possible to discern differing standpoints to policy on local governance guided by the application of ideological values towards the institution. These positions clearly differ among the mainstream political parties, and within these groups, especially the Conservative Party, there are significantly differing standpoints that mirror the ideological cracks within the party. The dominant Disraelian Tory values of the Conservative Party in the late nineteenth century harboured support for the institution of local government as a means by which territorially based political elites, the county gentry, could locally wield power and potentially progress to national political prominence. As chronicled by Lee in his study of county council government in Cheshire (Lee, 1963), many of the country gentry could claim that those fitted to rule through birth, education and ownership of landed property could be leaders and arbiters of local needs and customs. This attitude, perhaps most redolent in the politics of Burke and the younger Disraeli, argues for slow incremental change to society, best mediated by locally based leaders who governed in the national interest on behalf of their constituents. This ideology may remain in a few lost corners of the Conservative Party, but in terms of national policy-making it was replaced by New Right values and global capitalist interest, perhaps tempered to some degree by a 'one nation' conservatism which has come to prominence along with the concern for 'levelling up'. The last substantive success for the Burkean-Disraelian Tory values in the context of local government was perhaps the challenge faced by Peter Walker's attempts to impose the Redcliffe-Maud recommendations for single-tier local government units that were based on city centres and their dependent rural hinterlands.

Disraelian policies during the early twentieth century modernised into, to use Norton and Aughey's (1981) term, 'progressive

Toryism'. This was at its most influential after the Conservatives' shock defeat in the 1945 general election, which pushed forward the views of reformist-minded Conservatives, particularly R. A. Butler and Harold Macmillan, to ensure the party acknowledged and retained many aspects of the emerging welfare state and nationalisation of industries such as rail transport, gas and electricity production and telecommunications. Several of these initiatives, and especially utilities, had been pioneered by local authorities but transferred by the Attlee administration to state control under the belief that their importance to society could only be handled by central government. Both mainstream Conservatives and Labour leaders considered that the economy and individual welfare should be subservient to private sector interests, fortified when necessary with arm's-length public agencies established under government control but managed using private sector techniques as profitable, or at least break-even, enterprises. As outlined in Chapter 2 and by Chandler (2007), this consensus created a major revision in the role of local governments, requiring them to opt out of advancing productive wealth-creating industries to become agencies for welfare and regulation that was distributive in nature. This division in the perceived role of local government for many in the Conservative Party and the Labour Party was widely identified in Saunders's (1981) conception of the 'dual state'.

The old Tory knights of the shires, concerned with agriculture and estate management, gave way to new leaders concerned with industrial and financial growth within a private–public partnership at national rather than local level. The central leadership of the party became in many cases indifferent to local and community issues. The Liberal Democrats, like their predecessors in the Liberal Party, may be viewed as the continuing embodiment of the post-war public–private, dual state consensus. Within the Liberal Democrats there has been uneasily slotted into their centrist rhetoric factions that demand more autonomy for local government (Huhne, 2007) based on a concern to ensure greater individual liberty. Much of this stance finds support in communitarian thought, but also in the successful practice of winning parliamentary by-elections by emphasising local grievances and mobilising volunteers to support and communicate local concerns (Cyr, 1977: 260).

Expedient agencies of central government

The partnership model was by the 1980s challenged within the Conservative Party by New Right thought, with its antipathy to social justice and hence the welfare state and public community-based provision of services. Emphasis was given to the arguments of Hayek or Friedman that privatised competitive provision generated greater efficiency and that a trickle down of wealth would benefit the poor more than the socialist belief in redistributive taxation. This trend, set in motion by the Thatcher governments, included the privatisation of many public services such as gas and electricity distribution and water supply and drainage, that had begun their life as municipal services, and also services that were currently being provided by local authorities such as council housing and refuse collection. Later, under the Major governments, backroom services such as auditing, and collecting rates and taxes were required to be put out to competitive tender and were in many cases handed to private companies.

New Right ideology also favours cutting taxation and local government income to create balanced budgets and, in theory, create more efficient services. This demand led the Thatcher government into legal battles with several left-wing authorities that refused to make cuts in their budget and sought to increase local taxation to enhance the quality of their social commitments. Following the Rates Acts of 1984 and 1988, loopholes in earlier legislation were largely closed and locally raised expenditure became a relatively small fraction of locally raised income as councils became increasingly dependent on central grants. The 2008 bankers' crash, created in part by the application of New Right economic thought, gave the New Right politicians the excuse for imposing government austerity which reduced the resources flowing to local government. New Right ideology, if taken to its extreme, perceives government – and hence the public sector – as a threat to individual freedom. It can justify the creation of what has been termed the enabling local authority, in which locally elected councillors meet to assign and call to account, if necessary, private contractors and other agencies who carry out the responsibilities in the gift of the local authority. Such a scenario has been practised in a few towns in the United States but so far has been rarely taken to its limits in Britain. The application and influence of New Right ideology can be clearly identified as central to the move to the near destruction of local government which we have set out, given that many of its less privatisable services are also hived off to non-elected regulated agencies and to setting the path towards creating central governance of local services as opposed even to local governance (Barnett and Chandler, 2018). As we noted in Chapters 2 and 3, it has remained influential, although in rhetorically different clothing, in the 'advanced liberal' techniques associated with the localist agenda of the Coalition and subsequent governments.

The more contrasting ideologies of the Conservatives and the Labour Party began, however, to at least converge in their attitudes to local government. In its earlier years the Labour Party had a cohort of leading policymakers interested in the potential capacity for local government to secure the goals of social democracy. Many of its stalwarts such as the Webbs, George Bernard Shaw or Lansbury began their careers as enthusiasts for municipalisation of the means of production. Following the lead of Joseph Chamberlain in Birmingham, if not the ideological interests behind his ideas, it was apparent that big cities could municipalise productive services and ensure that these were provided equitably to all in their communities. These ideas were further developed by, among others, G. D. H. Cole (1947) and William Robson (1931), as has been discussed earlier in Chapter 2. By 1945 their values on efficiency and effectiveness, if not democracy, were widely implanted in the minds of many in the party leadership. However, because of both technological considerations and pressure from private and public leaders of these industries, it appeared to many reformers that regional if not national solutions rather than localised policies were the only way forward. The party tended to take on board the modernisers' view that there should be a single tier of larger executive local authorities, but not the idea that local authorities should have greater freedom from central control and more substantive entrepreneurial powers in the sphere of productive as opposed to redistributive services. Although the Labour Party after 1945 was characterised largely by indifference to the role of local government as a means of securing equality of ownership in the means of production, the institutions were nevertheless expedient in dealing with aspects of social service provision, many of which could trace their origins back to the poor law. A declining group of local enthusiasts, for example Morrison or, outside Westminster, academic specialists in local governance such as Cole, Robson and more latterly Stewart and Jones, supported the continuing role of local authorities as a means of supplying a range of social and educative services.

A second consideration harboured particularly among the left wing of the party is a tendency to value equality over local freedom. There is a strong argument that inequality in capitalist societies can only be assuaged by a central parliament that will lay down rules and means to ensure fairer provision of services. This dilemma troubled the Webbs (Webb and Webb, 1975), who proposed in their later writings that one of two new national parliaments of Britain should lay down minimum standards that must be implemented by each local government. This concern to secure equity in public provision is still held by many on the left of the Labour Party as the following intervention of Jeremy Corbyn during the second reading of the 2011 Localism Bill attests.

> To describe the Bill as one of the great historical Bills put before the House is to take historical hyperbole to new heights. It is ludicrous. There are more than 100 caveats on the powers that are devolved to local government, and the Conservative and Liberal Democrat Members who keep on about the joy that they have from the freedom for their local authorities will be back in the Chamber in two or three years complaining that the fire standards are worse in Dorset than they are in Warwickshire, that homeless people are more generously treated than they are in Bristol and so on. National Government have a responsibility to ensure that there are some national standards in what is done. It is important that Government Members understand that. (Hansard, HoC, Series 6, 17 January 2011, Vol. 521, cols 617–618)

The concern for minimum standards and equality is not, however, solely a left-wing one, but was also an element guiding aspects of the more centralist New Labour Blair governments' imposition of the complex catalogue of performance targets that were laid on local authorities. Indeed, as noted in Chapter 2, New Labour, despite localist rhetoric, continued to emphasise central control while accepting much of the New Right's premises, developing a stance towards local government in which social welfare was deemed to be inextricably linked to global economic competitiveness.

Ethical theory

What should be of serious concern is that there is little evidence that the core policymakers harbour strongly principled ethical values on the structuring, roles or procedures for local governments. In the next chapters we will argue that we believe there to be a necessary, if not substantive, moral right for citizens to determine policy for their communities, as outlined in Chapter 2, recognising that this would require a substantial change in the structuring of institutions of local governance. We argue that, as opposed to many European nations or the United States, Britain's lack of a widely accepted ethical basis for local government seriously compromises the stability of the institution as an essential element in its, albeit unwritten, constitution. At this point in our core argument in this volume, we will only point out that ethics and morality does not, however, appear to be a significant element in the development from the twentieth century to the present day in the evolution of the systems of British governance.

Reference in parliamentary debate to publications on the purpose and value of local government is rare. A search through House of Commons transcripts from 1970 to 2018 for 'Jones' and 'Stewart' and 'local' found only seven references to the writings of the two academics concerning local government, and almost all references were to comments they made in the *Local Government Chronicle* supporting specific criticisms of government Bills that were progressing through the legislature. None refer to the status and value of local government. W. A. Robson is referred to seven times in House of Commons debates concerning local government since 1930, largely centring on the debates on the status of the City of London. This is by no means a new phenomenon. For example, John Stuart Mill is only mentioned twice in the six days of parliamentary debates in the House of Commons on the 1888 Local Government (England and Wales) Bill that created elected county councils. Parliamentary debate on the ethical or even expediential status of local government as highlighted in the preceding chapter appears to operate in a wholly parallel universe to the ideas of academic commentary concerning the institution. Such may well be the fate of this study, and is perhaps to be expected, but it is clear that in public discourse among policymakers there is little more than lip service paid, conveniently, to the 'goodness' of the local and the value of local government.

It is possible, on occasion, to superficially obtain evidence from political speeches and debates that show some sense, over and above the generic, rhetorical use of 'local' to equate to a rather vague 'good thing', that the institution enhances democratic values in society but, especially in recent years, this appears to serve to disguise increasing dismemberment of local and community government through privatisation, austerity and boundary changes. Typical of this attitude is the 2011 Localism Act which was presented by the then Secretary of State Eric Pickles, with the idea that

> The Bill will reverse the centralist creep of decades and replace it with local control. It is a triumph of democracy over bureaucracy. It will fundamentally shake up the balance of power in the country, revitalising local democracy and putting power where it belongs in the hands of the people. (Hansard, HoC, Series 6, 17 January 2011, Vol. 728, col. 148)

It is, as shown in previous chapters, difficult to reconcile this intention with the subsequent unprecedented cuts in funding for local government and ad hoc development of subregional governments dominated by executive mayors. As David Blunkett observed in the debate on the second reading of the Bill, 'the Government are centralising power and decentralising pain' (Hansard, HoC, Series 6, 17 January 2011, Vol. 728, col. 569).

Perhaps it may be possible after the next general election, scheduled for 2024–25, to generate a parliamentary majority willing to promote more than the rhetoric for decentralisation of power, but the reality of decentralisation. As this book goes to press, the resurgent Labour Party has published its report on constitutional reform chaired by former Prime Minister Gordon Brown, which broadly advocates moving substantial powers from central government to the national parliaments and to unitary and regional tiers of subgovernment in England (Labour Party, 2022). There are suggestions in the report that there should be further devolution of power to local authorities, but it is far from clear that this would move to a neighbourhood level, and little in the report about what community or neighbourhood may entail. Considerable volumes of water will flow under Westminster Bridge before these hints of change become, if at all, a reality, but at least there is a recognition within central government that change is needed if the potential for local government can be realised.

Concluding comments

We have argued in the preceding chapters that the system of local government in Britain has evolved to approach an arrangement in which local governments neither govern nor are local. It has been shown in this chapter that attitudes to the institutions of local government and the architecture of subsidiarity among governing elites are composed of several intertwined and opposing factors. It is difficult, by its nature, to identify self-interest, but the broad evidence suggests that in Whitehall and Westminster local government is not seen as a means of enhancing status or careers. The ministerial post overseeing local government has, as noted, steadily been demoted to the junior ranks. The influence of ideology at times can clearly be identified, with broad acceptance of social democratic welfarism, and later the principles of New Right economics, dominating postwar attitudes to local government. However, ethical principles have been absent. Bereft of any strong ethical foundation in the mindset of central ruling factions, local government is an institution that lacks substantive roots. It has its uses and its disadvantages to differing groups and individual players at the level of central government, but these factors can often be contradictory and are also moulded to particular passing problems faced by the centre. The result is that local government is viewed as an expediential tool for central government, pushed into servicing differing roles for different situations, to serve differing ideological perspectives and used malleably to suit particular interests or views, or circumstances.

Among parliamentarians in the Commons, such attitudes appear to be grouped into a large faction of the indifferent and a much smaller group that has been most influential in changing the shape of the system, who are social democratic modernisers or New Right opponents of public sector communal enterprise. Perhaps the most serious issue in relation to the positioning of local government in the mindset of political leaders is the lack of attention to the role that local democracy may have in sustaining liberal democratic principles, especially at a time when several liberal democracies are currently facing a potential return to authoritarianism. The lack of a considered ethical case for local government also means that we have to add to it our picture of a dispiritingly low starting point and the considerable hurdles to overcome if we are to actually bring about change grounded on principle rather than expediency. Given this, can we build on what hope, 'gaps' and spaces which *may* be available to form the basis of an alternative, and will they be enough? We turn to these challenges in the next chapter.

9

Is there any possibility of change?

In the preceding chapters we have traced the decline in local government's powers and set them in the context of a centrally dominated polity which has consistently viewed local government in expedient terms. This has so far largely paralleled a number of recent academic studies charting the declining fortunes of local governance in Britain, but has also updated this trajectory up to 2022 into the May and Johnson governments, the very short time in office of Liz Truss and the early days of the Sunak government. Many of the recent studies that we have cited, such as Leach et al. (2018), Wills (2016), Latham (2017), Copus et al. (2017), Atkinson (2012) and Wilson and Game (2011), have dedicated their closing chapters to a review of the possible changes that may be pursued to ameliorate the present growth in centralising of state control. As shown in Chapter 7, there is no lack of ideas within British local governments, or from global experimentation stemming from the 'new municipalism' or the 'Fearless Cities' movement (Barcelona En Comu, 2019). But are these diverse strategies to bring power to localities likely to be taken up as policy and scaled up within the next few decades of the twenty-first century in Britain? As we have emphasised in the Introduction and in Chapter 8, the barrier to substantive liberalisation of the local governance systems of Britain lies not in local governments themselves but in need for restructuring and cultural support for the practices of democracy in local governance.

Any attempt to restructure central government to accommodate the interests of supporters of local government is in any regime what may be termed a 'big ask'. Demands for piecemeal changes in a constitution are rightly major issues in any nation, and when these include a requirement to restructure the institutional framework, let alone the ideologies supporting the governance of a nation, the demand is all the more revolutionary, and likely to be either unrecognised or challenged by those in positions of power. However, such challenges are being widely made in Western Europe and the Americas as increasingly the traditional intellectual supports for liberal democracy – as developed through theories of pluralism by writers such as Schumpeter or Dahl in the United States, or Mill and Oakshott in a British context – are subject to criticism, questioning Winston Churchill's view that 'democracy is the worst form of Government except for all the other forms that have been tried from time to time' (Hansard, HoC, Series 5, 11 November 1947, Vol. 444, Cols 206–207).

The crisis in representative liberal democracy

At root, it may be claimed that liberal democracies are generally liberal in character but place far more emphasis on this value than that of democracy. In practice only an elite few within the national population have any substantial role in the determination of public policy and the retention of existing institutions and traditions to facilitate changes in the rules of the political game. The critiques of the founders of elite theories of representative liberal democracy, such as Michels (1968), Mosca (1939) or Pareto (1976), have never been effectively answered by the later theorists, such as Schumpeter, Dahl or Downs (1957). Viewing the style of policy-making in Britain over recent decades, this elitist model is the one which we would accept offers the most realistic account of policy formulation, but that no one model can capture the whole story, and we will outline this interpretation below.

It can be argued that policy is determined firstly by the dominant gatekeepers who comprise core executives of government, that is the inner Cabinet of politicians who finally reject or accept policy proposals. Policy demands that are seriously considered by the gatekeepers emanate from a wider circle of party politicians, the leaders of national and global economic businesses and the controllers of the national media. Outside these circles, more outlying orbits of political concerns circulating within civic society get considerably less attention (Chandler, 2017). It may be countered that the liberal values of liberal democracies oblige core executives to tolerate opposition and to compromise. However, when choices are to be made between differing policies that emerge from what Kingdon (1995) described as the policy soup of ideas circulating in a society, it is the policy gatekeepers who have the resources, powers and skills to promote their own preferences. Moreover, when unwelcome change is necessary to secure longevity in power, this is achieved largely through a process of making small adjustments to their ideas in a form of muddling through (Braybrooke and Lindblom, 1963).

Although it is maintained that public policy should be made in a democratic context, in practice governance in any polity that has a significant population falls far short of any such ideal. The leaders of dominant political parties in liberal democracies have a considerable number of means to stack decisions in their favour. Firstly, this is a consequence of the size of most governed communities. The policy gatekeepers who determine which of many policies to prioritise and develop can only concern themselves with a few issues at any one time; it is impossible for them to give weight to the interests and comments of each member of the polity affected by a policy issue. Thus they are in conversation largely with a relatively small coterie of advisors, senior civil servants and leading interest groups in determining which of many competing pressures require their attention. Many policy decisions also require specialised theories and research, which empowers the groups who have acknowledged expertise in these issues. Policy decisions on specific technical areas such as in healthcare or education at either local or national level are, therefore, greatly influenced by the views of professionals, given their authority to represent accepted wisdom on technical issues (Fischer, 2009).

While policy-making elites may co-opt into their advisory networks agencies and groups that have been largely courting public opposition to policymakers, it is often at the cost of the group having to bend their behaviour to the rules of discourse expected from them by the policy-making fraternity. There is a tendency for favoured interests to pursue paths that may be acceptable in government circles through closed channels of communication within the dominant governing networks rather than by courting public opinion. Thus, many groups within the supportive inner network of policymakers, even when they are seriously harmed by central government policy, are reluctant to seek more confrontational public support through, for example, mass demonstrations or wider publicity campaigns. In this context, local governments in Britain, as represented by the LGA and its predecessors, have long thought themselves part of the advisory network that can communicate directly with senior policymakers in Whitehall and Westminster (Chandler, 1988: 83–87; R. A. W. Rhodes, 1986: 410–413; Wilson and Game, 2011: 196–197). Hence, although critical of governments and engaged in lobbying for their interests, they remain reluctant to push for change through more public channels of communication for the wider public despite the many changes in structure and the austerity that local authorities have faced in recent decades.

The capacity for public policy to be determined democratically is further undermined by the underlying difficulty of reconciling the value of liberalism, as seen in the context of a right to property, with that of democracy. This discrepancy in democratic efficacy stems largely from the interpretation of what liberalism entails. There are many debates concerning the extent to which any claim to have a right of freedom may always be damaging to the liberty of others, and while it is true that liberal democracies have sought to an extent to reconcile democracy with more egalitarian forms of social welfare, in practice in liberal democracies the dominant influence has been from 'classical' liberal values as promulgated by John Locke: that individuals have a right to life, liberty and – problematically for democracy – a right to property.

The inequalities between people's resources to obtain power in any society largely relate to the capacity and also the good fortune to amass and pass on to others their wealth. Through inheritance, these inequalities flow through generations to further widen inequalities in liberal democratic societies. As argued by Piketty (2014) or Putnam (2020) among others, with the wide acceptance of neoliberal and New Right thought, the gap between riches and poverty is widening in liberal democratic states. In liberal democracies those with property in terms of fixed and disposable assets have the resources to be significantly more dominant in the policy-making process. Many political leaders that rise to elite positions in competitive political parties obtain their position of power through the patronage of existing members of a core executive who had in their turn reached this position through a similar process. Although democracy may in theory equalise access to influence, in practice the opportunity to exercise it is profoundly imbalanced. This circle has been squared in liberal social democracies with education and welfare policies in a compromise to 'level up' these opportunities, but fundamentally there is a tension always in play, a dilemma in liberalism between this and limitations on restriction to personal freedoms, wealth and property. It may thus be argued that although personal liberty afforded by liberal democracies does in theory allow every citizen to seek out influence, in practice few can be chosen to reach political heights, and those that do succeed, such as the first Labour Party Prime Minister, Ramsey Macdonald, will frequently adopt the mannerisms and values of the life world – or to use Bourdieu's (1998) term, 'habitus' – of their newly acquired elite status. In contrast, the vast majority realise or accept that attempting to become the gatekeepers or successful advocates of policy is beyond their resources and they are restricted to little or no interest in the policy process.

A liberal polity of this nature ensures that views in opposition to a governing party leadership can be expressed, but are only likely to be adopted if elections place a new party in power or it is seen by government elites that they will be vulnerable to electoral defeat if they do not (as in the example of the poll tax revolt of 1988) at least to some extent bow to public pressure. Policy-making elites may often have deep differences, but they nevertheless join together in corporate alliances to ensure their grip on power by preventing change that may weaken their collective hold over the levers of decision-making (Jenkins-Smith and Sabatier, 1994; Lembruch and Schmitter, 1982). As Davies (2011: 152) argues, 'instead of inclusion and enrolment, we see exclusion and network closure – the incremental resolution of collaborative structures into relatively impermeable hierarchies'. Thus, communication networks such as the press, television and to a lesser extent social media can bring their collective prestige and expertise to ensure their influence over the policymakers by publishing views that are favourable to their mutual self-interest. Minority groups are also given legitimate avenues to let off steam without running the danger of having their personal and group liberties curtailed, and can sometimes have further value for policy-making elites by identifying and on occasion providing remedies for policy failures using strategies of piecemeal evolution rather than revolutionary and destabilising opposition to the system of governance. Moreover, by allowing the co-option of able individuals and interest groups from non-elite backgrounds, who are bought into this national view of political and civic culture, they can renew the efficacy of the core of central policymakers and create the illusion of change and opportunity. Only with luck can the more determined or privileged become part of, or even close to, the ruling elite. However, luck, in this context, only shines its beneficence on a relatively small cohort in any substantial society, and these are largely those who have inherited greater resources of wealth, education and networked connections from their families.

The result is not in liberal democracies to create a monolithic autocracy as today in Russia or China, but a situation in which several groups battle for political supremacy and if they are to succeed must appeal for popular support from civic society. However, the ideas and values of civic society are influenced, as observed in the preceding paragraph, by elites in business, the arts of communication or professionalised interest groups. As a result a chasm begins to form between the more elite policy-making and the lives of the large majority of the population. The political elites make choices whose implications are not fully understood by many in the broader civil society. At the same time, most members of civil society, as a consequence of centralisation and consequent disengagement from local governance, are also unable to seriously influence their sense of place and the shaping of the environment in which they live.

The condition of democracy in Britain does seem to reflect this broadly elitist perspective. Policymakers are influenced by a relatively small group of networked interests working through predominantly autocratic arrangements, such as political parties and the public media. This makes it easier for policy elites to claim and manipulate within a civic culture a widespread view that the majority of citizens have little interest in the problems of, or capacity to understand, public issues. The idea of developing a more vibrant democracy in a complex society is not thought, seriously, to be realistic, with policies aimed at increasing participation or democratic renewal being only tactical or rhetorical devices. This view is, moreover, ingrained in the system of education, which is not designed to produce a society that is fully literate in political, social and economic understanding. It is also reinforced by a widespread view among policy elites that most citizens lack the capacity to understand policy problems, giving rise to, at best, what might be termed a 'thin' form of elected representative democracy, supported by views, following Schumpeter, that such are the only appropriate means for governing democracies.

The local democratic malaise

This brief overview of the elitist perspective, together with a lack of concern for ethical principles, offers an explanation of how it has been possible for local government to be treated expediently. It correlates with a broad overview of how policy-making has operated in practice to exclude local voices. However, can democratic 'gaps' still be found and built on at local level? For example, Saunders's (1986) dual state theory suggested a different, more pluralistic politics taking place at local level, and policy-making by local agencies, it can be argued, should be more amenable to access to influence by a wider range of interests. At the same time, local government is highly constrained by and embroiled in central government policy: how far does this exclude alternatives, or provide space for them to be built upon? We have covered these issues in Chapter 7 with respect to service delivery and alternative visions from councils. Here we examine further the democratic potentialities of localism and possible alternative trajectories. What are the possibilities given the seemingly perilous picture of liberal democracy as it has come to be practised? We would, as ever, have to start from where we are, giving a 'chicken and egg' aspect to any such aspirations;

Is there any possibility of change?   225

the conditions necessary to develop and sustain a more democratic path are, paradoxically, the very ones whose deficiencies it would be intended to address. Thus we would have to accept an inevitably developmental approach, as part of an ongoing 'mission' of renewal (Wills, 2016: 204), and identify the practices on which we can build.

The elitist critique of liberal democratic practice set out above is consistent with the 'British political tradition' of polity dominated by Westminster, with a strong central executive and policy towards local government being determined by shifting central elite attitudes to the 'low politics' of local affairs. As we have seen in the preceding chapters, local government has been tossed around by the forces of state rescaling in line with party political expediency and the responses deemed necessary to macro-economic forces, and increasingly to whatever has been determined to best enhance 'competitiveness'. More broadly, local government has reached this point at a time when it seems less straightforward for us to simply reach for some traditional defences, dust them off and reuse them. The faith in representative government responding to changes in the opinion of an informed and rational electorate that dominated much Western political thought from the 1940s to 1980s has been seriously eroded. This necessitates a consideration of local government's potential relationship to alternative perspectives and democratic practices. Taking full advantage, then, of the 'promise' of local government will require not only some fundamental polity-wide change, but re-establishing, revisiting and clarifying arguments for it as a necessary and desirable foundation for meeting these democratic challenges.

A further look at the current context so far as local government is concerned lays bare the extent of the challenge. Firstly, political and societal pressures have increasingly seemed to undermine local government's credibility, as falling turnouts for local elections have served to undermine its legitimacy as a political unit. Amidst frustration with the perceived failings of representative democracy and absence of voice for citizens, alternative sources of participation and resistance have been foregrounded by those who are active, and the gap between local government and local politics has widened. Any assumed synergies between local politics and local government have been increasingly hard to pin down. This is particularly reflected in debates about council boundaries as large-scale unitary authorities replace those with more historically recognised boundaries. Further, in previous chapters we have also seen how local government has lost power over a range of services and in effect become one player in a complex system of local governance, which has left elected representatives with at best indirect influence over significant local issues. Councillors now operate amidst a local landscape populated by private providers, citizens who have direct choice and who often participate via co-production or other forms of direct engagement, and multiagency partnerships of agencies. As noted in Chapter 5, Sweeting and Copus (2012) thus identified representative, market, network and participatory forms of local democracy as being present in the governance of localities, but, given the overriding dominance of central government gatekeepers and a weak civic culture, the more participatory forms have been unable to establish and maintain sufficient citizen engagement and policy impact.

There *are* various types of democracy and democratic claims 'rubbing up against each other' at local level, which have the potential to make headway into the elitist scenario which has been painted above, and which have a 'less comfortable' relationship with liberal democracy than the traditional representative form (Tormey, 2022: 24). These however, in turn, pose fundamental questions which seem to destabilise the primacy of local government's democratic claims. Arguably, formal political units, territorially defined, are increasingly not synchronised with the scope of the issues to be dealt with and deliberated (Hajer, 2003), leaving a low degree of 'jurisdictional integrity' (Skelcher, 2005) or a 'loose coupling' of issues to administrative boundaries (Klijn and Skelcher, 2007). Raco and Flint (2001) referred to this as the space–place tension, with 'space' being the formally defined administrative unit and 'place' the actual lived experience of democratic and deliberative engagement. Consideration has thus turned to how networks and complex governance arrangements could be 'anchored' democratically (Sorensen and Torfing, 2005). The adequacy of 'traditional' modes of representative democracy, via elected local councils, in this environment is questioned, as seen in the calls for councillors to take on new roles as 'facilitators', noted in Chapter 5. This requires a rethinking of who is legitimately to be included in local decision-making. Who is affected by the issues at hand, and what constitutes the political unit? Such questions generate a need to readdress the connections between geography and democracy (Barnett and Bridge, 2013: 1036). Moreover, while they may seem to provide light in the elitist tunnel, in doing so they undermine local government's claim to local democratic primacy, it seems.

There are also questions posed by broad societal change, as democracy is required to respond to 'evolutionary and sociological' pressures (Tormey, 2022: 18). An ageing population and a mismatch between needs and resources have added to pressures stemming from long-term shifts in citizens' expectations and calls for more direct relationships with service providers. New technology and customer-centric trends in the private sector, including the use of social media, have led to calls for 'connected' councils, providing constant interaction and feedback. In this revised 'Relational State' model, citizens do more of the 'heavy lifting' themselves (Carr-West, 2013). At best, the sum of these pressures would culminate in a need for an alternative local government to operate in radically different ways, and take on more broadly conceived political roles as facilitators or 'convenors of conversations' (Zacharzewski, 2013). At worst, local government is again seen to potentially have just one claim to democratic legitimacy amidst a plethora of more 'direct' personal engagement.

In order to understand local government's current malaise fully, then, it is clear we have to set our consideration in the context not only of the elite and central government domination of the polity, but the whole sweep of social, economic and democratic change. What we have sketched out in the paragraphs above is recognition that local government has been subject to what some have portrayed as a broad 'crisis' of liberal democracy. Although there was never a 'golden age' of political trust and engagement, a mood of 'anti-politics' has increased in Britain in the post-war period (Clarke et al., 2017), focussed in particular on representative democracy and the institutions associated with it, which are the subject of increasingly negative attitudes and decline in engagement. This is reflected in reduced voter turnout and political party membership, and a long-term trend of decline in trust in politicians and interest in politics (Clarke et al., 2017; Quilter-Pinner et al., 2021; Tormey, 2014; Wood et al., 2020), leaving representative democracy looking and feeling 'exhausted' (Tormey, 2014). Three in five Britons say that democracy is losing its effectiveness as a form of government (Edelman Trust Barometer, 2021). Concerns are further raised by international evidence that these trends are occurring disproportionately among less educated and lower social classes, while alternative forms of political engagement are practised more by upper social status groups (Dalton, 2017).

Flinders (2016: 182) notes that despite the 'crises' in its practice, support for democracy remains high and it persists as one of the enduring ideas which are central to modern life; the disaffection and lack of interest is with politics as it is currently practised, in particular with representative democracy, and not with democracy per se. As Wood (2020: 149) points out, 'anti-political' sentiment need not necessarily lead to passive withdrawal. The disenchantment has, in fact, been a driver for the rise of a very influential type of anti-elite populism in the success of 'alternatives' offered, for example, by the Five Star Movement in Italy, and Donald Trump in the USA. However, it can also be associated with what Wood (2020) calls 'participatory anti-politics' – a desire to 'do politics differently' via a revival in interest in more participatory and discursive methods of engagement, and with debate concerning a range of progressive avenues, focussing on strengthening alternative forms of social organisation, including social movements and other radically idealistic ways of organising politics. These can be interpreted as reactions to the range of social, economic and environmental pressures which have undermined 'traditional', representative-based liberal democracy and left its institutions no longer 'fit for purpose'.

Some, like Streeck (2013), for example, alternatively point to pressures emanating from a changing global economic order, the increasing influence of market logics and a subsequent increase in individualism and decline in civic culture. Globalisation in particular is associated with a waning of the utility of traditional, territorially based political institutions, most notably the nation-state, with citizens recognising that 'the action is elsewhere' (Tormey, 2014). Urbanti and Warren (2008: 391) thus argue that 'the spaces for representative claims and discourses are now relatively wide open' and that 'In complex and broadly democratic societies, representation is a target of competing claims.' This 'liquidity' with respect to territory is reflected in the increased interconnectedness and complexity of issues, which 'increasingly strain the powers of representative agents' (Urbanti and Warren, 2008: 391). Here, more horizontal, 'flatter' forms of interaction are driven by 'Everyday Makers' who 'relate to political authority in terms of co-governance rather than hierarchy' (Bang and Sorensen, 1999: 335). Tormey (2014: 108) notes 'a revolution in terms of the manner and style of political mobilization away from people and parties that represent, toward styles and forms of politics that seek to draw attention to and contest injustices'. Drawing on the work of Ulrich Beck, Tormey thus associates this 'post-representative' politics with a more diverse, reflexive citizenry, engaging in 'sub-politics' beyond the formal political arena and maintaining a critical/sceptical distance from formal institutions. Such concerns are further developed by more 'critical' democratic perspectives, which privilege 'DIY Democracy', anti-institutional activity outside of formal settings (Blaug, 2002: 108) and alternative forms of participation which call into question conventional notions of what constitutes the appropriate form of political representation (Hendriks, 2009: 107).

Thus, more radical, 'post-representative' views stress the formation of alternative political identities and a range of forms of engagement in the public sphere outside of formal political arenas. These may have broader democratic potential consistent with liberal democracy while others have characteristics built on and adapted to an overarching democratic system. Others still find hope from within the broad but flawed architecture of representative democracy, arguing that the 'crisis' narrative has been overstated or misdiagnosed (Achen and Bartels, 2016; Hibbing and Theiss-Morse, 2002), and that democracy faces a series of challenges or stresses rather than crisis (Giovannini and Wood, 2022). Stoker (2006b) recognises that democratic systems are 'creaking' as collective forms of engagement have declined, but locates political disenchantment in the inevitable 'designed in disappointment' of politics (Stoker, 2006b: 66). Such views identify an 'expectations gap' left by the 'inflationary pressure' (Flinders, 2012: 48) of increasing demands and overpromising of delivery by gatekeepers keen to appease and win votes. The problem here, then, is seen to lie in a fundamental misunderstanding of the nature of, and subsequent disappointment with, the political process, which consists of negotiating settlements between competing interests and demands. Flinders and Dommett (2013) similarly argue that more emphasis should be put on expectations management, underpinned by a 'more honest and pragmatic account of politics' (Flinders, 2012: 41), or on addressing the 'output' side of politics with more effective policy-making (Marsh, 2014). Stoker and others recognise that times are challenging but not impossible to address by 'starting from where we are', reforming and supplementing existing institutions to facilitate greater 'listening' capacity by policymakers and communication channels for citizens. In short, here democracy's perceived shortcomings are seen as the result of a lack of awareness of its inevitable tensions and weaknesses, and restoring its health requires greater recognition that it is a pragmatic exercise in problem-solving in admittedly difficult circumstances.

This, admittedly brief, analysis of the health and suitability of liberal democracy reveals a range of opinions on the extent and causes of the 'crisis' of democracy, but whatever the diagnosis, there is consensus recognising the need to rethink methods of political engagement and the institutional frameworks necessary for its expression in response to both pragmatic pressures and theoretical challenges.

Can local government be the basis for reviving democracy?

What part can, or should, local government play in addressing the 'negative' aspects of anti-politics, overcoming the essentially elitist perspective embodied in the 'British political tradition' and re-engaging citizens in democratic practices? Secondly, to what extent can, or should, local government be the basis for 'regrounding' what appear to be increasingly complex and delocalised democratic forms of engagement? Why should local government be seen as a means to address both weaknesses of liberal representative democracy and demands for alternative means of engagement? Despite its claims to be 'closer' to people's concerns and still responsible for key services affecting their lives, local government as a 'traditional' elected institution has not been immune from anti-political sentiment, as evidenced in falling electoral turnouts and difficulties in recruiting candidates to stand for election. It does retain more public trust than central government (APSE, 2020), but we have to reconsider if there continue to be qualities in the local as a site for democratic practices which justify our pinning hopes for a healthier democracy on it.

In addressing these challenges, we can accept the arguments concerning both 'anti-political' sentiment and the more fragmented, diverse local environment, while also recognising the ongoing pragmatic need for collective decision-making and legitimate means of settling common concerns which emerge from living together. We see that we need to harness some of the power of the 'alternative' democratic practices outlined above, while also accepting Stoker's pragmatism and the need to work on improving formal systems of representation. A critique of 'post-representative' politics is that it does not pay enough attention to how it is to be institutionalised and accommodate a collective decision-making capacity, to deliver at least 'good enough', acceptable decisions from a range of competing claims (Lowndes and Paxton, 2018). Flinders and Wood (2018) thus portray a need to connect 'new' and 'old' forms of engagement, with important connections being located at the nexus of the two – and, we argue, any encroachment on the elitist polity-making architecture requires both.

We would argue, then, that local government is best suited as the primary unit to provide a pragmatic balance between the 'porosity' implied by new forms of engagement and the 'fixity' required of a recognised institutional site which carries the legitimacy to make collective decisions, to pragmatically bridge this 'space/place' tension. The local is where issues of much broader scale 'touch down' and are experienced in lived space; this mediated nature gives the possibility for political agency (Allen, 2004: 20). Here the 'local' does matter because it provides 'situated places of transactional intensity' (Barnett and Bridge, 2013: 1036), where challenges to meanings and contests are seen visibly and flows are temporarily halted. Local settings thus act as 'generators of democratic energy', and serve as reminders of the stakes which are present in living and contesting amidst difference (Amin, 2004: 43). Moreover, the local represents the level at which two contrasting requirements for democratic life can best, if not perfectly, be captured. We have noted in previous chapters how 'the local' has been used by successive governments as a form of 'spatial liberalism' (Clarke and Cochrane, 2013) in attempts to 'govern at a distance' and co-opt local actors into government projects. However, we can also see 'spatial liberalism' as accommodating, as far as possible, the push and pull of the need to provide for both individual freedom and commitment to a collective polity (Wills, 2016), for reconciling the freedom of self-governing communities with a recognition of their wider responsibilities to others (Magnusson, 2015), and for achieving the benefits of both feelings of shared connection with neighbours and the recognition of wider sets of interests (Miller, 2009).

Locality can, then, provide a focus for 'democratic mending', the linking of a variety of forms of democracy (Hendriks et al., 2020) and also the improved listening and communication required to address the misunderstandings identified by Stoker, Flinders and others. Taking a 'systemic' approach to democracy (Hendriks, 2016), it should be the cornerstone feature in enhancing a system involving a range of types of democracy. As Saward (2003) points out, democracy is many faceted and can encompass a range of practices, such as direct discursive, deliberative, delegative or representative, and a range of associated mechanisms to secure their delivery, with each one potentially contributing one or other democratic 'good', which hopefully can be complemented by others. Warren (2017) similarly evaluates democratic mechanisms by asking what kind of democratic problems they address, judging them against criteria of inclusion, democratic agenda-setting and collective decision-making. Having more, and smaller units of local government within a wider system would multiply the numbers of institutions, enhancing communicative capacity to both aid problem-solving and connect communities with shared interests and concerns (Schwarzmantel, 2007).

In addition, while we accept that current local government structure leaves a lot to be desired, as outlined in previous chapters, local government provides a pragmatic 'starting place'.

Reform cannot be entirely 'ahistorical'. Localities have existing institutional histories and place attachments (Tormey, 2014; Wills, 2020) which provide a starting point for a debate concerning boundaries and scales, again serving to ground 'post-representative' trends in material and practice. This is not to say that local government institutions would be set in stone or could perfectly capture all the relevant social and economic relations in a given area, and their boundaries and status would be open to continual contestation. In this light, Blanco, Griggs and Sullivan (2014), for example, argue that 'the local is not local government, but local government is the institutional expression of it'. Also, we have argued in earlier chapters that in order to generate sufficient motivation for citizens to get involved, and to meet the requirements of output democracy, local government has to matter in that it provides valued services for a community and serves to further and protect their interests. Models of local governance in which councils are merely 'convenors' or 'facilitators' do not match these criteria (Stoker, 2011a).

Local governments, then, as service providers will always to some extent be 'Janus-faced' – both service provider and agitator – and there is an inevitable limit on the extent to which it can act as a 'dual intermediary' (Barnett, 2011). A local government system would need to be structured with the aim of getting as close as possible to the 'sweet spot' of balancing governing capacity and popular engagement, allowing the maximum amount and variety of democratic input compatible with pragmatic decision-making and service delivery. An exact match will always be elusive, and the subject of an ongoing search, but our point here is that increasingly the balance has been tipped in favour of a now much reduced service delivery role, with even that, moreover, being largely determined according to the expedient requirements of central government. In addition, the necessary 'revisability' (Stoker, 2006a), 'experimental governance' (Morgan and Sabel, 2019) and institutional redesign implied by this 'ongoing search' is stymied by central government's control over structures and scales, and its prescription and control of the types of democratic innovations which local government can promote.

As an underpinning in the search for a local government system which approximates, as far as possible, to the requirements set out above, attention should turn to the contribution which small, primary units can make. Living in proximity and sharing public space and collective services provides a basis for more direct, discursive and face-to-face political engagement within communities that are sufficiently small in number for their members, should they wish, to meet together to discuss issues that concern them jointly. It is the basis for 'the politics of the everyday' (Rosenblum, 2016) as people negotiate and make accommodations with those with whom they share proximity. Many may not recognise this as political problem-solving, although most individuals experience these practices constantly throughout their lives; in effect, this changes assumptions about where we find politics – of where the space of the political is (Magnusson, 2015).

In practice, this could only apply to small scales, as the potency in allowing freedom for individuals to express their preferences would decline in respect to size of the organisations involved and their capacity for both the time and the numbers of individuals to meet and discuss. An issue which arises from this is how such small units of governance can be designated. Should they, like current parish and town governments in Britain, be structured as liberal democratic representative governments with small, elected councils, or allow all adults to participate in the formation of policy, in a form of direct discursive democracy similar to the Rousseauian vision or the New England townships praised by de Tocqueville (1994), as discussed in Chapter 2? It could be claimed that the capacity for citizens to develop such discursive communities is today more advanced with the use of digital communication, but many problems would also be faced here in determining, for example, who are eligible attendees of virtual meetings, and whether the resources and capabilities to participate are sufficiently distributed.

However, a framework of deliberative decision-making is not impossible to imagine in communities, and one such model continues to be practised in the New England township meetings that were much admired by de Tocqueville (1994) and advocated by Benjamin Barber (1984) as a means of reinvigorating democracy in the USA. In this setting, direct discursive democracy aims to institutionalise the democratic right for those in a community to resolve problems they share between themselves, as we have suggested in Chapter 2. Moreover, the practice of what we are here labelling 'direct' or 'discursive' democracy at the local level can, as Mill stressed, have a significant educative role in developing a knowledgeable civil culture within a polity by allowing individuals to embrace a culture for reasoned argument, and give and take, in finding a way forward through the 'policy soup'. As local governments have become larger in terms of both area and population, and are shoehorned into subregional unitary authorities with fewer powers or resources, local government has, as is shown in Chapter 5, become less democratic as it is enmeshed in the liberal democratic malaise which affects the whole polity. In Britain there has been a decline in the percentage of citizens voting in local elections, and it is also far lower than in comparable liberal democracies (Chandler, 2007: 233, 321). In contrast to policy-making at a national or regional level, a community's policies could, as Toulmin Smith was aware, be determined by the views of citizens of a small locality who will be more aware of the specific environment of their area than most elite experts.

Still it could be argued that, given the size of the task and the problems identified earlier, a focus on the micro-level or on 'everyday politics' could, taking into account social economic imbalances, even prove to be counterproductive. We could see this, then, as a vicious circle, by which the very qualities needed for such a polity are the ones which we seem to be increasingly short of. Following Jacques Rancière it could be argued that true political emancipation and democracy requires a 'rupture' in consciousness which must occur independently of the political system (Purcell, 2013). However, this would be to dismiss as unimportant all of the current communal political activity of the kind which we saw providing support at local level during the COVID-19 pandemic, and also the myriad of local organising which takes place at local level outside of the 'formal' political channels. For example, the provision of food banks during the pandemic (Taylor and Wilson, 2020), along with a range of activity during that crisis led Wargent and Talen (2021: 89) to conclude that

> Even though everything a localised social grouping might be based on may seem to have lost relevance long before the pandemic – extended

families living in the same locale, face-to-face communication as the main form of social connection, the close integration of work and residence, daily shopping at the corner market – neighbourhoods continue to matter in all kinds of ways.

Such voluntary activity, it can be argued, would occur anyway, independently of local government, and in some cases would actually prefer to do so. However, local community government will add value by facilitating knowledge sharing, contributing skills, facilities and resources and identifying overlap, making best use of community assets. The interventions may be small-scale, but they would allow for a high level of engagement and a greater perception of efficacy by those participating.

There are many reservations, though, to be considered which might be said to render any such thinking to be wholly impractical 'pie in the sky', and we can only offer a brief sketch here of the practical and theoretical terrain which is opened up. Firstly, arguably, a radical change in British civic culture would be required. Parvin (2015) notes the increased demands which high levels of active engagement and discursive forms of democracy place on individuals, and points out that, from a relatively low base, the necessary habits and norms to sustain such practices need a long time to develop, with no guarantee that they would. Further, any assumption that open discussion necessarily results in consensus is met with the criticism that politics is, in essence, about conflict, power and interests (Shapiro, 1999). Thus *direct* democracy does not assume that those taking part will not simply seek to promote their own interests, but only that all can have their voices heard. Moreover, the skills, confidence and dispositions associated with participating in public arenas, necessary for the equal representation of all voices, are not themselves distributed equally, and indeed tend to reflect broader inequalities; as Mansbridge (in Bryan et al., 2019: 3) notes, thus 'the open door is not enough'. Therefore, more direct forms of democracy cannot be bracketed to stand outside of broader social and economic conditions (Barnett, 2011), nor can imbalanced power relations be neutralised (Bagg, 2018). *Deliberative* democracy sets an even higher bar, being premised on the assumption that participants are willing to adjust their views and accommodate those of others and that, if all affected persons are heard, decisions will be reached by consensus based on the strength of the better argument (Barnett, 2011). Thus, to avoid issues of inequality, deliberative forums need to be carefully designed and facilitated 'mini publics' to ensure fair hearings of all voices, and the issue then arises of how to link these to actual sites of decision-making, without which they are simply 'deliberation without power' (Leighninger, 2019: 5). Also, applying such principles to small, local, place-based decision-making, how would all affected interests be included, as by nature members would be selected by means of residence alone?

It may be questioned, then, whether such a reawakening of local politics either assumes participation or agreement; whether it might be detached from sites of broader decision-making, or whether it overvalues the importance of residence in decision-making. In response, it must firstly sit within a broader set of ethical standards and rights. In arguing for a right to democratic government at the community level, we recognise that this is a necessary but not substantive right. Such local units will not have 'exclusive jurisdiction' over everything which happens within their boundaries (Magnusson, 2015). As we noted in the Introduction, the localities are not closed entities but are embedded in wider, distanciated relations nationally and indeed globally, requiring their voice to be heard in a range of spaces of engagement, while in turn requiring them to be aware of their effects on others (Clarke and Cochrane, 2013). We agree with those, as mentioned above, who argue for the strengthening of existing representative democracy, being pragmatic and seeking to enhance the 'transmission' capacity between scales of engagement (Boswell et al., 2016), in turn arguing that this process should be more 'bottom-linked' (Bianchi, 2022). There is nothing inconsistent in arguing for small self-governing units while recognising the requirement for larger scales (Magnusson, 2015) and this should not be seen as a 'zero-sum' equation but one of mutual reinforcement; there is not one simple trade-off to be made between democratic engagement and system effectiveness, but rather governance arrangements should recognise and facilitate 'a participative division of labour' (Lowndes and Sullivan, 2008: 67).

There thus need to be intermediate larger councils or single purpose agencies for determining policies that affect several communities: national or global organisations, that because of their size would be representative, must be present to resolve issues of ethical principle and efficiency affecting the relationships between centre and periphery. These must safeguard the integrity of the small primary units of governance. There would need to be means and guarantees to ensure that local democracy does not descend into local autocracy or favour solely a specific racial or cultural group. However, means should be found to ensure that smaller primary units of governance can have the right to have their concerns in this context debated with other groups. Institutions and practices that determine principles of wider concern should not, if local government is to have a measure of independence, be able – as is largely the case at present – to be determined with little reference to community concerns. It may be speculated that a reformed Upper House of Parliament could be restructured as a House of Communities to represent local institutions and values, and create a link between local and nation policy-making.

Moreover, we have noted the enduring resonance of place, and of proximity, and, in the Introduction, that it is in shared, lived spaces where we find a congruence of both material and imagined, or affective, interests. Overconcentration on either one or the other results in an unsatisfactory arrangement whereby, in theory, either isolated individuals would recognise themselves as a collective only at times of discourse over shared interests, or, on the other hand, as a highly bonded unit with shared affect and emotions but with no material reason to form a political community. Mansbridge (1983), for example, talks of 'unitary' democracy which has at its basis common bonds and unified interests, with people meeting to reach agreement, and 'adversary' democracy, where differing interests ensure that such agreement cannot be reached. She argues that both are required: unitary democracy to generate, as far as possible, common interests, but where agreement cannot be reached, decision-making mechanisms – voting, elections and others – for the democratic settlement of disputes.

In turn, the questions of 'who should be included?' and 'who decides who should be included?' have not only dogged local government policymakers and scholars, but appear to produce a paradox in democratic theory (Goodin, 2007). In practice, in

Is there any possibility of change? 239

Britain the basic primary units for establishing community governments based on direct democratic principles are present in rural areas and smaller urban areas within the existing structures of parish, community and town governments, and it is often recognised in cities that smaller units for neighbourhoods can be discerned in their boundaries as electoral wards or school or doctors' catchment areas. For practical purposes, these can be used unless there is widespread objection, and a pragmatic view can be taken on the site and boundaries of small primary councils dependent on the views of residents on the geography and traditions of their neighbourhoods, as far as possible. This would require some external body to determine who should be included in any such determination of the desired local polity. Nevertheless, while in many areas the demarcation of local boundaries may fit existing boundaries, especially in large cities where there are few localised governance institutions, the issue may in some areas be a matter of contention and systems will be needed to adjudicate on settling such differences. This suggestion, of going for the best possible approximation of the confluence of sense of belonging and objective interests, could be criticised for being in effect simply a replication of the approach taken by previous local government reviews, notably the process attempted by the Redcliffe-Maud and Banham Commissions. This is correct, in that such trade-offs are more or less inevitable. Again, however, our point here is they have been settled historically predominantly on the side of the perceived extent of objective interests and efficiency.

An obvious objection may be, given that we have argued that local governments need responsibilities for delivery of outcomes which matter, 'what could small primary units do?' We only have space to discuss this in the context of two of the major issues facing us currently: climate change and social services. Firstly, climate change poses what seems to be the biggest challenge to a turn to the small-scale, as the scope and urgency of necessary change requires action at a global scale. Attempting to firstly agree, let alone implement, global targets on carbon emissions, for example, has proven elusive. However, a 'localised' approach has been advocated for some time – what Fischer (2017: 227) has called an 'environmentalism of everyday life' based around community initiatives, from promotion of local produce via farmers' markets to local low-carbon schemes and community gardening. Such initiatives, in turn, need connecting to other levels of governance if they are to 'scale up', without losing their local knowledge-based independence and innovation (Ostrom, 2010; Shaw and Cumbers, 2018). Democratic theory and practice around climate concerns has developed from focussing on issues of global and regional collaboration to embrace a 'new materialist' approach, drawing on local initiatives and based on micro-scale 'everyday life' practices, such as improving community commons, community markets and renewable energy schemes. Such innovations can lack durability and be episodic without some institutional support, without which scaling up becomes more difficult (Eckersley, 2020). The National Association of Local Councils (NALC, 2021) representing parish and town councils has declared that there is a climate emergency and 37 per cent of their members have made a similar statement. A NALC survey of their membership identified a wide variety of schemes established by parish and town councils including generating sustainable energy or organising charging points for electric vehicles, but the most popular response from 64 per cent of their respondents concerned tree planting and for 54 per cent rewilding schemes. NALC (2020) has also published a survey of a wide range of briefly described case studies of schemes by its members to ameliorate the threat of climate change for their communities. However, currently the relationship between central and local governments on the issue of climate change is itself in crisis. A National Audit Office Report from 2021–22 stresses that there is still little evidence of effective working on climate change issues between central and local government (NAO, 2021a).

In dealing with the problems of social services and healthcare for the elderly or less abled, local community authorities may also be able to foreground caring, being able to tap into and help direct qualities which stem from neighbourliness and what Hankins (2017) calls 'the quiet politics of the everyday'. For example, they could encourage those with empathetic skills to visit people in their community who are socially isolated by age or illness; local gardeners or handy persons may similarly aid those with health and financial problems to improve their home environment. This could be, and is, done on a voluntary basis by groups and individuals, but community councils may coordinate such roles using local knowledge of unmet needs and requirements for help, and might choose to employ full- or part-time carers. This does not in any way downplay the urgent need to systematically address the huge immediate and long-term issues facing in particular adult social care, nor the extent of informal care which now increasingly falls onto family members and friends – needs which must be addressed in an equitable way that provides acceptable levels of care and dignity for all. However, caring involves relationships 'within a range of formal and informal spaces and practices' (Hall and McGarrol, 2013: 695), and innovative practices developed in local communities can not only help individuals, but 'recast [care] as set of social interrelationships and actions in "caring about" a group of people and a place' (Hall and McGarrol, 2013: 699). As such, they can help to reconnect isolated individuals to a sense of place and belonging, strengthening other sources of support by demonstrating a 'powerful ethic of "caring about" a local community' (Hall and McGarrol, 2013: 702).

Conclusion

There is, we conclude, no shortage of ideas on how local government can have a more democratic profile, greater concern for neighbourhood issues, and greater powers and resources. But it seems that they would not be entertained by central government unless they can fit within the prevailing notion that the institution is expedient to the needs of Whitehall and Westminster, and for Scotland, Holyrood. Attempts to break out of the depressed state of local government historically in Britain, as we show in Chapter 1, are not unprecedented. Indeed, locally promoted innovations in the early nineteenth century led to more effective and democratic local governance. As we have shown in Chapters 3 to 7, however, recent years have seen austerity in local government finances, major changes in local government boundaries that have reduced their number and increased their size in terms of population, and a continuing wilting away of local government powers and internal democracy. In such a context it is unlikely that in the foreseeable future the British government is likely to accept legislation, let alone alternative perspectives, that allow local government greater autonomy to pursue separate policies that counter the values of the ruling parties. In his later writing, Copus and his collaborators' conclusion is pertinent but rather bleak:

> Given a local acceptance of the centralist narrative, or at least a willingness to act in its confines, it is unlikely that emergence of an independent and autonomous local government will develop from the bottom up, or from a local government revolution. (Copus et al., 2017: 180)

We accept this sentiment, and recognise the extent of the task: the problems of local government are, we recognise, inextricably linked to the predominating policy formulation styles and wider problems faced by liberal democracy on a national and global scale. However, we also argue that there is value in continuing to hope and to push for a democratically re-energised local government along the lines we have sketched out above.

Conclusions and reflections

Local governments in Britain are ceasing to be local, and increasingly administer policy on behalf of central government rather than governing. 'The local' is a malleable term which can be enlisted for a variety of purposes and political projects; its geographical scope is necessarily contestable and impossible to pin down precisely. However, it has a 'common-sense' meaning in which it conveys a sense of physical proximity combined with some meaningful shared and common interest. We have shown that local government, apart from what remains of parish government, does not fit the description of local in most everyday usages of the term. Since the Herbert and Redcliffe-Maud Reports in the 1950s and 1960s, there has been an insidious progress towards creating a single tier of principal authorities that undertake the major tasks assigned to local government, covering what should be termed subregional rather than local authorities, in the principal meaning of the term 'local'. Unitary authorities such as Northumbria or Shropshire, covering some 60 miles north to south, can scarcely be thought of as local, let alone North Yorkshire, a unitary county-wide authority created by combining seven district authorities abolished without any clear failures on their part. The large cities such as Sheffield, Manchester or Southampton are, with the exception of Greater London, similarly bundled into single-tier arrangements. While cities and towns do represent historical communal attachments, within these unitary authorities there are limited attempts to decentralise to their many separate localities. In addition, in conurbations, even larger subregional authorities have been placed under the control of elected mayors. Britain has, as a consequence, far fewer principal subnational authorities than other comparable liberal democracies outside the British Isles, as is shown in Table 1 (see Appendix 1).

Not only are the principal local authorities ceasing to be local, but they are also losing much of their responsibility to govern what were once widely seen as locally relevant services. Since the Second World War, as shown in Chapter 1, responsibility for many of the potentially profitable services that were once implemented by local authorities has been undertaken by private or arm's-length agencies regulated by central government. This was already the lot of electricity and gas supply, telecommunications and water distribution and drainage before 1980. Subsequently, the traditional role of local policing outside London has been stripped from local government, in an incremental process, culminating in the creation of a reduced number of police forces accountable to an elected commissioner who is not directly accountable to local authorities. Similarly, the hollowing out of local government by the creation of ad hoc agencies has befallen several local government responsibilities such as transport services, flood control and probation services. Chapter 4 explains in greater detail how more formerly redistributive services such as social services, education and social services have often been operated on a profit-making basis by private companies, subsidised by central government or as non-local consortia, which in many cases provide higher salaries to their managers than may be secured in public sector employment. Many potentially less profitable local functions such as the provision of public libraries, allotments or local parks are, given years of austerity, frequently run outside of local control in isolation from other services needed by the community.

The loss of local government control over local services and the development of subregional authorities can in itself produce a loss of local democratic efficacy for individuals and groups, but this consequent democratic deficit is further promoted, as discussed in Chapter 5, by the centrally imposed restructuring of local authority constitutions. The authorities in charge of local services have been increasingly governed in a corporate style by leaders or executive mayors and Cabinets that, for most citizens, are more remote and unapproachable. The decline of the local, and even regional, press ensures that their activities are poorly publicised and beyond the knowledge of most citizens. A vote for an executive mayor or a police commissioner will often mirror the electorate's view of the fortunes of the political party in charge of central government and the leading members of the opposition parties rather than that of their local stewardship. A survey in 2021 found that only in Manchester and London could more than 50 per cent of respondents name the mayor of their city (Centre for Cities, 2021). Moreover, popular opinion concerning the behaviour of central government and opposition parties will be for many voters a reflection of the influence exercised by national pressure groups, national consortia and, perhaps, the coteries of successful celebrity self-appointed bloggers on the internet.

As shown in Chapter 4, these local authorities have, since 2010, taken the burden of cuts in the drive by central government for austerity. In such straitened circumstances many of them have struggled to deliver adequately those services over which they have some control. But failures can, as in the case of the bankruptcy of Northamptonshire County Council, be wholly blamed by central government on their local managers. A further consequence of this is that, while it is hard see any overall benefit for communities from these developments in the local government system, or even the several local public and private agencies delivering local services, it will continue to be the poorest authority areas with the worst symptoms of social deprivation that will suffer the greatest poverty and destitution. The 'levelling up' agenda revealed in 2022 was far from adequate to address the spatial inequalities and imbalance in investment and productivity which exist between, for example, the south-east and north-east regions of England. Moreover, the United Kingdom's withdrawal from European Union membership has exacerbated the problem, removing access to the programmes that have been a major contributor to regeneration in northern England and the south of Wales. Addressing these issues in the long run requires an underpinning 'shift away from central direction to local power and control' (Fahnbulleh et al., 2022: 2).

We do not, however, argue in this book that local government is, let alone should be, just an agency of central government, only able to undertake tasks at the demand of Westminster and Whitehall or the Scottish, Welsh or Northern Ireland governments. Chapter 7 outlines how local authorities have sought to use their capacity for innovation to seek new roles and ventures within the confines of the right to self-competence, despite the austerity and legislation that confines these powers. The chapter shows that many local authorities can be innovative despite the restrictions applied from above, and as such remain a vital agency to make government work effectively in delivering services. Such activity demonstrates that properly managed local authorities with cognisance of local need and capable of generating local resources and expertise could, like the Birminghams and Manchesters of the nineteenth century, if allowed, be capable of developing and shaping their communities more effectively than is currently possible.

In Chapter 8 we consider the view of devolved local governance from the point of view of core executives. There are, we argue, strong reasons why in a centralising state the centre requires a measure of devolved administration, if not governance. Delegating detailed tasks to local government avoids overloading the capacity of central government to make policy on matters of principle. Local administration through elected agencies can also be used as a means of resolving local or regional problems that have evaded the competence of central agencies, and may provide valuable scapegoats for policy failures that, especially at a time of financial austerity, should be laid at the door of central politicians. Finally, and crucially, the presence of something called local government is an important element in the belief that Britain's liberal democracy is sufficiently democratic to secure individual and community freedom and liberty. Appeals to the value of 'local democracy' thus continue to emanate from politicians across the political spectrum despite the practical implications of their policies, and it is called upon as a useful prop to justify all manner of reforms which are neither local nor democratic.

It could be argued by those at the extreme edges of advocacy for reducing the size of the public sector that private sector enterprise can supply the collective needs of citizens (Nozick, 1974), but it makes little sense to venture very far down this route. There is no question that in a democratic civic culture there must be, in any substantial polity, local decentralised administrations to coordinate the policies required by its central government and its citizens. Atomised and often conflicting private agencies are highly unlikely to develop the joined-up working necessary to establish policies that work in the interest of society as a whole rather than an elite of wealthy consumers and entrepreneurs. In addition, as we argue in Chapter 9, a fragmented local polity requires an institutional form through which to make collective decisions.

In the penultimate Chapter 9 we argue that the centralisation of policy-making in Britain is a retrograde development for a number of interlinked reasons. Most predominantly it is an unethical trend undermining the principles of liberal, let alone direct, democracy, which could be an essential foundation of a moral political society. It is argued in Chapters 1 and 2 that until the nineteenth century there was a widespread and informed view that individual liberty should not be secured solely, if at all, by national government. With the growth in academic support for a philosophical grounding supporting liberal democracy, particularly in the works of John Stuart Mill, there is a firm rationale for continuing the maintenance of local democracy as a necessary, if not sufficient, right for communities (Chandler, 2010). Such was the ideal if not always the practice. In Chapter 2 we show that Mill himself on balance emphasised that central government should have dominance over matters of principle, to leave local governments with the determination of matters of detail.

In this study we conclude with two related issues concerning local government in Britain and its relationship to the state. Firstly, that increasingly local government is being used as an expedient agency of central government, as opposed to an institution that provides an important right for citizens to determine the issues that affect them as a community but do not seriously impinge on the rights of others. Secondly, consideration of this plight needs to be set within the context of the condition of liberal democratic policy-making. Despite the austerity and legislative chains that have been attached to the system, local governments, as indicated in Chapter 7, still show capacity to innovate in the most difficult of circumstances. The problem, or rather the crisis, of local government is to be found in the working mindset, elitism and state of liberal democracy at the centre of national government. Without restructuring of national government and a reinvigoration of the democratic polity, no solution to the present decline of democracy is likely to be secured.

The question that this evisceration of local government raises is whether such an institution has any remaining value to central government, and whether it is being driven down the road to virtual extinction. The complete abolition of local government, however, is extremely unlikely. As Peter John (2014) has argued, local government may indeed be the 'Great Survivor', even if this is based on it continuing to prove useful for central government, as is the case in Britain.

Reflections

Although we parallel and update many of the concerns that have been emphasised in recent studies of local government in the United Kingdom, this volume differs from many of these works in that we have highlighted the possibility, derived from John Stuart Mill's writing, of a normative reason for the existence and structuring of local government. We argue that a system primarily based on community governments is more ethically democratic in terms of ensuring popular and well-considered policies affecting individual citizens and in encouraging a more politically literate civil society. George Monbiot (2022: 3) observes that 'we need ... radical devolution to the lowest possible levels at which decisions can be made accompanied by deliberative participatory democracy'. There has been renewed interest in forms of direct democracy coming from many quarters in recent years. As we noted in the Introduction, the 'new municipalism' has reawakened interest in Murray Bookchin's advocacy of direct municipal forums (Bookchin, 2015), which itself draws on Hannah Arendt's 'council democracy' (Arendt, 2009). Interest was also generated by the 'self-organising' and 'horizontal' collective practices of movements like Occupy and others around the globe following the financial crisis of 2008–10 (Graeber, 2011). In conjunction with this there has been renewed interest in John Dewey's perception of democracy as a way of life, or a form of society, which has to be experienced and practised, a consequence of living together which should be facilitated, as far as possible, by direct communication in a constant process of learning and adjustment, meaning that we have to 'plunge deeper' to uncover democratic practices (Frega, 2019). Small, primary local government units allow for this, while being the appropriate level for a 'politics of the everyday' which builds up via neighbourly connections, trust and reciprocity, and aids the forging of relationships for the discovery of shared goals (Rosenblum, 2016; Stears, 2011).

If we fully accepted this view, local government should have a primary foundation in smaller units that can develop, following Barber (1984), into more deliberative forums as regards local issues and also express with other localities concerns of city, county, regional and national significance. Similarly, the views of other localities may be heard when there are particular issues in which there is an 'overspill' of interest. Of course, there may be a range of other, non-geographical sites of collective engagement which could also be further democratised and integrated into an overall democratic ecology, around specific services or issues (Fung and Wright, 2001). This extends also to other potentially radical forms of self-organisation which position themselves outside of, or alongside, formal political structures (Cumbers, 2015), and to work-based and forms of economic democratisation. Fung and Wright, and Paul Hirst (1993), via his concept of associative democracy, are among those who have proposed means of institutionalising these various forms of social and economic democratisation and creating what Cohen and Sabel (1997) labelled a 'polyarchy' of directly deliberative forms. It is outside the scope of this study to pursue these issues further and more thought is needed to draw out and investigate how place-based democratisation potentially fits together with other forms, including workplaces. However, we have focussed here on the essential place of locality in decision-making over collectively shared services and in representing, as far as practically possible, the grounded experience of shared space.

We accept Blaug's point that innovations in democratic design need to have an awareness of how and where they *fit in*, and that we need to 'learn how to walk first' (Blaug, 2000: 148). As he points out, organisations based on direct forms of engagement have a tendency to 'fizzle out'; they can be ephemeral and face, at a certain point, dangers of co-optation or overformalisation when coming into contact with state institutions and decision-making. Blaug (2002) argues that we should not attempt to 'engineer' democracy, but that it must emerge via its own energies. In contrast, we agree with Barber (1984) and others in thinking that democratic practice is a learning process which can be facilitated and helped along. Institutional support is needed. Thus Mansbridge, for example, once a critic of the domination and exclusion she found in open town meetings in the United States (Mansbridge, 1983), later suggested means by which they could be better facilitated and laced with greater realism. Bryan (1995), while recognising some disappointment in levels of engagement and other issues, noted that on a range of democratic 'goods', town meetings delivered to a greater extent than the current alternatives of voting and participating in elections, and argued that

> If we conclude that talk democracy is essential to the building of citizens capable of using representative structures to govern a complex nation, there is only one choice, I would argue, open to us. We must re-empower our citizens to do the work of governance again. Town meeting is neither electric or elastic. It cannot be stretched out to govern the whole. The trick is to re-establish and re-empower governments of human scale. (Bryan, 1995: 42)

Unless we are to do nothing, then, we need to at least offer some hope that there may be a gap in the 'vicious circle' of attempting to generating vibrant democratic renewal in somewhat hostile circumstances. While local government sits amidst an inhospitable social and economic environment, there is a need for what William Connolly has called 'interim visions' (Howarth, 2011). Wright (2010) similarly promotes the value of 'Real Utopias', visions for the future which are fully cognisant of the pragmatism in moving towards them. As Mansbridge (2003: 195) notes, 'Pushing the ideal increases the pressure on the system, and that pressure often makes the underlying relations clearer, the way clenching your fist makes the veins stand out from the flesh.' Direct democracy at a micro level could, then, be seen as democratic experimentation, a place to start, potentially expansive in terms of producing effects which enrich other democratic forms of engagement, and initially giving, at minimum, a chance for all the people 'to govern themselves in at least some public matters at least some of the time' (Barber, 1984: xxii).

A vision needs to be adopted which sets local government properly in the context of how local primary units of government may underpin an overall democratic envelope of governance in Britain and thus link a local perspective into the many concerns that have now surfaced over the theory and practice of democracy. There should be a more balanced relationship between local communities and Westminster and Whitehall. This is not in itself a new idea, and indeed linking local discursive decision-making to national or global policy-making and values has been analysed since at least the sixteenth century through theorists such as Althusius (1995), and was current in early nineteenth-century thought and emphasised in the works of de Tocqueville, Toulmin Smith and John Stuart Mill. In the later twentieth century it was present in the works of others such as Habermas and Bourdieu. Among more liberal democratic-minded theorists, connecting local and national policy-making is a central theme of Benjamin Barber's (1984) concept of Strong Democracy and is also reflected in D. E. Ashford's (1982) too often overlooked study of the contrasting cultures in local governance between Britain and France. We have, if briefly, drawn attention to recent democratic practices and theorising and considered their implications for local government, and would argue that these serve to infuse the traditional debates with interesting new insights and possibilities. However, we note the enduring contribution in particular of Mill's thinking in providing us with an ethical grounding on which to move forward.

There are many issues that require further thought on how local government should evolve in the twenty-first century, and many arguments that need to be clarified as to how this should progress to produce a more balanced relationship between local neighbourhood or local communities and Westminster and Whitehall. We are aware that we have pulled at many threads in the argument, and that some require further exploration, so exactly how this can be achieved would take another volume to further develop the ideas that have been outlined in this study. We hope, however, that we have provoked some questions and provided some signposts as to how we might move towards a local government which can do justice to the energies and innovative capacities which can be found in localities.

Appendix 1

Table 1 Average population size of lowest executive tiers of local government

Belgium	19,600	Communes
Denmark	59,592	Municipalities
Eire	160,561	Municipalities
France	1,843	Communes
Germany	6,862	Gemeinden
Italy	7,639	Comune
Netherlands	49,893	Municipalities
Poland	15,269	Gmina
Portugal	33,428	Municipalities
Spain	5,824	Municipalities
United States	9,216	Municipalities and townships
United Kingdom	165,338	Principal authorities

Source: Wikipedia, national data on local government for each country, 2021.

Appendix 2

Table 2 1974 local government structures

	England outside London	London	Wales	Scotland
1st tier County councils (39)	Metropolitan councils (6)	Greater London Council	Counties (8)	Regions (8) Island councils (3)
2nd tier Districts (296)	Metropolitan districts (36)	London boroughs (32)	Districts (37)	Districts (53)
3rd tier Parish/town councils	Parishes/town councils (approx. 10,000)	None	Community councils (approx. 730)	Community councils (approx. 1,300)

References

Achen, C. and L. Bartels (2016) *Democracy for Realists: Why Elections do not Produce Responsive Results*. Princeton, NJ: Princeton University Press.
Agnew, J. A. (1987) *Place and Politics: The Geographical Mediation of State and Society*. London: Allen and Unwin.
Allen, J. (2004) 'The whereabouts of power: Politics, government and space', *Geografiska Annaler*, 86B:1, 19–32.
Althusius, J. (1995) *Politica*, translated and edited by F. Carney. Indianapolis: Liberty Fund.
Amin, A. (2004) 'Regions unbound: Towards a new politics of place', *Geografiska Annaler*, 86B:1, 33–44.
APSE (Association for Public Service Excellence) (2014) *Two Tribes?* Manchester: APSE.
APSE (2019a) *Ensuring the Leadership of the New Municipalism*. Manchester: APSE.
APSE (2019b) *Rebuilding Capacity: The Case for Insourcing Public Contracts*. Manchester: APSE.
APSE (2020) *Selling Services to Schools: Facing the Future*: Manchester: APSE.
APSE (2021) *Local by Default: Final Report of the APSE Local Government 2030 Commission*. Manchester: APSE.
Arendt, H. (2009) *On Revolution*. London: Penguin Classics.
Arnold, S. and A. Stirling (2019) *Councils in Crisis: Local Government Austerity 2009/10–2024/25*. London: New Economics Foundation.
Arrieta, T. (2022) 'An assessment of the resilience of local government in England: Was it well-equipped to overcome the Covid-19 pandemic?', *Political Quarterly*, 93:3, 408–415.
Ashford, D. E. (1982) *British Dogmatism and French Pragmatism*. London: George Allen & Unwin.
Ashworth, R. and S. Snape (2010) 'An overview of scrutiny: A triumph of context over structure', *Local Government Studies*, 30:4, 538–556.

Atkinson, H. (2012) *Local Democracy, Civic Engagement and Community*. Manchester: Manchester University Press.

Atkinson, H. and S. Wilks-Heeg (2000) *Local Government from Thatcher to Blair*. Cambridge: Polity Press.

Audit Commission (1990) *We Can't Go on Meeting Like This*. London: Audit Commission.

Ayres, S., M. Flinders and M. Sandford (2018) 'Territory, power and statecraft: Understanding English devolution', *Regional Studies*, 52:6, 853–864.

Bache, I. and M. Flinders (2004) *Multi-Level Governance*. Oxford: Oxford University Press.

Bagg, S. (2018) 'Can deliberation neutralise power?', *European Journal of Political Theory*, 17:3, 257–279.

Bailey, N. and M. Pill (2011) 'The continuing popularity of the neighbourhood and neighbourhood governance in the transition from the "Big State" to the "Big Society" paradigm', *Environment and Planning C: Government and Policy*, 29:5, 927–942.

Bailey, N. and M. Pill (2015) 'Can the state empower communities through localism? An evaluation of recent approaches to neighbourhood governance in England', *Environment and Planning C: Government and Policy*, 33:2, 289–304.

Bailey, D. and W. Wood (2017) 'The Metagovernance of English devolution', *Local Government Studies*, 43:6, 966–999.

Bains, M. (1972) *The New Local Authorities: Management and Structure*. Working Group on Local Authority Management. London: HMSO.

Ball, S. (2018) 'The tragedy of state education in England: Reluctance, compromise and muddle – a system in disarray', *Journal of the British Academy*, 43: 207–238.

Bang, H. and E. Sorensen (1999) 'The everyday maker: A new challenge to democratic governance', *Administrative Theory & Praxis*, 21:3, 325–341.

Banham, J. (1994) *The Anatomy of Change: Blueprint for a New Era*. London: Orion.

Barber, B. (1984) *Strong Democracy: Participatory Politics for a New Age*. Berkeley, CA: University of California Press.

Barcelona En Comu (2019) *Fearless Cities*. Oxford: New Internationalist Publications.

Barnett, C. (2014) 'What Do Cities Have to Do with Democracy?', *International Journal of Urban and Regional Research*, 38:5, 1625–1643.

Barnett, C. and G. Bridge (2013) 'Geographies of radical democracy: Agonistic pragmatism and the formation of affected interests', *Annals of the Association of American Geographers*, 103:4, 1022–1040.

References

Barnett, N. (2003) 'Local government, New Labour and active welfare: A case of "self responsibilisation"?', *Public Policy and Administration*, 18:3, 25–38.
Barnett, N. (2011) 'Local government at the nexus', *Local Government Studies*, 37:3, 275–290.
Barnett, N. and J. Chandler (2018) 'Local government as governance for localities', paper presented to the Political Studies Association Annual Conference, University of Cardiff.
Barnett, N., S. Griggs, S. Hall and D. Howarth (2019) 'Whatever happened to councillors? Problematising the deficiency narrative in English local politics', *Political Studies*, 67:3, 775–794.
Barnett, N., S. Griggs, S. Hall and D. Howarth (2022) 'Local agency for the public purpose? Dissecting and evaluating the emerging discourses of municipal entrepreneurship in the UK', *Local Government Studies*, 48:5, 907–928.
Bartlett, D., P. Corrigan, P. Dibben, S. Franklin, P. Joyce and A. Rose (1999) 'Preparing for Best Value', *Local Government Studies*, 25:2, 102–118.
Bauman, Z. (2000) *Liquid Modernity*. Cambridge: Polity Press.
Beer, A. and T. Clower (2014) 'Mobilizing leadership in cities and regions', *Regional Studies, Regional Science*, 1:1, 5–20.
Bello, B., J. Downe, R. Andrews and S. Martin (2018) 'Does austerity drive public service innovation?', *Public Money & Management*, 38:2, 131–138.
Beswick, J. and J. Penny (2018) 'Demolishing the present to sell to the future?', *International Journal of Urban and Regional Research*, 42:4, 612–632.
Bianchi, I. (2022) 'Empowering policies for grassroots welfare initiatives: Blending social innovation and commons theory', *European Urban and Regional Studies*, 30:3, 107–120.
Blakeley, G. and Quilter-Pinner, H. (2019) *Who Cares?: The Financialisation of Adult Social Care*. London: IPPR.
Blanco, I., S. Griggs and H. Sullivan (2014) 'Situating the local in the neoliberalisation and transformation of urban governance', *Urban Studies*, 51:15, 3129–3146.
Blanco, I., Y. Salazar and I. Bianchi (2019) 'Urban governance and political change under a radical left government', *Journal of Urban Affairs*, 42:1, 18–38.
Blaug, R. (2000) 'Outbreaks of democracy', *Socialist Register*, 36, 145–160.
Blaug, R. (2002) 'Engineering democracy', *Political Studies*, 50:1, 102–116.
Blunkett, D. and K. Jackson (1987) *Democracy in Crisis*. London: Hogarth Press.
Bookchin, M. (2015) *The Next Revolution*. London: Verso.

Boswell, J., C. M. Hendriks and A. S. A. Ercan (2016) 'Message received? Examining transmission in deliberative systems', *Critical Policy Studies*, 10:3, 263–283.

Bottom, K. and C. Game (2012) 'Fewer councillors on super-sized councils: the UK's formula for increasing local democracy – not!', paper presented to the IPSA 22nd World Congress of Political Science, Madrid, 8–12 July.

Bourdieu, P. (1998) *Practical Reason*. Stanford, CA: Stanford University Press.

Bradley, Q. (2015) 'The political identities of neighbourhood planning in England', *Space and Polity*, 19:2, 97–109.

Branson, N. (1979) *Poplarism 1919–1925*. London: Lawrence and Wishart.

Braybrooke, D. and C. E. Lindblom (1963) *A Strategy of Decision*. New York: Free Press.

Brenner, N., J. Peck and N. Theodore (2010) 'Variegated neoliberalization: Geographies, modalities, pathways', *Global Networks*, 10:2, 182–222.

Brent, J. (2009) *Searching for Community*. Bristol: Policy Press.

Brien, P., M. Sandford and M. Keep (2020) *Local Government Finance Settlement 2020–21*, House of Commons Briefing Paper No. 08818. London: House of Commons.

Broadhurst, K. (2018) 'In the pursuit of economic growth: Drivers and inhibitors of place-based partnerships', *Regional Studies, Regional Science*, 5:1, 332–338.

Brogan, H. (2006) *Alexis DeTocqueville: A Life*. New Haven, CT: Yale University Press.

Bryan, F. M. (1995) 'Direct democracy and civic competence', *The Good Society*, 5:3, 36–44.

Bryan F., Keith W., Kloppenberg J., Mansbridge J., Morrell M. and Smith G. (2019) 'Collective interview on the history of town meetings', *Journal of Public Deliberation*, 15:2, 1–15.

Bua, A. and O. Escobar (2018) 'Participatory-deliberative processes and public policy agendas: Lessons for policy and practice', *Policy Design and Practice*, 1:2, 126–140.

Bulpitt, J. (1983) *Territory and Power in the United Kingdom*. Manchester: Manchester University Press.

Butler, P. (2020) 'Former "red wall" areas could lose millions in council funding review', *Guardian*, 25 January.

Butler, P. (2022) 'Thurrock council admits disastrous investments caused £500m deficit', *Guardian*, 29 November.

Cameron, D. (2011) Speech to the Local Government Association Annual Conference, ICC Birmingham, 28 June 2011, available at www.politics.co.uk/comment-analysis/2011/06/28/david-camerons-lga-speech-in-full/ (accessed 22 January 2015).

Carr, R. (2015) *Commercial Councils: The Rise of Entrepreneurialism in Local Government*. London: Localis.

Carr-West, J. (2013) 'Introduction: Putting the local jigsaw together' in *Connected Localism*. London: LGiU, 1–10.

Carr-West, J. (2022) 'Levelling up White Paper fails to meet its own challenge', *Local Government Chronicle*, 7 February.

Centre for Cities (2021) 'What do the public think about devolution and the metro mayors?', available at www.centreforcities.org/data/what-do-the-public-think-about-devolution-and-the-metro-mayors/ (accessed 6 August 2022).

Chandler, J. A. (1988) *Public Policy for Local Government*. London: Croom Helm.

Chandler, J. A. (1989) 'The Liberal justification for local government: Values and administrative expediency', *Political Studies*, 37:4, 604–611.

Chandler, J. A. (2007) *Explaining Local Government: Local Government in Britain since 1800*. Manchester: Manchester University Press.

Chandler, J. A. (2008) 'Liberal justifications for local government: The triumph of expediency over ethics', *Political Studies*, 56:2, 355–373.

Chandler, J. A. (2009) *Local Government Today*, 4th edn. Manchester: Manchester University Press.

Chandler, J. A. (2010) 'A rationale for local government', *Local Government Studies*, 36:1, 5–20.

Chandler, J. A. (2017) *Public Policy and Private Interest*. Abingdon: Routledge.

Chisholm, M. (2000) *Structural Reform of British Local Government: Rhetoric and Reality*. Manchester: Manchester University Press.

Chisholm, M. and S. Leach (2008) *Botched Business: The Damaging Process of Reorganising Local Government 2006–2008*. Coleford: Douglas McLean Publishing.

Chisholm, M. and S. Leach (2011) 'Dishonest government: Local government reorganisation in England 2006–2011', *Local Government Studies*, 37:1, 19–41.

Christophers, B. (2019) 'Putting financialisation in its financial context', *Transactions of the Institute of British Geographers*, 44:3, 571–586.

Clark G. (2016) Greg Clark's speech to the LGA conference, 5 July, available at https://tinyurl.com/2xn7xanw (accessed 17 June 2021).

Clarke, N. and A. Cochrane (2013) 'Geographies and politics of localism: The localism of the United Kingdom's Coalition government', *Political Geography*, 34, 10–23.

Clarke, N., W. Jennings, J. Moss and G. Stoker (2017) 'Changing spaces of political encounter and the rise of anti-politics: Evidence from Mass Observation's general election diaries', *Political Geography*, 56, 13–23.

Clegg, N. (2010) 'Forword', *Decentralisation and the Localism Bill: An Essential Guide*. London: HMSO.
CLES (Centre for Local Economic Strategies) (2020a) 'Manchester City Council spend analysis 2018/19', available at https://tinyurl.com/2p8e88be (accessed 7 April 2022).
CLES (2020b) *Own the Future*. Manchester: CLES.
Coaffee, J. and N. Headlam (2007) 'Pragmatic localism uncovered: The search for locally contingent solutions to national reform agendas', *Geoforum*, 39:4, 1585–1599.
Cobbett, W. (1834) *Cobbett's Legacy to the Labourers*. London: Cobbett.
Cochrane, A. (2007) *Understanding Urban Policy: A Critical Approach*. Oxford: Blackwell.
Cockburn, C. (1977) *The Local State: Management of Cities and People*. London: Pluto Press.
Cohen, J. and C. Sabel (1997) 'Directly-deliberative polyarchy', *European Law Journal*, 3:3, 313–342.
Cole, G. D. H. (1947) *Local and Regional Government*. London: Cassell.
Cole, M. and G. Boyne (1996) 'So you think you know what local government is?', *Local Government Studies*, 21:2, 1091–1202.
Cole, M. and L. McAlister (2015) 'Evaluating and theorising committee scrutiny: A UK comparative perspective', *Local Government Studies*, 41:2, 220–239.
Cooper, D. (2016) 'Retrieving the state for radical politics – a conceptual and playful challenge', *Journal of Social Policy Studies,* 14:3, 409–422.
Copestake, P. (2011) 'New public servants needed', in F. Boardman (ed.), *Making Policy in an Age of Austerity*. London: Chartered Institute of Public Finance and Accountancy, 43–52.
Copus, C. (2006) *Leading the Localities: Executive Mayors in English Local Governance*. Manchester: Manchester University Press.
Copus, C. (2008) 'English councillors and mayoral governance: Developing a new dynamic for political accountability', *Political Quarterly*, 79:4, 590–604.
Copus, C. (2010) 'The councillor: Governor, governing, governance and the complexity of citizen engagement', *British Journal of Politics and International Relations*, 12:4, 569–589.
Copus, C. (2013) 'Elected mayors: An idea whose time has not yet come does not make it a bad idea', *Policy and Politics*, 41:1, 128–131.
Copus, C. and M. Dadd (2014) '"It's a proper job": process, people and power in an English city', *Public Money and Management*, 34:5, 323–330.
Copus, C., M. Roberts and R. Wall (2017) *Local Government in England: Centralisation, Autonomy and Control*. Basingstoke: Palgrave.

Copus, C., D. Sweeting and M. Wingfield (2013) 'Why we need councillors and councils', *Policy and Politics*, 41:3, 389–408.
Copus, C. and R. Wall (2017) *The Voice of the Councillor: The Final Report of the De Montfort University and Municipal Journal Councillor Commission*. Leicester: De Montfort University.
Corrigan, P. (1979) 'The local state: The struggle for democracy', *Marxism Today*, July, 203–209.
Council of Europe (1985) *European Charter of Local Self-Government*, Strasbourg: European Council, available at https://rm.coe.int/168007a088 (accessed 10 March 2022).
Coyle, H. and L. Ferry (2022) 'Financial resilience! A comparative study of three lower tier authorities in England', *Financial Accountability & Management*, 38:5, 686–701.
Craig, G. (1989) 'Community work and the state', *Community Development Journal*, 24:1, 3–18.
Crawford, M., B. Maxwell, J. Coldron and T. Simkins (2022) 'Local authorities as actors in the emerging "school-led" system in England', *Educational Review*, 74:4, 788–804.
Cretu, C. (2020) 'New operating models and COVID-19: A catalyst for change?' (Part I: Initial findings – NESTA, project update), available at https://tinyurl.com/47z7w6ej (accessed 5 December 2021).
Crick, M. (1997) *Michael Heseltine: A Biography*. London: Hamish Hamilton.
Crossman, R. H. S. (1975) *The Diaries of a Cabinet Minister, Vol. 1*. London: Hamish and Jonathan Cape.
Cumbers, A. (2015) 'Constructing a global commons in, against and beyond the state', *Space and Polity*, 19:1, 62–75.
Cumbers, A. and S. Becker (2018). 'Making sense of remunicipalisation: Theoretical reflections on and political possibilities from Germany's Rekommumalisierung process', *Cambridge Journal of Regions, Economy and Society*, 11:3, 503–517.
Curato, N., J. S. Dryzek, S. A. Ercan, C. A. Hendriks and S. Niemeyer (2017) 'Twelve key findings in deliberative democracy research', *Daedalus*, 146:3, 28–38.
Cusak, R. (2018) 'Updated: Unitary size steer as Northants faces commissioners', *Local Government Chronicle*, 27 March.
Cyr, A. (1977) *Liberal Party Politics in Britain*. London: Calder.
Dagdeviren, H. and E. Karwowski (2022) 'Impasse or mutation? Austerity and (de)financialisation of local governments in Britain', *Journal of Economic Geography*, 22:3, 685–707.
Dahl, R. A. (1961) *Who Governs? Democracy and Power in an American City*. New Haven, CT: Yale University Press.
Dalton, R. J. (2017) *The Participation Gap: Social Status and Political Inequality*. Oxford: Oxford University Press.

Davies, J. S. (2002) 'The governance of urban regeneration: A critique of the "governing without government" thesis', *Public Administration*, 80:2, 301–322.
Davies, J. S. (2008) 'Double-devolution or double dealing? The local government White Paper and the Lyons Review', *Local Government Studies*, 34:1, 3–22.
Davies, J. S. (2011) *Challenging Governance Theory: From Networks to Hegemony*. Bristol: Policy Press.
Davies, J. S. and E. Thompson (2016) 'Austerity realism and the governance of Leicester', in M. Bevir and R. A. W. Rhodes (eds), *Rethinking Governance*. Abingdon: Routledge, 144–161.
Davoudi, S. and P. Cowie (2013) 'Are English neighbourhood forums democratically legitimate?', *Planning Theory and Practice*, 14:4, 562–566.
Deas, I. (2013) 'Towards post-political consensus in urban policy? Localism and the emerging agenda for regeneration under the Cameron government', *Planning Policy and Practice*, 28:1, 65–82.
Deas, I. (2014) 'The search for territorial fixes in subnational governance: City-regions and the disputed emergence of post-political consensus in Manchester, England', *Urban Studies*, 51:11, 2285–2314.
Deloitte (2018) *Policing 4.0: Deciding the Future of Policing in the UK*. London: Deloitte.
Denters, B., M. Goldsmith, A. Ladner, P. E. Mouritzen and L. E. Rose (2014) *Size and Local Democracy*. Cheltenham: Edward Elgar.
DCLG (Department for Communities and Local Government) (2006) *Strong and Prosperous Communities: The Local Government White Paper*, Cm 6939. London: HMSO.
DCLG (2008a) *Communities in Control: Real People, Real Power*. London: DCLG.
DCLG (2008b) *Duty to Promote Democracy (Impact Assessment)*. London: DCLG.
De Tocqueville, A. (1994) *Democracy in America* (ed. J. P. Mayer). London: Fontana Press.
DoE (Department of Environment) (1993) *Community Leadership and Representation*. London: HMSO.
Doogan, K. (1999) 'The contracting out of local government services', in G. Stoker (ed.), *The New Management of British Local Governance*. Basingstoke: Macmillan, 62–78.
Dorset County Council (2016) Minutes of the County Council, 10 March, available at https://moderngov.dorsetcouncil.gov.uk/Data/255/2016031 01000/Agenda/Exploring%20Options%20for%20the%20Future%20 of%20Local%20Government%20in%20Bournemouth,%20Dorset %20and%20Poole.pdf (accessed 28 May 2023).

Downs, A. (1957) *An Economic Theory of Democracy*. New York: Harper & Row.

DTLR (Department of Transport, Local Government and the Regions) (2001) *Strong Local Leadership – Quality Local Services*, White Paper, CM 5237. London: HMSO.

Dunleavy, P. (1980) *Urban Political Analysis: The Politics of Collective Consumption*. London: Macmillan.

Dunleavy, P. (1984) 'The limits to local government', in M. Boddy and C. Fudge (eds), *Local Socialism?* London: Macmillan, 49–81.

Durose, C. and V. Lowndes (2010) 'Neighbourhood governance: Contested rationales within a multi-level setting – a study of Manchester', *Local Government Studies*, 36:3, 341–359.

Durston, C. (2001) *Cromwell's Major-Generals*. Manchester: Manchester University Press.

Earle, J., J. Froud, S. Johal and K. Williams (2018) 'Foundational economy and foundational politics', *Welsh Economic Review*, 26:38, 38–45.

Eckersley, R. (2020) 'Ecological democracy and the rise and decline of liberal democracy: Looking back, looking forward', *Environmental Politics*, 29:2, 214–234.

Edelman Trust Barometer (2021) available at www.edelman.com/trust/2021-trust-barometer (accessed 30 November 2021).

Egner, B., D. Sweeting and J.-P. Klok (2013) 'Local councillors in comparative perspective: Drawing conclusions', in B. Egner, D. Sweeting and J.-P. Klok (eds), *Local Councillors in Europe*. Springer: Weisbaden, 255–262.

Elledge, J. (2020) 'The British government wants more mayors and fewer councils in England', *City Monitor*, 30 July, available at https://tinyurl.com/2p8n5hen (accessed 30 August 2020).

Entwistle, T., V. Guarneros-Meza, S. Martin and J. Downie (2016) 'Reframing governance: Competition, fatalism and autonomy in central–local relations,' *Public Administration*, 95:4, 897–914.

Escobar, O. (2017) 'Pluralism and democratic participation: What kind of citizen are citizens invited to be?', *Contemporary Pragmatism*, 14:4, 416–438.

Etherington, D. and M. Jones (2016) 'The city–region chimera: The political economy of metagovernance failure in Britain', *Economy and Society*, 9:2, 371–389.

Etzioni, A. (1993) *The Spirit of Community*. London: Fontana Press.

Etzioni, A. (1996) *The New Golden Rule*. London: Profile Books.

Fahnbulleh, M., E. Kiberd and A. Pendleton (2022) *Closing the Divide: How to Really Level Up the UK*. London: New Economics Foundation.

Farnworth, A. (2021) 'Plans for a new "community bank" in Lancashire have moved a step forward', *Lancashire Telegraph*, 24 March, available at https://tinyurl.com/2p96mvjk (accessed 30 March 2022).

Faulkener, P. (2022) 'Preston City Council budget 2022: Labour hails "miraculous" performance, but opposition say progress is too slow and criticise "ideology"', *Lancashire Post*, available at https://tinyurl.com/4cyzc9xb (accessed 12 November 2022).

Fenwick, J. and H. Elcock (2014) 'Elected mayors: Leading locally?', *Local Government Studies*, 40:4, 581–599.

Fenwick, J., H. Elcock and S. Lilley (2003) 'Out of the loop? Councillors and the new political management', *Public Policy and Administration*, 18:1, 29–45.

Fenwick, J. and L. Johnston (2020b) *Public Enterprise and Local Place*. Abingdon: Routledge.

Ferry, L., R. Andrews, C. Skelcher and P. Wegorowski (2018) 'New development: Corporatization of local authorities in England in the wake of austerity, 2010–2016', *Public Money & Management*, 38:6, 477–480.

Finer, H. (1945) *English Local Government*, 2nd edn. London: Methuen.

Fischer, F. (2009) *Democracy and Expertise: Re-Orienting Policy Enquiry*. Oxford: Oxford University Press.

Fischer, F. (2017) *Climate Crisis and the Democratic Prospect: Participatory Governance in Sustainable Communities*. Oxford: Oxford University Press.

Flinders, M. (2012) *Defending Politics*. Oxford: Oxford University Press.

Flinders, M. (2016) 'The problem with democracy', *Parliamentary Affairs*, 69:1, 181–203.

Flinders, M. and K. Dommett (2013) 'Gap analysis: Participatory democracy, public expectations and community assemblies in Sheffield', *Local Government Studies*, 39:4, 488–513.

Flinders, M. and M. Wood (2014) 'Rethinking depoliticisation beyond the governmental', *Policy and Politics*, 42:2, 135–149.

Flinders, M. and M. Wood (2018) 'Nexus politics, conceptualising everyday political engagement', *Democratic Theory*, 5:2, 56–81.

Foot, M. (1962) *Aneurin Bevan*, Vol. 1. London: Macgibbon and Kee.

Frega, R. (2019) *Pragmatism and the Wide View of Democracy*. Cham, Switzerland: Palgrave Macmillan.

Fuller, C. (2012) 'Urban politics and the social practices of critique and justification: Conceptual insights from French pragmatism', *Progress in Human Geography*, 37:5, 639–657.

Fuller, C. and M. Geddes (2008) 'Urban governance under neoliberalism: New Labour and the restructuring of state-space', *Antipode*, 40:2, 252–282.

Fung, A. and Wright, E. O. (2001) Deepening democracy: Innovations in empowered participatory governance, *Politics & Society*, 29:1, 5–41.

Fyans, J., G. Newcombe and Z. Qureshi (2022) *Mapping a Route to Clean Local Growth*. London: Localis.

Fyans, J., B. Roughley and Z. Qureshi (2019) *Hitting Reset: A Case for Local Leadership*. London: Localis.

Gains, F., S. Greasley, P. C. John and G. Stoker (2007) *Does Leadership Matter?: A Summary of Evidence on the Role and Impact of Political Leadership in English Local Government*. London: Department of Housing, Communities & Local Government.

Gains, F., P. C. John and G. Stoker (2005) 'Path dependency and the reform of English local government', *Public Administration*, 83:1, 25–45.

Game, C. (2019) 'Local elections 2019: Gone missing – 500 councillors', *Democratic Audit*, available at https://tinyurl.com/yc3bm78j (accessed 6 July 2020).

Gaskell, J. and G. Stoker (2020) 'Centralised or decentralised: Which governance systems are having a "good" pandemic?', *Democratic Theory*, 7:2, 33–40.

Geddes, M. (2006) 'Partnership and the limits to local governance in England: institutionalist analysis and neoliberalism', *International Journal of Urban and Regional Research*, 30:1, 76–97.

Geddes, M. and H. Sullivan (2011) 'Localities, leadership and neoliberalization: Conflicting discourses, competing practices', *Critical Policy Studies*, 5:4, 391–413.

Gill, S. (2020) *William Wordsworth: A Life*, 2nd edn. Oxford: Oxford University Press.

Giovannini, A. and M. Wood (2022) 'Understanding democratic stress', *Representation*, 58:1, 1–12.

Goodin, R. E. (2007) 'Enfranchising all affected interests, and its alternatives', *Philosophy & Public Affairs*, 35:1, 40–68.

Goodwin, M. (1989) 'The politics of locality', in A. Cochrane and J. Anderson (eds), *Politics in Transition*. London: Sage, 160–171.

Goodwin, M. (2009) 'Can we promote cohesion through contact? Intergroup contact and the development of community cohesion', in C. Durose, S. Greasley and L. Richardson (eds), *Changing Local Governance, Changing Citizens*. Bristol: Policy Press.

Goodwin, M., S. Duncan and D. S. Halford (1993) 'Regulation theory, the local state, and the transition of local politics', *Environment and Planning D: Society and Space*, 11:1, 67–88.

Goodwin, M. and J. Painter (1996) 'Local governance, the case of Fordism and the changing geographies of regulation', *Transactions of British Geographers*, 21:4, 635–648.

Gore, T., E. Bimpson, J. Dobson and S. Parkes (2021) *Local Government Responses to the COVID-19 Pandemic in the UK: A Thematic Review*. Sheffield: Sheffield Hallam Centre for Regional Economic and Social Research, Sheffield Hallam University.

Graeber, D. (2011) 'Occupy and anarchism's gift of democracy', *Guardian*, 15 November.
Gray, C. (1994) *Government Beyond the Centre: Sub-National Politics in Britain*. Basingstoke: Macmillan.
Gray, M. and A. Barford (2018) 'The depth of the cuts: The uneven geography of local government austerity', *Cambridge Journal of Regions, Economy and Society*, 11:3, 541–563.
Griffith, J. A. G. (1966) *Central Departments and Local Authorities*. London: Allen & Unwin.
Griggs, S. and M. Roberts (2012) 'From neighbourhood governance to neighbourhood management: A "roll-out" neo-liberal design for devolved governance in the United Kingdom?', *Local Government Studies*, 38:2, 183–210.
Guarneros-Meza, V. and M. Geddes (2010) 'Local governance and participation under neoliberalism: Comparative perspectives', *International Journal of Urban and Regional Research*, 34:1, 115–129.
Guinan, J. and O'Neill, M. (2019) *The Case for Community Wealth Building*. Cambridge: Polity Press.
Gunn, S., E. Brooks and G. Vogor (2015) 'The community's capacity to plan: The disproportionate requirements of the new English neighbourhood planning initiative', in S. Davoudi and A. Madanipour (eds), *Reconsidering Localism*. Abingdon: Routledge, 147–167.
Gurr, T. R. and D. S. King (1987) *The State and the City*. Chicago: University of Chicago Press.
Hadley, R. and S. Hatch (1981) *Social Welfare and the Failure of the State*. London: Allen & Unwin.
Hain, P. (1976) 'The future of community politics', in P. Hain (ed.), *Community Politics*. London: John Calder.
Hajer, M. (2003) 'Policy without polity? Policy analysis and the institutional void', *Policy Sciences*, 36:2,175–195.
Hale, S. (2006) *Blair's Community: Communitarian Thought and New Labour*. Manchester: Manchester University Press.
Hale, S. (2013) 'Education for modernisation?', *Local Government Studies*, 39:4, 541–561.
Hall, E. and S. McGarrol (2013) 'Progressive localism for an ethics of care: Local area co-ordination with people with learning disabilities', *Social & Cultural Geography*, 14:6, 689–709.
Hambleton, R. (2016) *Place-Based Leadership*, Royal Society of Arts, Comment, available at www.thersa.org/comment/2016/11/place-based-leadership (accessed 6 June 2021).
Hambleton, R. (2019) 'The new civic leadership: Place and the cocreation of public innovation', *Public Money and Management*, 39:4, 271–279.

Hammersmith and Fulham LBC (2020) *Neighbourhood Planning Forum and Area Refusal Statement*, Decision Notice, 11 May, available at https://tinyurl.com/3r3cp538 (accessed 17 July 2020).

Hancox, D. (2019) 'Great British sell-off: How desperate councils sold £9.1bn of public assets', *Guardian*, 5 March.

Hankins, K. (2017) 'Creative democracy and the quiet politics of the everyday', *Urban Geography*, 38:4, 502–506.

Hanretty, C. (2021) 'The pork barrel politics of the Towns Fund', *Political Quarterly*, 92:1, 7–13.

Hanson, R. (2021) 'Council to create new trading company to deliver key services', *Lowestoft Journal*, December, available at https://tinyurl.com/2p887xep (accessed 5 January 2022).

Harris, T., L. Hodge and D. Phillips (2019) *English Local Government Funding: Trends and Challenges in 2019 and Beyond*. London: Institute for Fiscal Studies.

Harrison, J. (2012) 'Life after regions? The evolution of city-regionalism in England', 46:9, 1243–1259.

Harvey, B. (1989) 'From managerialism to entrepreneurialism', *Geografiska Annaler: B*, 71:1, 3–17.

Hastings, A., N. Bailey, M. Gannon, K. Besemer and G. Bramley (2015) 'Coping with the cuts? The management of the worst financial settlement in living memory', *Local Government Studies*, 41:4, 601–621.

Haughton, G., I. Deas, S. Hinks and K. Ward (2016) 'Mythic Manchester: Devo Max, the Northern Powerhouse and rebalancing the English economy', *Cambridge Journal of Regions, Economy and Society*, 9:2, 355–370.

Haus, M. and J. E. Klausen (2011) 'Urban leadership and community involvement: Ingredients for good governance?', *Urban Affairs Review*, 47:2, 256–279.

Hay, C. and A. Payne (2015) *Civic Capitalism*. Cambridge: Polity Press.

HCLGSC (House of Commons Housing, Communities and Local Government Select Committee) (2019) *Local Government Finance and the 2019 Spending Review: Eighteenth Report of Session 2017–19*. London: HMSO.

Headlam, N. and P. Hepburn (2017) 'What a difference a mayor makes. A case study of the Liverpool mayoral model', *Local Government Studies*, 43:5, 731–751.

Hendriks, C. M. (2006) 'Deliberation: Reconciling civil society's dual role in deliberative democracy', *Political Studies*, 54:3, 486–508.

Hendriks, C. M. (2009) 'The democratic soup: Mixed meanings of political representation in governance networks', *Governance*, 22:4, 689–715.

Hendriks, C. M. (2016) 'Coupling citizens and elites in deliberative systems: The role of institutional design', *European Journal of Political Research*, 55:1, 43–60.

Hendriks, C. M. and A. W. Dzur (2021) 'Citizens' governance spaces: Democratic action through disruptive collective problem-solving', *Political Studies*, 70:3, 680–700.

Hendriks, C. M., S. A. Ercan and J. Boswell (2020) *Mending Democracy: Democratic Repair in Disconnected Times*. Oxford: Oxford University Press.

Heseltine, Lord M. (2012) 'No stone unturned in pursuit of growth'. London: Department for Business, Innovation and Skills.

Hibbing, J. R. and E. Theiss-Morse (2002) *Stealth Democracy: Americans' Beliefs about How Government Should Work*. New York: Cambridge University Press.

Hildreth, P. (2011) 'What is localism and what implications do different models have for managing the local economy?', *Local Economy*, 26:8, 702–714.

Hill, D. M. (2000) *Urban Policy and Politics in Britain*. Basingstoke: Macmillan.

Hill, J. (2020) 'Updated: £4bn "levelling up" fund unveiled', *Local Government Chronicle*, 25 November.

Hill, J. (2021) 'Gove signals "redistribution" of funding to support poorer councils', *Local Government Chronicle*, 9 November.

Hill, J. (2022a) 'Exclusive: County devo talks descend into "dog's breakfast"', *Local Government Chronicle*, 17 June.

Hill, J. (2022b) 'Value of Spelthorne's out of borough investments slides by £70m', *Local Government Chronicle*, 30 August.

Hill, J. (2022c) 'Intervention: What happens when the government sends in commissioners?', *Local Government Chronicle*, 13 September.

Hirst, P. (1993) *Associative Democracy: New Forms of Economic and Social Governance*. Cambridge: Polity Press.

HM Government (2010a) 'Local enterprise partnerships'. Letter to local authority leaders and business leaders from the Secretaries of State for Business, Innovation and Skills, and Communities and Local Government, 29 June, available at https://tinyurl.com/y7mpwd2x (accessed 20 May 2021).

HM Government (2010b) *The Coalition: Our Programme for Government*. London: HMSO.

HM Government (2011) *Unlocking Growth in Cities*. London: HMSO.

HM Government (2020) *Levelling Up the United Kingdom*. London: HMSO.

HM Treasury and UK Cabinet Office (2004) *Devolving Decision Making: Delivering Better Public Services: Refining Targets and Performance Management*. London: HM Treasury.

HM Treasury, DBERR (Department for Business, Enterprise and Regulatory Reform) and DCLG (Department for Communities and Local

Government) (2007) *Review of Sub-National Economic Development and Regeneration*. HMSO: London.

Hobhouse, L. T. (1904) *Democracy and Reaction*. London: T. Fisher and Unwin.

Hobhouse, L. T. (1924) *Social Development*. London: George Allen & Unwin.

Hoggett, P. and R. Hambleton (eds) (1987) *Decentralisation and Democracy: Localising Public Services*. Bristol: School of Advanced Urban Studies, Bristol University.

Holtby, W. (1936) *South Riding*. London: Collins.

Hope, N. and N. Wanduragala (2010) *New Model Mayors*. London: NLGN.

Hoppe, R. (2011) 'Institutional constraints and practical problems in deliberative and participatory policy making', *Policy & Politics*, 39:2, 163–186.

House of Commons Communities and Local Government Committee (2013) *The Balance of Power: Central and Local Government: Sixth Report of Session 2008–09*. London: House of Commons.

House of Commons Communities and Local Government Committee (2017) *Effectiveness of Local Authority Overview and Scrutiny Committees: First Report of Session 2017–19*. London: House of Commons.

House of Commons Health and Social Care Select Committee (2020) *Social Care: Funding and Workforce: Third Report of Session 2019–21*. London: House of Commons.

House of Commons Public Administration and Constitutional Affairs Committee (2022) *Governing England: Third Report of Session 2022–23*. London: House of Commons.

House of Lords Public Services Committee (2020) *A Critical Juncture for Public Services: Lessons from COVID-19: 1st Report of Session 2019–20*. London: House of Lords.

Housing Maintenance and Management (2020) *LGA Responds to Local Government Ombudsman Report on Homelessness*, available at https://housingmmonline.co.uk/news/lga-responds-to-local-government-ombudsman-report-on-homelessness/ (accessed 28 May 2023).

Howarth, D. (2011) 'Reimagining capitalism and Christianity today: Articulating and negotiating contestable faiths in a minor key', *Political Theology*, 12:2, 210–225.

Hudson, B. (2018) 'Adult social care: Is privatisation irreversible?', LSE Politics and Policy Blog, 14 February, available at https://tinyurl.com/35rumtdk (accessed 14 June 2020).

Huhne, C. (2007) 'The case for localism: The liberal narrative', in D. Brack, R. Grayson and D. Haworth, *Reinventing the State: Social Liberalism for the 21st Century*. London: Politicos, 241–254.

Hunt, J. (2018) Speech delivered to the World Social Work Day Conference, London, 20 March, available at https://tinyurl.com/25t24mf6 (accessed 14 July 2020).

Hunt, T. (2004) *Building Jerusalem*. London: Weidenfeld and Nicolson.

IFS (Institute for Fiscal Studies) (2019) Written evidence submitted by the Institute for Fiscal Studies [FSR 090] to the Housing, Communities and Local Government Committee's Local Government Finance and the 2019 Spending Review inquiry. London: HCLGCLG/HMSO.

James, S. and E. Cox (2007) *Ward Councillors and Community Leadership*. York: Joseph Rowntree Foundation.

Jardin, A. (1988) *Tocqueville: A Biography* (trans. Lydia Davies). London: Peter Halban.

Jenkins-Smith, H. and P. Sabatier (1994) 'Evaluating the Advocacy Coalition Framework', *Journal of Public Policy*, 14:2, 175–203.

Jennings, W., L. McKay and G. Stoker (2020) 'The politics of levelling up', *Political Quarterly*, 92:2, 302–311.

Jessop, B. (2002) *The Future of the capitalist State*. Cambridge: Polity Press.

John, P. (2014) 'The great survivor: The persistence and resilience of English local government', *Local Government Studies*, 40: 5, 687–704.

Jones, G. and J. Stewart (1983) *The Case for Local Government*. London: George Allen & Unwin.

Jones, M. (2019) *Cities and Regions in Crisis: The Political Economy of Subnational Economic Development*. Cheltenham: Edward Elgar.

Jones, M. and K. Ward (2002) 'Excavating the logic of British urban policy: Neoliberalism as the "crisis of crisis-management"', *Antipode*, 34:3, 473–494.

Karlsson, D. (2013) 'The hidden constitutions: How informal political institutions affect the representation style of local councils', *Local Government Studies*, 39:5, 681–702.

Keil, R. (2009) 'The urban politics of roll-with-it neoliberalization', *City*, 13:2–3, 230–245.

Keith-Lucas, B. (1980) *The Unreformed Local Government System*. London: Croom Helm.

Kentish, B. (2017) 'Council housing numbers hit lowest point since records began', *Independent*, 16 November.

Kenyon, M. (2021a) 'County proposes "Pan-Hampshire" combined authority', *Local Government Chronicle*, 8 October.

Kenyon, M. (2021b) 'Finance round up: Job cuts planned at Cornwall, Croydon and Derby', *Local Government Chronicle*, 13 December.

Kenyon, M. (2022) 'Devon to propose non-mayoral combined authority', *Local Government Chronicle*, 15 February.

Kingdon, J. W. (1995) *Agendas, Alternatives and Public Policies*, 2nd edn. New York: Harper Collins.

Klein, P., J. Mahoney, A. McGahan and A. Pitelis (2010) 'Toward a theory of public entrepreneurship', *European Management Review*, 7:3, 1–15.

Klijn, E.-H. and C. Skelcher (2007) 'Democracy and governance networks: Compatible or not?', *Public Administration*, 85:3, 587–608.

Knight, K. (2013) *Facing the Future: Findings from the Review of Efficiencies and Operations in Fire and Rescue Authorities in England*. London: Department for Communities and Local Government.

Labour Party (2022) *New Britain: Renewing our Democracy and Rebuilding our Economy: Report of the Commission on the UK's Future*. London: Labour Party.

Ladner, A., K. Keuffer and H. Baldersheim (2016) 'Measuring local autonomy in 39 countries 1990–2014', *Regional and Federal Studies*, 26:3, 321–357.

Laffin, M. (2009) 'Central–local relations in an era of governance: Towards a new research agenda', *Local Government Studies*, 35:1, 21–37.

Larner, W. (2003) Neoliberalism?', *Environment and Planning D: Society and Space*, 21:5, 509–512.

Latham, P. (2017) *Who Stole the Town Hall?* Bristol: Policy Press.

Lauermann, J. (2016) 'Municipal statecraft: Revisiting the geographies of the entrepreneurial city', *Progress in Human Geography*, 42:2, 205–224.

Lawler, J. (2008) 'Individualization and public sector leadership', *Public Administration*, 86:1, 21–34.

Lawson, N. (2020) *From Paternalism to Participation: How one London Borough Dealt with the Covid Crisis and Built a New Collaborative Institution*. London: Compass.

Layfield, F. (chair) (1976) *Report of the Committee of Enquiry into Local Government Finance*, Cmnd. 6453. London: HMSO.

Leach, R. and J. Percy-Smith (2001) *Local Governance in Britain*. Basingstoke: Palgrave.

Leach, S. (1996) *Enabling or Disabling Local Government: Choices for the Future*. Buckingham: Open University Press.

Leach, S. and C. Copus (2004) 'Scrutiny and the political party group in UK local government: New models of behaviour', *Public Administration*, 82:2, 331–354.

Leach, S. and C. Copus (2021) 'Unitary authorities: The larger local government becomes, the greater the damage to local democracy', LSE British Politics and Policy Blog, 6 September, available at https://tinyurl.com/2p9ycwxe (accessed 30 October 2021).

Leach, S., J. Stewart and G. Jones (2018) *Centralisation, Devolution and the Future of Local Government in England*. Abingdon: Routledge.

Lee, J. M. (1963) *Social Leaders and Public Persons: A Study of County Government in Cheshire since 1888*. Oxford: Oxford University Press.

Lee, N. (2019) 'Inclusive growth in cities: A sympathetic critique', *Regional Studies*, 53:3, 424–434.

Lee, S. and R. Woodward (2002) 'Implementing the third way: The delivery of public services under the Blair government', *Public Management*, 22:4, 49–56.

Leicestershire County Council (2018) *Views to be Sought on Unitary Options*, Leicestershire County Council, 17 October, available at https://tinyurl.com/mpsxfbac (accessed 30 December 2020).

Leighninger, M. (2019) 'What we can learn from town meetings', *Journal of Deliberative Democracy*, 15:2, 1–6.

Lembruch, G. and P. Schmitter (1982) *Patterns of Corporatist Policy Making*. London: Sage.

Lemprière, M. and V. Lowndes (2019) 'Why did the North East Combined Authority fail to achieve a devolution deal with the UK government?', *Local Economy*, 34:2, 149–166.

Lepine, E. and H. Sullivan (2010) 'Realising the public person', *Local Government Studies*, 36:1, 91–107.

Liddle, J. (2010) 'Twenty-first-century public leadership within complex governance systems: Some reflections', *Policy and Politics*, 38:4, 657–663.

Liddle, J. (2016) 'Introduction: Public sector entrepreneurship: Key issues, challenges and developments in theory and practice', in J. Liddle (ed.), *New Perspectives on Research, Policy & Practice in Public Entrepreneurship*. Contemporary Issues in Entrepreneurship Research, Vol. 6. Bingley: Emerald Group Publishing Limited, 11–34.

Liddle, J. and G. McElwee (2019) 'Theoretical perspectives on public entrepreneurship', *Journal of Entrepreneurial Behaviour & Research*, 25:6, 1308–1320.

Lloyd, J. and A. Randle (2019) *Introducing New Operating Models for Local Government*. London: NESTA.

LGA (Local Government Association) (2017) *Enterprising Councils: Supporting Councils' Income Generation Activity*. London: LGA.

LGA (2018a) *Local Government Funding: Moving the Conversation On*. London: LGA.

LGA (2018b) *National Census of Local Authority Councillors 2018*, available at www.local.gov.uk/sites/default/files/documents/Councillors%27%20Census%202018%20-%20report%20FINAL.pdf (accessed 18 June 2018).

LGA (2019a) *Report of the Councillors Census 2018*. London: LGA.

LGA (2019b) 'Right to Buy rules undermining council efforts to boost housebuilding', 24 August, available at https://tinyurl.com/yckrmndv (accessed 20 September 2020).

LGA (2021) *Provisional Local Government Finance Settlement 2022/23: On-the-Day Briefing*, 30 December, available at https://tinyurl.com/2p8f9skz (accessed 5 January 2022).
LGA (n.d.) 'Shared services', available at https://tinyurl.com/3xw5zk4d (accessed 20 March 2020).
LGiU (Local Government Information Unit) (2013) *The Future Town Hall: How will Local Government be Different 30 years from Now?: A Collection of Ideas to Mark the 30th Anniversary of the LGiU*. London: LGiU.
LGiU (2018) 'People not politics', seminar, 15 February, available at https://tinyurl.com/5xker39r (accessed 15 June 2020).
Lodge, G. (2012) 'Mayors for all major English cities? A democratic argument', *Open Democracy* blog, available at https://tinyurl.com/32u95dm6 (accessed 25 June 2020).
Lorimer, K. (2022) 'The price of freedom – has local government commercialisation succeeded?', *Public Finance*, 11 February.
Loughlin, M. (1996a) 'The constitutional status of local government', in L. Lowndes, L. Pratchett and D. Wilson (eds), *Local Government and Democracy*. Basingstoke: Palgrave, 38–61.
Loughlin, M. (1996b) 'Understanding central–local relations', *Public Policy and Administration*, 11:2, 48–65.
Lowndes, V. (1999) 'Rebuilding trust in central/local relations: Policy or passion?', *Local Government Studies*, 25:4, 116–136.
Lowndes, V. (2002) 'Between rhetoric and reality: Does the 2001 White Paper reverse the centralising trend in Britain?', *Local Government Studies*, 34:1, 135–147.
Lowndes, V. and A. Gardner (2016) 'Local governance under the Conservatives: Super-austerity, devolution and the "smarter state"', *Local Government Studies*, 42:3, 357–375.
Lowndes, V. and K. McCaughie (2013) 'Weathering the perfect storm?', *Policy & Politics*, 41:4, 533–549.
Lowndes, V. and M. Paxton (2018) 'Can agonism be institutionalised? Can institutions be agonised? Prospects for democratic design', *British Journal of Politics and International Relations*, 18:3, 693–710.
Lowndes, V. and L. Pratchett (2012) 'Local governance under the Coalition government: Austerity, localism and the Big Society', *Local Government Studies*, 38:1, 21–40.
Lowndes, V., L. Pratchett and G. Stoker (2006) 'Local political participation: The impact of rules-in-use', *Public Administration*, 84:3, 539–561.
Lowndes, V. and M. Roberts (2013) *Why Institutions Matter* Basingstoke: Palgrave.
Lowndes, V. and H. Sullivan (2008) 'How low can you go? Rationales and challenges for neighbourhood governance', *Public Administration*, 86:1, 53–74.

Lyall, S, M. Wood and D. Bailey (2016) *Democracy: The Missing Link in the Devolution Debate*. London: New Economics Foundation.

Lyons, M. (2007) *Place Shaping: A Shared Ambition for the Future of Local Government: Lyons Final Report*. London: HMSO.

Mabbett, D. (2021) 'Rolling out the pork barrel', *Political Quarterly*, 92:2, 169–171.

Mackenzie, W. J. M. (1961) *Theories of Local Government*. London: London School of Economics.

Macleod, G. (2011) 'Urban politics reconsidered: Growth machine to post-democratic city?', *Urban Studies*, 48:12, 2629–2660.

Magnusson, W. (2015) *Local Self-Government and the Right to the City*. Montreal: McGill Queens University.

Maille, S. and P. Hoggett (2001) 'Best Value and the politics of pragmatism', *Policy and Politics*, 29:4, 510–519.

Mangan, C., C. Needham, K. Bottom and S. Parker (2016) *The 21st Century Councillor*. Edgbaston: University of Birmingham.

Mansbridge, J. (1983) *Beyond Adversary Democracy*. Chicago: University of Chicago Press.

Mansbridge, J. (2003) 'Practice–Thought–Practice', in A. Fung and E. O. Wright (eds), *Deepening Democracy: Institutional Innovations in Empowered Participatory Governance*. London: Verso, 175–199.

Marinko, P. (2019) 'Brokenshire in unitary unanimity move', *Municipal Journal*, 23 July.

Marsh, A. (2012) 'Is it time to put the dream of elected mayors to bed?', *Policy and Politics*, 40:4, 607–611.

Marsh, D. (2014) 'What is the nature of the crisis of democracy and what can we do about it?', *Democratic Theory*, 1:2, 37–46.

Martin, J. (2002) 'The state and sovereign subjectivity', in A. Finlayson and J. Valentine (eds), *Politics and Post-Structuralism*. Edinburgh: Edinburgh University Press, 52–65.

Massey, D. (1995) *Spatial Divisions of Labour: Social Structures and the Geography of Production*. London: Macmillan.

Massey, D. (2005) *For Space*. London: Sage.

Maud, Sir J. (1967) *Report of the Committee on the Management of Local Government, Vol. 2*. London: HMSO.

Maver, I. (2000) *Glasgow*. Edinburgh: Edinburgh University Press.

Mayo, M. (2000) *Cultures, Communities, Identities*. Basingstoke: Palgrave.

McInroy, N. (2018) 'The everyday economy: Framing a new political economy in the UK', *Political Quarterly*, 89:4, 614–617.

McKinley, S., M. Lawrence and M. Brett (2020) *Democratic by Design: A New Community Wealth Building Vision for the British Economy after COVID-19*. Ohio: Common Wealth and Democracy Collaborative.

Melo, M. A. and G. Baiocchi (2006) 'Deliberative democracy and local governance: Towards a new agenda', *International Journal of Urban and Regional Research*, 30:3, 587–600.

Merrick, N. (2019) 'PWLB hike: A rise too far?', *LocalGov*, available at https://tinyurl.com/32cb6ae7 (accessed 20 March 2020).

Merrick, N. (2020) 'Is outsourcing falling out of favour with local government?', *Public Finance*, 11 February.

MHCLG (Ministry for Housing, Communities and Local Government) (2018) *The Proposed Reorganisation of Local Government in Northamptonshire*. London: MHCLG.

Michels, R. (1968) *Political Parties: A Sociological Study of Oligarchical Tendencies of Modern Democracies*. New York: Free Press. First published 1911.

Mill, James (1828) 'Essay on government', in J. Lively and J. Rees (eds), *Utilitarian Logic and Politics*. Oxford: Clarendon Press, 1978, 53–96.

Mill, J. S. (1969) *Autobiography* (ed. H. Laski). Oxford: Oxford University Press.

Mill, J. S. (1975) *John Stuart Mill on Liberty, Representative Government and the Subjection of Women* (ed. Richard Wollheim). Oxford: Oxford University Press.

Miller, D. (2009) 'Democracy's domain', *Philosophy & Public Affairs*, 37:3, 201–228.

Monbiot, G. (2022) 'The dire truth is that Rishi Sunak's Britain is already broken', *Guardian*, 26 October.

Morgan, K. and C. Sabel (2019) *The Experimentalist Polity*. London: NESTA.

Morphet, J. (2016) 'Local authorities build housing again', *Town and Country Planning*, May, 170–177.

Morphet, J. (2019) 'Why are councils returning to direct delivery of housing?', *Planning, Building and Construction Today*, 5 August, available at https://tinyurl.com/3kcj38hm (accessed 14 July 2021).

Morphet, J. (2021) *The Impact of Covid-19 on Devolution*. Bristol: Bristol University Press.

Morphet, J. (2022) 'Deals and devolution: How the UK government is using local deals to undermine devolved decision making', paper presented to the Political Studies Association Annual Conference, 11–13 April, York.

Morphet, J. and B. Clifford (2017) *Local Authority Direct Provision of Housing*. London: Royal Town Planning Institute.

Morphet, J. and B. Clifford (2021) *Reviving Local Authority Housing Delivery*. Bristol: Policy Press.

Mosca, G. (1939) *The Ruling Class*. New York: McGraw-Hill.

Mossberger, K. and G. Stoker (2001) 'The evolution of urban regime theory: The challenge of conceptualization', *Urban Affairs Review*, 36:6, 810–835.

Mulgan, G. (2012) 'Government with the people', in G. Cooke and R. Muir (eds), *The Relational State*. London: IPPR, 20–34.

Munro, J. and I. Burbidge (2020) *Seizing the Moment*. London: RSA.

NALC (National Association of Local Councils) (2020) *Case Studies: Climate Change*. London: NALC.

NALC (2021) *What can Local Councils do on Climate Change*. London: NALC.

NAO (National Audit Office) (2017) *Mayoral Combined Authorities – Interactive Guide*, available at https://tinyurl.com/4rurszfk (accessed 19 May 2020).

NAO (2018) *Financial Sustainability of Local Authorities*. London: Ministry of Housing, Communities and Local Government.

NAO (2020) *Local Authority Investment in Commercial Property*. London: Ministry of Housing, Communities & Local Government.

NAO (2021a) *Local Government and Net Zero in England*. London: HM Government.

NAO (2021b) *Local Government Finance in the Pandemic: Report by the Comptroller and Auditor General, Session 2019–21*, HC 1240. London: NAO.

Newman, J. (2005) 'Enter the transformational leader: Network governance and the micro-politics of modernization', *Sociology*, 39:4, 717–734.

Newman, J. (2014a) 'Landscapes of antagonism: Local governance, neoliberalism and austerity', *Urban Studies*, 51:15, 3290–3305.

Newman, I. (2014b) *Reclaiming Local Democracy*. Bristol: Policy Press.

NLGN (New Local Government Network) (2018) 'Three headlines from NLGN's latest Leadership Index', available at https://tinyurl.com/2ybr5r9v (accessed 12 June 2021).

Norton, P. and A. Aughey (1981) *Conservatives and Conservatism*. London: Temple Smith.

Nozick, R. (1974) *Anarchy, State and Utopia*. Oxford: Basil Blackwell.

O'Connor, J. (1973) *The Fiscal Crisis of the State*. London: St Martin's Press.

Odgers, W. B. and E. J. Naldrett (1909) *Local Government*, 2nd edn. London: Macmillan.

ODPM (Office of the Deputy Prime Minister) (2004) *The Future of Local Government: Developing a 10 Year Vision*. London: HMSO.

ODPM (2005) *Vibrant Local Leadership*. London: ODPM.

OECD (Organisation for Economic Co-operation and Development) (2017) *Government at a Glance, 2017*. Paris: OECD.

Ogden, K., D. Phillips, L. Sibieta, M. Warner and B. Zaranko (2022) *Does Funding Follow Need? An Analysis of the Geographic Distribution of Public Spending in England*, IFS Report R224. London: Institute for Fiscal Studies.

Oglethorpe, K. (2021) 'Citizens Assemblies: Fashionable focus groups or the great hopes of democracy?', *New Local*, available at www.newlocal.org.uk/articles/citizens-assemblies/ (accessed 10 November 2021).

O'Neill, M. and T. Howard (2018) 'Beyond extraction', *Renewal*, 26:2, 46–53.

ONS (Office for National Statistics) (n.d.) *Population Estimates*, available at https://tinyurl.com/a3pn9nt5 (accessed 5 May 2021).

O'Reilly, D. and M. Reed (2010) '"Leaderism": An evolution of managerialism in UK public service reform', *Public Administration*, 88:4, 960–978.

Orr, K. (2009) 'Local government and structural crisis: An interpretive approach', *Policy and Politics*, 37:1, 39–55.

Ostrom, E. (2010) 'Polycentric systems for coping with collective action and global environmental change', *Global Environmental Change*, 20:4, 550–557.

Ottewill, R. (2008) 'The establishment of parish councils in Hampshire', *Southern History*, 30, 43–77.

Owen, D. and G. Smith (2015) 'Survey article: Deliberation, democracy, and the systemic turn', *Journal of Political Philosophy*, 23:2, 213–234.

Paine, T. (1969) *Rights of Man* (ed. H. Collins). London: Penguin Classics.

Parekh, B. (ed.) (1973) *Bentham's Political Thought*. London: Croom Helm.

Pareto, V. (1976) *Sociological Writings* (ed. S. E. Finer). London: Pall Mall Press.

Parker, G., T. Lynn and M. Wargent (2015) 'Sticking to the script? The co-production of neighbourhood planning in England', *Town Planning Review*, 86:5, 519–536.

Parker, G., T. Lynn and M. Wargent (2017) 'Contestation and conservatism in neighbourhood planning in England: Reconciling agonism and collaboration?', *Planning Theory and Practice*, 18:3, 446–465.

Parker, G. and E. Street (2015) 'Planning at the neighbourhood scale: Localism, dialogic politics and the modulation of community action', *Environment and Planning C: Government and Policy*, 33:4, 794–810.

Parker, G., M. Wargent, K. Salter, M. Dobson, T. Lynn, A. Yuille and Navigus Planning (2020) *Impacts of Neighbourhood Planning in England: Final Report to the Ministry of Housing, Communities and Local Government*. Reading: University of Reading.

Parker, S. (2013) 'Connected localism and the challenge of change', in *Connected Localism*. London: LGIU, 53–67.

Parkinson, J. (2007) 'Localism and deliberative democracy', *Good Society*, 16:1, 23–29.

Parvin, P. (2015) 'Is deliberative democracy feasible? Political disengagement and trust in liberal democratic states', *Monist*, 98:4, 407–423.

Peck, J. (2012) 'Austerity urbanism: American cities under extreme economy', *City*, 16:6, 626–655.

Peck, J. and J. Tickell (2002) 'Neoliberalizing space', *Antipode*, 34:3, 380–404.

Phelps, N. A. and J. T. Miao (2020) 'Varieties of urban entrepreneurialism', *Dialogues in Human Geography*, 10:3, 304–321.

Phillips, D. (2018) 'Equalisation, incentives and discretion in English local public service provision', in *Governing England: Devolution and Funding*. London: The British Academy, 35–53.

Pickard, J. (2021) 'At least 12 English councils in rescue talks as Covid shatters local finances', *Financial Times*, 8 February.

Pike, A. (2017) *Metro-Mayors: Claims and Evidence*, Newcastle University, Centre for Urban and Regional Development Studies, 4 April, available at https://tinyurl.com/4ew26pum (accessed 7 May 2020).

Pike, A., D. Marlow, A. McCarthy, P. O'Brien and J. Tomaney (2015) 'Local institutions and local economic development: The local enterprise partnerships in England 2010–', *Cambridge Journal of Regions, Economy and Society*, 8:2, 185–204.

Pike, A. and J. Tomaney (2009) 'The state and uneven development: The governance of economic development in England in the post-devolution UK', *Cambridge Journal of Regions, Economy and Society*, 2:1, 13–34.

Piketty, T. (2014) *Capital in the Twenty-First Century*. Cambridge, MA: Harvard University Press.

Plüss, L. and D. Kübler, D. (2013) 'Coordinating community governance? Local councillors in different governance network arrangements', in B. Egner, D. Sweeting and P.-J. Klok (eds), *Local Councillors in Europe*. Weisbaden: Springer, 203–219.

Poole, K. P. and B. Keith-Lucas (1994) *Parish Government 1894–1994*. London: National Association of Local Councils.

Pope, T., S. Hoddinott, M. Fright, N. Davies, P. Nye and G. Richards (2022) *What Does the Autumn Statement Mean for Public Services?*, Institute for Government Insight. London: Institute for Government.

Pratchett, L. (2004) 'Local autonomy, local democracy and the "new localism"', *Political Studies*, 52:2, 358–375.

Priestley, J. B. (1947) *The Inspector Calls: A Play in Three Acts*. London: Heinemann.

Public Finance (2021) 'Gove calls time on 75% business rates retention', *Public Finance*, 8 November.
Purcell, M. (2004) 'Urban democracy and the local trap', *Urban Studies*, 43:11, 1921–1941.
Purcell, M. (2013) 'The right to the city: The struggle for democracy in the urban public realm', *Policy and Politics*, 41:3, 311–327.
Putnam, R. (2020) *The Upswing*. London: Swift Press.
Pycock, G. (2020) 'London governance and the politics of neighbourhood planning: A case for investigation', *Town Planning Review*, 91:1, 1–20.
Quilley, S. (2000) 'Manchester first: From municipal socialism to the entrepreneurial city', *International Journal of Urban and Regional Research*, 24:3, 601–615.
Quilter-Pinner, H., R. Statham, W. Jennings and V. Valgarðsson (2021) *Trust Issues: Dealing with Distrust in Politics*. London: IPPR.
Raco, M. (2005) 'Sustainable development, rolled-out neoliberalism and sustainable communities', *Antipode*, 37:2, 324–347.
Raco, M. (2013) *State-Led Privatisation and the Demise of the Democratic State*. Abingdon: Routledge.
Raco, M. and J. Flint (2001) 'Communities, places and institutional relations: Assessing the role of area-based community representation in local governance', *Political Geography*, 20:5, 585–612.
Rao, N. (2000) *Reviving Local Democracy*. Bristol: Policy Press.
Redcliffe-Maud, Lord (chair) (1969) *Royal Commission on Local Government in England*, Vol. III, Cmnd. 4040. London: HMSO.
Rees, J. and A. Lord (2013) 'Making space: Putting politics back where it belongs in the construction of city regions in the North of England', *Local Economy*, 28:7–8, 679–695.
Rhodes, G. (1970) *The Government of London*. London: Weidenfeld and Nicolson.
Rhodes, G. (1976) 'Local government finance, 1918–1966', in F. Layfield (chair), *Report of the Royal Commission on Local Government Finance*, Cmnd. 6453, Appendix 6. London: HMSO.
Rhodes, R. A. W. (1981) *Control and Power in Central–Local Government Relations*. Farnborough: Gower.
Rhodes, R. A. W. (1986) *The National World of Local Government*. London: Allen & Unwin.
Rhodes, R. A. W. (1988) *Beyond Westminster and Whitehall*. London: Unwin Hyman.
Rhodes, R. A. W. (1995) 'From prime ministerial power to core executive', in R. A. W. Rhodes and P. Dunleavy (eds), *Prime Minister, Cabinet and Core Executive*. Basingstoke: Macmillan, 11–37.
Rhodes, R. A. W. (1997) *Understanding Governance*. Buckingham: Open University Press.

Rhodes, R. A. W. (1999a) 'Foreword: Governance and networks', in G. Stoker (ed.), *The New Management of British Local Governance*. Basingstoke: Macmillan, xii–xxvi.

Rhodes, R. A. W. (1999b) *Control and Power in Central–Local Relations*, 2nd edn. Aldershot: Ashgate.

Richards, D. and M. J. Smith (2015) 'In defence of British politics against the British political tradition', *Political Quarterly*, 86:1, 41–51.

Richardson, L. (2012) 'Handing over the reins of power', *Political Insight*, 3:3, 32–4.

Roberts, J. (2020) 'The leadership of place and people in the new English combined authorities', *Local Government Studies*, 46:6, 995–1014.

Robson, W. A. (1931) *The Development of Local Government*. London: George Allen & Unwin.

Robson, W. A. (1939) *The Government and Misgovernment of London*. London: George Allen & Unwin.

Robson, W. A. (1954) *The Development of Local Government*, 3rd edn. London: George Allen & Unwin.

Rosenblum, N. L. (2016) *Good Neighbors: The Democracy of Everyday Life in America*. Princeton, NJ: Princeton University Press.

Rudgewick, O. (2020) 'Back in the fold: Barnet's experience bringing services back in house', *Public Finance*, 8 November.

Rudgewick, O. (2022) 'Capital receipt loophole was a "longstanding concern"', *Public Finance*, 4 August.

Rummens, S. (2012). 'Staging deliberation: The role of representative institutions in the deliberative democratic process', *Journal of Political Philosophy*, 20:1, 23–44.

Russell, B. (2019) 'Beyond the local trap: New municipalism and the rise of the Fearless Cities', *Antipode*, 51:3, 989–1010.

Rustin, S. (2020) *Beyond Radical Neighbourliness: The Case for Micro Democracy*. Lawrence and Wishart *Soundings* blog, available at https://lwbooks.co.uk/soundings-blog-beyond-radical-neighbourliness-the-case-for-micro-democracy (accessed 28 May 2023).

St Helens Cares (n.d.) *What is St Helens Cares?*, available at www.sthelenscares.co.uk/what-is-st-helens-cares/ (accessed 30 March 2021).

Sandel, M. J. (2009) *Justice: What is the Right Thing to Do?* New York: Farrar, Straus & Giroux.

Sandford, M. (2017) 'Intervention in local government', *Insight*, 10 August.

Sandford, M. (2019) *Local Government: Alternative Models of Service Delivery*, House of Commons Briefing Paper No. 05950. London: House of Commons.

Sandford, M. (2020a) *Local Government in England: Structures*, House of Commons Briefing Paper No. 07104. London: House of Commons.

Sandford, M. (2020b) 'Giving power away? The "de- words" and the downward transfer of power in mid-2010s England', *Regional and Federal Studies*, 30:1, 25–46.

Sandford, M. (2020c) *Reviewing and Reforming Local Government Finance*, House of Commons Briefing Paper No. 07538. London: House of Commons.

Sandford, M. (2021) *Directly Elected Mayors*, House of Commons Briefing Paper No. 05000. London: House of Commons.

Sasse, T., S. Nickson, C. Britchfield and N. Davies (2020) *Government Outsourcing: When and How to Bring Public Services Back into Government Hands*. London: Institute for Government.

Saunders, P. (1981) *Social Theory and the Urban Question*. London: Hutchinson.

Saunders, P. (1982) 'Why study central–local relations?', *Local Government Studies*, 8:2, 55–66.

Saunders, P. (1986) *Social Theory and the Urban Question*, 2nd edn. London: Hutchinson.

Saward, M. (2003) 'Enacting democracy', *Political Studies*, 51:1, 161–179.

Scharpf, F. W. (1999) *Governing in Europe: Effective and Democratic?* Oxford: Oxford University Press.

Schumpeter, J. A. (1943) *Capitalism, Socialism and Democracy*. New York: Harper.

Schwarzmantel, J. (2007) 'Community as communication: Jean-Luc Nancy and "Being-in-Common"', *Political Studies*, 55:2, 459–476.

Scott, A. and J. Pitt (2015) *Local Government Knowledge Navigator: Local Government Funding*, review number six of the Local Government Knowledge Navigator, available at https://tinyurl.com/dekmnw8m (accessed 20 May 2020).

Sen, A. (2009) *The Idea of Justice*. London: Penguin.

Seyd, P. (1990) 'Sheffield: From socialism to entrepreneurialism', *Political Studies*, 38:2, 335–345.

Shafique, A., B. Antink, A. Clay and E. Cox (2019) *Inclusive Growth in Action: Snapshots of a New Economy*. London: RSA.

Sharman, L. (2021) 'Council launches new placemaking company', *LocalGov*, 10 November, available at https://tinyurl.com/yckkbduz (accessed 30 January 2021).

Shapiro, I. (1999) 'Enough of deliberation: Politics is about interests and power', in S. Macedo (ed.), *Deliberative Politics: Essays on Democracy and Disagreement*. Oxford: Oxford University Press, 28–38.

Shapps, G. (2010) 'Councillors being given more powers than ever to become local champions', 7 December, available at https://tinyurl.com/2p8ekrhh (accessed 17 November 2020).

Sharpe, L. J. (1970) 'Theories and values of local government', *Political Studies*, 18:2, 153–174.
Shaw, D. and Cumbers, A. (2018) 'The work of community gardens: Reclaiming place for community in the city', *Work, Employment and Society*, 32:1, 133–149.
Shaw, K. and M. Tewdwr-Jones (2017) '"Disorganised devolution": Reshaping metropolitan governance in England in a period of austerity', *Raumforschung und Raumordnung: Spatial Research and Planning*, 75, 211–224.
Shearmur, R. and V. Poirier (2017) 'Conceptualising non-market municipal entrepreneurship', *Urban Affairs Review*, 53:4, 718–751.
Skelcher, C. (2005) 'Governing communities: Parish-pump politics or strategic partnerships?', *Local Government Studies*, 29:4, 1–16.
Skelcher, C. (2017) 'An enterprising municipality?', *Local Government Studies*, 43:6, 927–945.
Skerratt, S. and A. Steiner (2013) 'Working with communities of space, complexities of empowerment', *Local Economy*, 28:3, 138–151.
Slay, J. and J. Penny (2013) *Surviving Austerity: Local Voices and Local Action in England's Poorest Neighbourhoods*. London: New Economics Foundation.
Smart, B. (2002) *Michel Foucault*. London: Routledge.
Smith, G. (2010) *Designing Institutions for Citizen Participation*. Cambridge: Cambridge University Press.
Smith, J. T. (1851) *Local Self Government and Centralization*. London: John Chapman.
Smith, J. T. (1857) *The Parish*, 2nd edn. London: Sweet.
Smulian, M. (2021) 'Durham County deal bid could split North East region further', *Local Government Chronicle*, 4 October.
Smyth, C. (2020) 'More elected mayors and fewer councils to break Labour's red wall strongholds', *The Times*, 7 September.
Sorensen, E. and J. Torfing (2005) 'The democratic anchorage of governance networks', *Scandinavian Political Studies*, 28:3, 195–218.
Sorensen, E. and J. Torfing (2009) 'Making governance networks effective and democratic through metagovernance', *Public Administration*, 87:2, 234–258.
Sorensen, E. and J. Torfing (2019) 'Designing institutional platforms and arenas for interactive political leadership', *Public Management Review*, 21:10, 1443–1463.
Stacey, M. (1969) 'The myth of community studies', *British Journal of Sociology*, 20:2, 134–147.
Stears, M. (2011) *Everyday Democracy*. London: IPPR.
Stewart, J. (2000) *The Nature of British Local Government*. Basingstoke: Macmillan.

Stewart, J. (2003) *Modernising British Local Government*. Basingstoke: Palgrave Macmillan.
Stoker, G. (1998) 'Governance as theory: Five propositions', *International Social Science Journal*, 50:155, 17–28.
Stoker, G. (2002) 'Life is a lottery: New Labour strategy for the reform of devolved governance', *Public Administration*, 80:3, 417–434.
Stoker, G. (2004) *Transforming Local Governance: From Thatcherism to New Labour*. Basingstoke: Palgrave Macmillan.
Stoker, G. (2006a) 'Normative theories of local government and democracy', in D. King and G. Stoker (eds), *Rethinking Local Democracy*. Basingstoke: Palgrave Macmillan, 1–25.
Stoker, G. (2006b) *Why Politics Matters: Making Democracy Work*. Basingstoke: Palgrave Macmillan.
Stoker, G. (2011a) 'If town halls don't pay the piper then they can't really call the tune', *Parliamentary Brief*, 17 January.
Stoker, G. (2011b) 'Was local governance such a good idea?', *Public Administration*, 89:1, 15–31.
Stoker, G. and T. Travers (2001) *A New Account?: Choices in Local Government Finance*. York: Joseph Rowntree Foundation.
Streeck, W. (2013) *Politics in an Age of Austerity*. Cambridge: Polity Press.
Sullivan, H. (2004) 'Community governance and local government', in G. Stoker and D. Wilson (eds), *British Local Government into the 21st Century*. Basingstoke: Palgrave Macmillan, 182–198.
Sullivan, H. (2011) 'Governing the mix: How local government still matters', in J. Richardson (ed)., *From Recession to Renewal*. Bristol: Policy Press, 179–195.
Sweeting, D. and C. Copus (2012) 'Whatever happened to local democracy?', *Policy and Politics*, 40:1, 20–37.
Sweeting, D. and C. Copus (2013) 'Councillors, participation, and local democracy', in B. Egner, D. Sweeting and P.-J. Klok (eds), *Local Councillors in Europe*. Berlin: Springer, 121–137.
Sweeting, D. and R. Hambleton (2017) 'Mayoral governance in Bristol: Has it made a difference?', in D. Sweeting (ed.), *Directly Elected Mayors in Urban Governance: Impact and Practice*. Bristol: Policy Press, 19–34.
Sweeting, D. and R. Hambleton (2020) 'The dynamics of depoliticisation in urban governance: Introducing a directly elected mayor', *Urban Studies*, 57: 5, 1068–1086.
Sweeting, D., R. Hambleton, A. Marsh and J. Howard (2013) *The Prospects for Mayoral Governance in Bristol*. Bristol: University of Bristol.
Swyngedouw, E. (2018) *Promises of the Political: Insurgent Cities in a Post-Political Environment*. Cambridge, MA: MIT.
Talen, E. (2014) 'Do-it-yourself urbanism', *Journal of Planning History*, 14:2, 135–148.

Tam, H. (1998) *Communitarianism: A New Agenda for Politics and Citizenship*. Basingstoke: Macmillan.

Taylor, L., P. Haynes and M. Darking (2021) 'English local government finance in transition: Towards the "marketization of income"', *Public Management Review*, 23:7, 1081–1106.

Taylor, M. and M. Wilson (2020) *Locally Rooted: The Place of Community Organising in Times of Crisis*. Warminster: Community Organisers.

Thomas, A. and R. Clyne (2021) *'Responding to Shocks: 10 Lessons for Government'*. London: Institute for Government.

Thomas, H. and R. Imrie (1997) 'Urban development corporations and local governance in the UK', *Journal of Economic and Human Geography*, 88:1, 53–64.

Thompson, M., V. Nowak, A. Southern, J. Davies and P. Furmedge (2020) 'Regrounding the city with Polyani', *Environment and Planning A*, 52:6, 1171–1194.

Tiratelli, L. and S. Kaye (2020) *Communities vs Coronavirus*. London: New Local.

Tomaney, J. (2013) 'Parochialism – a defence', *Progress in Human Geography*, 37:5, 658–672.

Tomaney, J. (2016) 'Limits of devolution: Localism, economics and post-democracy', *Political Quarterly*, 87:4, 546–552.

Tomaney, J. and A. Pike (2020) 'Levelling up?', *Political Quarterly*, 91:1, 43–48.

Tormey, S. (2014) 'The contemporary crisis of representative democracy', *Democratic Theory*, 1:2, 104–112.

Tormey, S. (2022) 'Stresses and strains: Will we ever agree on what's going wrong with democracy?', *Representation*, 58:1, 13–26.

Travers, T. (1986) *The Politics of Local Government Finance*. Hemel Hempstead: Allen & Unwin.

Travers, T. (2022) 'Levelling up will continue to be run from SW1', *Public Finance*, 3 February.

Tressell, R. (1914) *The Ragged Trousered Philanthropists*. London: Grant Richards.

Tribillon, J. (2014) The Localism Act in London: Institutionalising urban divisions', *metropolitics*, available at https://metropolitiques.eu/The-Localism-Act-in-London.html (accessed 20 June 2021).

Turner, A. (2020) 'Children's trusts: Lessons from outsourcing "failing" council services', *Community Care*, 9 October.

Urbanti, N. and M. E. Warren (2008) 'The concept of representation in contemporary democratic theory', *Annual Review of Political Science*, 11, 387–412.

Vabo, S. I. and J. Aars (2013) 'New Public Management reforms and democratic legitimacy: Notions of democratic legitimacy among

West European local councillors', *Local Government Studies*, 39:5, 703–720.
Walker, D. and T. Tizard (2018) *Out of Contract: Time to Move on from the "Love in" with Outsourcing and PFI*. London: Smith Institute.
Wargent, M. (2020) 'Localism, governmentality and failing technologies: The case of neighbourhood planning in England', *Territory Politics Governance*, 9:2, 1–21.
Wargent, M. and E. Talen (2021) 'Rethinking neighbourhoods', *Town Planning Review*, 92:1, 89–95.
Warner, S., D. Richards, D. Coyle and M. J. Smith (2021) 'English devolution and the Covid-19 pandemic: Governing dilemmas in the shadow of the Treasury', *Political Quarterly*, 92:2, 321–330.
Warren, M. E. (2009) 'Governance-driven democratization', *Critical Policy Studies*, 3:1, 3–13.
Warren, M. E. (2017) 'A problem-based approach to democratic theory', *American Political Science Review*, 111:1, 39–53.
Webb, S. and B. Webb (1906) *English Local Government from the Revolution to the Municipal Corporations Act: The Parish and the County*. London: Longman Green and Co.
Webb, S. and B. Webb (1922) *English Local Government, Vol. 4: Statutory Authorities for Special Purposes*. London: Longman, Green and Co.
Webb, S. and B. Webb (1927) *English Local Government, Vol. 8: English Poor Law History, Part I: The Old Poor Law*. London: Longman.
Webb, S. and B. Webb (1929) *English Local Government, Vol. 8: English Poor Law History, Part II: The Last Hundred Years*, vol. 1. London: Longman.
Webb, S. and B. Webb (1975) *A Constitution for the Socialist Commonwealth of Great Britain*. Cambridge: Cambridge University Press. First published 1920.
Werran, J. (2022) '"Levelling up" White Paper: Brilliant analysis not matched by policy measures', *Public Finance*, February.
West, A. (2015) 'Education policy and governance in England under the Coalition government (2010–15): Academies, the Pupil Premium, and free early education', *London Review of Education*, 13:2, 21–36.
Whyte, W. (1925) *Local Government in Scotland*. Edinburgh: William Hodge.
Wickwar, W. H. (1970) *The Political Theory of Local Government*. Columbia, SC: Carolina University Press.
Widdicombe, D. (chair) (1986) *The Conduct of Local Authority Business*, Cmnd. 9797. London: HMSO.
Williams, A., H. Goodwin and P. Cloke (2014) 'Neo-liberalism: Big Society and progressive localism', *Environment and Planning*, 46:12, 2798–2915.

Wills, J. (2016) *Locating Localism: Statecraft and Democracy*. Bristol: Policy Press.
Wills, J. (2020) 'The Geo-constitution and responses to austerity: Institutional entrepreneurship, switching, and re-scaling in the United Kingdom', *Transactions of the Institute of British Geographers*, 45:4, 817–832.
Wilson, D. and C. Game (2011) *Local Government in the United Kingdom*, 5th edn. Basingstoke: Palgrave Macmillan.
Wilson, W., C. Murphy and C. Barton (2017) *The New Homes Bonus (England)*. Briefing Paper No. 05724. London: House of Commons Library.
Wintour, P. (2015) 'George Osborne offers devolution route to cities with elected mayor', *Guardian*, 14 May.
Wistow, G., M. Knapp, B. Hardy and C. Allen (1992) 'From providing to enabling: Local authorities and the mixed economy of care', *Public Administration*, 70:1, 25–47.
WLGA (Welsh Local Government Association) (2015) *Councils and Councillors: An Introduction*. Cardiff: WLGA.
Wolman, H. and M. Goldsmith (1990) 'Local autonomy as a meaningful analytic concept: Comparing local government in the United States and the United Kingdom', *Urban Affairs Review*, 36:1, 3–27.
Wood, B. (1976) *The Process of Local Reform*. London: George Allen & Unwin.
Wood, M. (2020) 'The political ideas underpinning political distrust: Analysing four types of anti-politics', *Representation*, 58:1, 27–48.
Wood, M., M. Flinders and J. Corbett (2020) 'Anti-politics and democratic innovations', in S. Elstub and O. Escobar (eds), *Handbook of Democratic Innovation and Governance*. Cheltenham: Edward Elgar, 148–160.
Wright, A. (2002) 'The curse of centralism', *Public Finance*, 28 June.
Wright, E. O. (2010) *Envisioning Real Utopias*. London: Verso.
Young, K. and N. Rao (1997) *Local Government since 1945*. Oxford: Blackwell.
Zacharzewski, A. (2013) 'Open, networked, democratic: A localist future', in *Connected Localism*', London: LGIU, 31–50.

Index

Acts of UK parliament 23, 24, 42, 54, 147, 206
Academies (2010) 99
Care (2014) 106, 165
Children (2004) 101
Cities and Local Government devolution (2016) 86
Education (2011) 99
Education Reform (1988) 38
Electoral Reform (1832) 25
Further and Higher Education (1992) 39
Greater London Authority (1999) 135
Homeless Reduction (2017) 108
Learning and Skills Act (2000) 98
Local Democracy, Economic Development and Construction (2009) 84, 130
Local Government 'Parish Councils Act (1894) 28, 29
Local Government (1988) 27, 43, 111
Local Government (1972) 32, 95
Local Government (1999) 45, 169
Local Government (2000) 127, 135
Local Government (2003) 186
Local Government Devolution (2016) 137
Local Government and Public Involvement Health (2007) 49, 127, 130
Local Government Finance (2018) 86
Local Government, Planning and Land Act (1980) 43
Local Government and Public Involvement in Health Act (2007) 75, 127, 130
Local Government and Elections (Wales) (2021) 82, 215
Localism (2011) 27, 36, 70, 85, 97–8, 99, 116, 130, 136, 152, 153, 157, 186
London Government (1899) 2, 27
Municipal Corporations (1835) 26
National Health Service and Community Care (1990) 105
Poor Law Amendment (1834) 56
Public Services (Social Value) (2012) 189
Rates (1984) 42, 205, 211
Rates (1988) 211
Well-being of Future Generations (Wales) (2015) 148
Addison, Christopher 41
adult social care 168, 192

allotments 29, 244
Althusius, Johannes 251
Anti-Centralization Union 56
Arendt, Hannah, 248
arms-length agencies 210
Ashford, D. E. 18, 68, 251
Association of County Councils 41
Association of Municipal
    Authorities 41
Association for Public Service
    Excellence (APSE) 6, 100,
    111, 113, 189
Attlee, Clement 208
  Governments of 31, 66, 82, 210,
    212
audit 12, 43, 45, 109–10, 116, 211
Audit Commission 43, 45, 126,
    152
  National Audit Office (NAO) 12,
    109, 116, 246
austerity 9, 86, 123, 142, 161, 171,
    172, 211, 246
  and innovation 182–3
  easing of austerity 163, 168
  effect of 6–7, 49, 70, 76, 93,
    104, 109–20, 123, 128,
    154–5, 171, 191, 194, 241
autocracy 223, 228

Banham, Sir John 33, 73–5, 81
banking crash (2008) 211
Barber, Benjamin 68, 234, 249,
    250–1
Barcelona 191
Barnsley Metropolitan District 88
Barnett, Clive 16, 227
Barnett, C. and Bridge, G. 231
Barnett, Neil 125, 126, 150, 196,
    212, 233, 236, 237
Bassetlaw District Council 88
Bauman, Zygmunt 15
Bentham, Jeremy 25, 54–6, 59, 62
best value 45

Bevan, Aneurin 30–1, 66, 208
Beveridge Report 30
'Big Society' initiative 150–1, 154,
    193, 194
Birmingham iv, 2, 36, 194, 212,
    246
  City Council and MBC 1, 2, 36
    194, 212
Blair, Tony 33, 68
  governments 34, 44, 49, 51, 213
Blaug, Ricardo 249–50
bloggers 245
Blunkett, David vii, 42, 215
boards of education 26
Bookchin, Murray 15, 248
Bourdieu, Pierre 222
Bradford City 26
Bradley, Q. 160
Branson, Noreen 20
Brexit, 8, 167
Bristol, 140, 191
Brokenshire, James 78
Brown, Gordon 215
  Government 44, 51
Bryan, F. M. 250
Buchanan, George 2
Buckinghamshire County 77
Bulpitt, Jim 147, 155, 169
burial boards 26
Burke, Edmund 53, 58, 125, 209
Burnham, Andy 12, 140
business elites 177, 199
Butler, Rab 210

Cambridge and Peterborough
    Combined Authority 87,
    137
Cameron, David 151, 203
  governments 150–5
Carillion 185
central government
  attitudes to community 193
  central-local relations 179–80

control of local government
146–70, 199–217
overseeing local government 148–9
Chadwick, Edwin 25–6
Chamberlain, Joseph 2, 212
Chandler, James A. 3, 18, 149,
207, 220
right to local self-government,
18, 62–3, 69, 149, 247
Chartered Institute for Public
Finance (CIPFA) 41, 117
Chesterfield Borough Council 88
chief constable 23
chief executives 35, 119, 185, 187,
208
chief officers 35, 119, 128, 185, 186
Chisholm, Michael 68, 75, 200
Churchill, Sir Winston 208
citizens' juries 188
City Challenge initiative 177
City Deals 85–90, 108, 116, 135,
139
City of London 27, 214
'civic capitalism' 191
civic society 223
Civil Service 42, 48, 199, 204,
208–9
attitudes to local government 30,
41–2, 154, 198, 206
Clarke, N. and Cochrane, A. 16,
48, 151, 157, 232, 237–4
clean energy initiatives 191
Cleveland, Ohio 191
climate change 239
climate emergency 190, 240
Coalition government (2010–15)
76, 99, 110, 130, 150, 151
Cockburn, Cynthia 175
Cohen, J and C. Sabel 249
Cole, G. D. H. 65, 66, 212, 213
Cole, M. and G. Boyne, George
3, 4
Cobbett, William 55–6

Combined Authorities (CAs)
79–80, 85–6, 89, 91, 108,
135–7, 169
commercial property acquisitions
40, 69, 116, 160, 164, 171,
185–6
commissions and inquiries
Local Authorities and Allied
Personal Social Services
(Seebohm Report 1968) 38
Local Government (Banham
Commission 1992) 33, 44,
73–4
Local Government Boundaries
(1947, 1956) 31
Local Government in England
(Redcliffe Maud, 1966–69)
32, 83, 125, 209, 243
Local Government Finance
(Layfield Committee 1976)
162
Local Government in Greater
London (Herbert, 1960) 74,
243
Management of Local
Government (Maud Report
1967) 127
Place Shaping (Lyons Inquiry
2007) 47
The Conduct of Local Authority
Business (Widdicombe
Report 1986) 42, 43, 122,
205
committee system for local policy
making 127, 130
communitarianism 68
community 2, 5, 14–18, 21, 44,
55, 57–9, 63, 64, 67, 71,
72, 88, 97, 141, 151,
157–8
champions 129, 134, 141
defined 15, 69, 199–200, 208,
235

community *(cont.)*
  empowerment 130, 172, 179, 184, 202
  leadership 173–4
  planning 159
  value of 236, 240, 248
  wealth building 36–7, 191–3
community councils 48, 97, 239
community infrastructure levy 112
comprehensive performance assessments (CPAs) 45, 126, 150
compulsory competitive tendering 43, 45, 173
Conservative Party 2, 76
  governments 31, 34, 36, 37, 38–40, 44, 84, 86, 109, 137, 139, 210
  Members of Parliament 203–4
  decline of landowning influence 49–50
  ideology 151, 209–12
  opposition to Redcliffe Maud Report 210
Copus, Colin 35, 68–9, 72, 82, 125, 129, 142–3, 166, 242
Corbyn, Jeremy 213
core executive 128, 198, 201, 205, 220, 222, 246
  defined 11, 219
Cornwall County Council 87, 91
council housing 37, 39–40, 41, 42, 101–3, 117–18, 189–20, 193
Council of Europe 58
council leaders 77, 83, 93, 126, 127, 139, 208, 244
council leadership 2, 11, 75, 77, 81, 84, 93, 126–9, 134–44, 150, 174
councillors 123, 131–2
  as facilitators 227
  backbench councillors 34–5, 128, 129, 132, 133–4, 139, 145
  changing roles 124–56
  decline in numbers 123, 133
  disciplining 42, 197
  managerial role 126, 128
  representative role 133–4
  workload 123, 132
county councils 2, 23, 27, 28, 30, 34, 37, 38, 75, 77, 79, 90, 92, 103
corporatism 222
corruption 208
COVID crisis 9–12, 111, 142, 167–8, 171, 183–4
  test and trace system 10
Cromwell, Oliver 53
Crossman, R.H.S. 31
Cumbria County Council 7, 79

Dahl, Robert 68, 219
Davies, Jonathan S. 47, 170, 171, 178, 222
decentralisation 48–9, 62, 151–2, 200–1, 215–16, 236, 243
democracy 9, 14, 23, 219–22, 230–49
  associative 249
  crisis in 219–30
  critics of a 'crisis' 229
  deliberative 133, 134, 188, 195, 226, 232, 234, 236, 249
  different forms of 124, 232
  direct 4, 21, 68, 144, 157, 227, 232, 234–6, 239, 247–51
  discursive 21, 228, 232, 234–5, 236, 251
  effectiveness in Britain 228
  innovations 194–5
  unitary 238
democratic deficit 127, 221, 244
democratisation of British Local Government 21, 27–30, 68–9, 139

Department of Communities and Local Government 200
Department of Transport Local Government and the Regions (DTLR) 45, 263
Derbyshire County Council 87, 88, 90–1, 138
devolution 148, 155, 166–7, 215–16
  deals 7, 79–82, 114, 116, 135, 136, 154, 155, 178, 216
  devolution to Scotland, Wales and Northern Ireland 98–9, 109, 110
  in Levelling Up White Paper 109, 110, 137–8, 156
  value to central government 201–2
Devon 104, 138, 270
Dewey, John 248
Disraeli, Benjamin 40, 56, 58, 68, 209–10
district councils 2, 28, 32, 35, 50, 58, 111, 200
  mergers and abolitions 72, 75, 76–80, 87–8, 119, 133, 243, 244
  metropolitan districts 33, 72
  Northern Ireland districts 81
  urban and rural differences 28
doctors 30, 239
Doncaster Metropolitan District 88, 104, 140
Dorset County Council 77, 79, 104
Downs, Anthony 219
drainage, powers over 27, 211, 244
dual state theory 210, 224
Durham County Council 87, 89, 91, 188
Dunleavy, Patrick 175, 176

East Midlands CA 138
East Riding 72

East Sussex 187
education boards 1, 26, 28–9
electricity boards 1, 82
electric vehicles 240
elite theorists 219
energy saving 190
energy supply 40, 119, 190, 193, 240
English sub-regionalism 82–95
equality and freedom 213
ethical status of local government 52–70, 207, 214–16, 247
Etzioni, Amitai 68
Europe 22, 48, 92, 132
European Charter for Local Self-Government 48
European Union 8, 83, 200, 245
  Brexit 8, 156, 245

Fabian Society 65
farmers' markets 240
'Fearless Cities' movement 191, 218
Fenwick, John and Howard, Elcock 135, 136
food banks 235
Foucault, Michel 3, 149–50
Finer, Herman 65
Flinders, Matthew 94, 228, 229, 230, 231, 232
France 198
  local government in 18, 21, 28, 54, 68, 251
  Revolution (1789) 55
franchise 21, 27–8, 49, 53, 55, 61
Framework for Devolution 156
Friedman, Milton 211
Functional Economic Area (FEA) 80, 89, 95, 144, 154
Fung, A. and Wright, E. O. 249
Future High Streets Fund 8

Game, Chris vii, 123
gas services 1, 24, 36, 37, 118–19, 193, 210, 211, 244
gatekeepers 219, 220, 222, 226, 230
Gateshead MDC 89
General Board of Health 26, 41, 61
Gladstone, William 41
Glasgow 1, 2, 110
globalisation, 6, 15, 17, 30, 140, 160, 174, 177–8, 196, 199–200, 214, 218, 228, 240
Goodwin, Mark 176
Goodwin Mark and Joe Painter 4–5
Gove, Michael 167
governance 4–6
government departments 161
  Communities and Local Government 200
  Education 99–100
  Housing and Local Government 42
  Ministry of Health 41, 42
  Treasury 12, 46, 83, 92–3, 103, 152, 161
Government Offices for the Regions 83
Gray, Clive 5
Greater London Authority 92, 103, 104, 135, 139
Greater London Council 31, 33, 35
Greater Manchester (CA) 104, 106, 108, 109, 137
Green paper, Strengthening Local Government (2018) 82
Green, Thomas Hill 64, 65
Grenfell Tower fire 204

Hale, Sarah 68, 126
Hambleton, Robin 140
Hampshire County Council 80
Hartlepool Neighbourhood Forum 158
Hayek, Friedrich von 211
health boards 61
Herbert, Edwin 31
Hendriks, C. M. 14
Hendriks, C. M. and A. W. Dzur 6
Heseltine, Michael 34, 43, 73
Hirst, Paul 249
Hobhouse, Lionel T. 64–5
Hogget Paul and Robin Hambleton 49
homelessness 108, 115, 118
hospitals 2, 26, 30, 37, 107
housing 33, 37, 39, 40, 41, 86, 101–3, 108, 160, 189–190
  management 43, 114, 117, 193
  privatisation 51, 185
  right to buy 102
Hull City 93
hundreds 22, 58

ideology 50, 52, 94, 206–7, 209–14
improvement trusts 24
industrialisation 24
industrialists 2, 25, 26, 52, 210
inequality 221
intergovernmental relations 42, 147–70, 172–4, 204–7
  contractual model 155
IT infrastructure 9, 43, 114, 119

Jenrick, Robert 80, 137
John, Peter 3, 171, 248
Johnson, Boris 7, 62, 208
  government 92, 112, 137, 154, 156, 164, 193, 218
Jones, George 3
Jones, George and John Stewart 67, 68, 213, 214
Jones, Martin 16, 17
justices of the peace 23, 27, 28, 61

Index

Kingdon, John 220

Labour Party 40, 50
  attitudes before 1945 to local government 2, 65, 208
  attitudes from 1945 to New Labour 30, 32, 37, 42, 72, 83, 84
  central control of local government 149–50
  constituencies 11, 110, 137
  devolution policy 215–16
  left wing 213
  New Labour 33, 39–40, 44–8, 68, 75–6, 98, 102, 126, 129–30, 135, 139, 173–4, 177, 179, 182, 213
  similarities with Conservatives 194, 206–7, 210, 212, 223
Laffin, Martin 147, 148
landed gentry 25, 28, 32, 50, 209, 210
Layfield, Sir Frank, 162
Leach Robert and Percy-Smith, Janie 5
Leach, Steve vii, 77, 129, 146, 149, 151, 152–3, 200
leadership 141–2, 144
Leicestershire County Council 77
levelling-up 7–8, 80, 90, 92, 109, 114, 117, 156, 168, 193, 245
Liberal Democrats 210
Liberal Party 151, 210
  support for more autonomous local government 211
liberal democracy vi, 18, 21, 59–64, 68, 69, 125, 145, 202, 219–30
  and inequality 222
Lindblom, Charles 220
liquid modernity 15, 229
Liverpool 12, 136, 137, 140, 193
  City Region 196

Livingstone, Ken 42
local 14–18
  as a potential democratic space 231–2
  ambiguities in use of the term 153–4
  meanings 3, 15–16, 153, 243
local education authorities (LEAs) 31, 38–9, 47, 100
Local Enterprise Partnerships (LEPs) 85–6, 89, 94, 182
Local Government Association, 12, 38–9, 47, 203, 221
local government
  autonomy 173, 174–5
  boundaries 6, 19, 28, 30–3, 71–96, 99, 107, 109, 116, 160, 197, 233, 239
  cabinet systems 34, 35, 127–8, 131, 138, 144–5, 156, 219, 244
  challenges to 6–8
  chief executives 35, 119, 208–9
  commercialisation 184–5, 189
  committee structure 33–4, 127–8, 130, 131, 143, 152
  community leader role 174
  compared with other liberal democracies 18, 21, 146, 162, 244
  decision making structures 127–8
  defined 3–4
  democracy in 202, 224–30, 244–6
  democratic innovations 161, 167, 188, 194–7, 233, 249–52
  difference in party attitudes to 207
  elections 9, 87, 222, 238, 250
  election turn out 9, 136, 137

294 *Index*

local government (*cont.*)
  ethical value 13–14, 18, 24, 52–70, 166
  expediential role 13, 198, 199–217, 247
  franchise 29, 55
  history (to 1832) 22–5
  history (1833–2010) 12–13, 19, 27–33
  hollowing out 147, 205, 226, 244
  innovation 190–3, 196, 246, 247
  insourcing 185, 187
  intergovernmental relations 19, 42, 161, 146–70, 218–40
  leisure services 1, 36, 43, 114, 121
  local government staff 9, 10, 35, 105, 129, 183
  local sourcing of goods and services 192
  means to revive liberal democracy 230–42
  parks 116, 121, 244
  partnership with private sector 147, 155, 177, 183
  powers 4, 9, 10, 97–109, 147–8, 152, 155, 190
  privatisation of roles 226, 244
  rebellion against central government 198
  redundancies 114, 116, 118
  refuse collection 2, 43, 187, 203, 211
  scapegoat role iv, 108, 203, 204, 246
  sharing services and management 76, 119
  socialism 42, 191, 200
  stewardship role 149
  theories of moral right to community governance 13–14, 18, 52–71, 181, 212–13, 214–16, 243, 248–52
Local Government Board 41, 208
local government finance
  austerity, 6, 7, 9, 49, 142, 150, 154, 161–70, 171, 191–204, 246
  consequences of 88, 93, 104, 109–20, 123, 178, 182, 191–204, 244
  bankruptcy 12, 111, 117, 245
  business rates 161–3, 164
  Business Rate Retention Scheme (BRRS) 163
  commercial revenue 187
  community charge (poll tax) 43, 198, 222
  council tax 12, 43, 45, 108, 110, 112–20, 152–3, 163–4, 167, 168, 203–4
  domestic rates 162
  'Fair Funding' 164, 166
  grants from central government 12, 38, 40, 45, 103, 110, 112, 162–4, 177, 194, 203, 211
  outsourcing local authority services 101, 106, 193
  profit making 189
  rates on agricultural land 40
  reduction in spending 110
  reserves 111
  revenue support grant 110
localised planning 157–6
Locke, John 221
London 27, 48, 90, 92, 135, 139, 202
  City of 214
  devolution 49
  guilds 22, 27, 53

Greater London Authority
(GLA) 33, 35, 103, 135
Inner London Education
Authority 31
London Boroughs 158
Borough of Poplar (London)
208
Barking and Dagenham 188
Barnet 185
Croydon 111
Hackney 158, 159
Islington 49
Lambeth 183
Kensington and Chelsea 204
Newham 188
Sutton 189
Tower Hamlets 49, 136, 188
London County Council 27, 31
lord lieutenant 23
Loughlin, Martin 4, 146, 149
Lowndes, Vivien 46, 147, 154

Macdonald, Ramsey 222
Mackenzie, W. J. M. 66, 71
Macmillan, Harold 210
magistrates 27, 28, 103
Major, Sir John 43
governments 51, 73, 74, 211
management theory 201
Manchester 24, 35, 243, 245,
246
City Council 192
Greater Manchester 12, 86, 89,
104, 106, 108–9
Greater Manchester Health
and Social Care Partnership
109
Mayor 140
Mansbridge, J. 236, 250
Marsh, A. 143
Massey, Doreen 15–16
May, Teresa
government 87

mayors 2, 34, 109, 127, 129–10
directly elected mayors (DEM)
35, 135–8, 142–4, 145, 152,
215, 243–4
lord mayors 34
of combined authorities 11, 86,
104, 106, 140, 208
Mayor of Greater London
Authority 35, 104, 139–40
media 52, 197–8, 206, 220, 223,
227
Members of Parliament 217
experience as local councillors
208
factions among 217
metropolitan authorities 33, 72,
84, 111
Metropolitan Board of Works 27,
61
Metropolitan Police 25, 103–4,
118, 244
Michels, Robertro 219
'Midlands Engine' initiative 86
Mill, James 55, 59
Mill, John Stuart 18, 59–64, 67,
214, 219, 235, 247, 248, 250
differences with Toulmin Smith
56, 60, 61
on the local franchise 61
on the role of central
government 62
value of local government 60, 235
minimum standards 165, 213
Ministers for
Decentralisation 151, 152
Health 41
Housing, Communities and
Local Government
(MHCLG) 78, 89, 131
Housing and Local Government
42
Intergovernmental Relations 149
Monbiot, George 248

Morphet, Janice 8, 10, 12, 78, 85, 87, 92–3, 156, 169, 180, 189–90
Mosca, Gaetano 219
muddling through 220
multi-area agreements 84
municipal banks 36–7, 193
Municipal Bonds Agency 189
municipalisation 1, 2, 26, 27, 36, 189, 194, 212, 244

Nancy, Jean-Luc 16
National Association of Local Councils (NALC) 240
nationalisation of local services 37, 50, 210
neighbourhood 14–15, 21, 68, 129, 151, 157, 216, 235, 239, 241
  definitions 15, 153
  planning forums 150, 158, 150, 157–61, 188
neoliberalism 180
Newcastle on Tyne 35, 89
New England 234
Newman, Innes 69, 180, 205, 180–1
new-municipalism 191, 195, 218
New Policy Institute 110
new public management (NPM) 34, 43, 126, 141, 155
new-right 42, 207, 209, 211–12, 216, 217, 221–2, 246
New Urban Left (NUL) 176, 182, 197
Norfolk County Council 187
North Ayrshire Council community empowerment initiatives 188
Northampton County Council 204, 245
  abolition 77–8
Northern Ireland 81, 89, 98–9, 131, 136, 202, 206

'Northern Powerhouse' initiative 86
North of Tyne Combined Authority 87, 89
Northumberland County Council 89
North Yorkshire 7, 79, 243
  Combined Authority (CA) 87, 88–9, 104, 138, 243
  County Council 7, 91, 118
  directly election mayor (DEM) 137
  Unitary Authority 7, 72, 79, 138, 202, 203
Nottingham City Council 91, 119, 187, 193
  Robin Hood Energy 119
Nottinghamshire County Council 87, 91, 119, 138
Nozick, Robert 246

Oakshott, Michael 219
Ofsted 39, 100
One Yorkshire CA proposal 79, 88–9, 91, 202
open vestries 1, 22, 27, 29, 57
Organisation for Economic Co-operation and Development (OECD) 109, 162, 182
Osborne, George 86–7, 109, 137, 154
Ottewill, Roger 29

Paine, Thomas 55
Pareto, Villfredo 219
parish 2, 3, 28–9, 32, 48, 58, 69, 97, 153, 157, 239, 240, 243
  councils 29
  meetings 22
  pre-1894 1, 22, 23–4, 27
  uncontested elections 29
Parkes, Joseph 55

Index

Parkinson, J. 134
Parliament of the UK 199, 205
participatory budgeting 188
Phillips, D. 164
Peel, Robert 25, 40
Peterborough 87, 111, 137
Pickles, Eric 78, 97, 151, 154, 215
Piketty, Thomas 221
place shaping 144, 223, 238, 249
planning 81, 112, 114, 157–61, 188
Plymouth 138
police 2, 24, 25, 52, 58, 86, 103–4, 133, 244, 245
political elites 19, 52, 53, 59, 93–4, 122, 198, 200, 209, 220, 222–4
policy decision making 219–21
policy gatekeepers 220, 222, 226
policy networks 222–4, 226
political parties
    attitudes towards local government 72, 120, 129, 137, 209, 212, 219, 225
    electoral advantage 137, 139, 142, 168, 225
    ideology 50, 65, 209–14
    structures 132, 142
    whips 34, 203
poor law 2, 23–5, 30, 40, 61, 213
    decline 28–9, 37
    National Poor Law Board 25, 41, 56
    local poor law boards 28
    Reform Bill 3
Poplarism 208
populism 57, 228
pork barrel politics 7
power-dependence model 205
Pratchet, Lawrence 173–4
Prescott, John 33, 83
Preston District Council 191–2, 193

Preston model 191
primary units of local government 14, 49, 63, 231, 234, 238–9, 249, 251
private acts of Parliament 24, 26, 27, 36, 41
privatisation 6, 40, 51, 186, 205, 211, 215, 244
public health 10, 30, 41, 104, 105, 107–9, 184, 205
Public Health England 10
public libraries 244
Putnam, Robert 221

quarter sessions courts 23, 27
Queen's Park parish 49

Raco, M. 178
Rancière, Jaques 235
Redcliffe-Maud, Lord 32, 73, 125, 127
referenda 136, 152
    for directly elected mayoral systems 136, 140
Regional Development Agencies (RDAs) 83, 85
regions 53, 82, 83, 85, 202, 205
    North East England 33, 245
Rhodes, Gerald 40
Rhodes, R. A. W. 5, 11, 205
rights of way 29
Robson, William 27, 65, 66, 68, 212, 213, 214
Rotherham Metropolitan District Council 88
Royal Charters 22, 36
rural districts 28, 30

Salford MBC 136
Salisbury, Lord, Robert 27, 40
Sandel, Michael 69
Sandford, Mark vii, 76, 86, 163, 185, 186, 187

Saunders, P. 175, 210, 224
Schumpeter, Joseph 68, 219, 224
Scotland 8, 11, 29, 33, 90, 99, 102, 106, 110, 131, 148, 202, 245–6
  county councils 27
  education administration 99
  local government finance 162, 192
  local government in the nineteenth century 22, 26
  National Performance Framework 148
  police 103–4
  regional councils 32
  Scottish Parliament 8, 104
  social care 107
  unitary authorities 73–4, 81, 89
Scottish Royal Burghs 26
scrutiny committees 16, 34–5, 92, 104, 127–9, 130, 139, 145, 156
self-interest 207
Sen, Amartya 69
Senior, Dereck (Memorandum of dissent to Redcliffe Maud Report) 83
Senior, Nassau 25
SERCO 10
Sharpe, L. J. 67, 68
Shared Prosperity Fund 8
Sheffield 26, 88, 131, 244
  City Region 88–9, 137
Sheriff 23
Single Regeneration Fund 177
Slough 111
Smith, Joshua-Toulmin 56–9, 61, 62, 63, 68, 235, 251
social deprivation 245
social justice 69, 166, 211
social services 30, 37, 38, 68, 101, 105–7, 130, 147, 165, 193, 213, 240–1, 244–5
  funding 112, 115, 163, 165

Somerset 7, 77, 79, 104
South Somerset District Council 49, 107
South Yorkshire 88, 137
space–place tension 226
Spelthorne District Council 117
Staffordshire county council 187
Staffordshire Highways 187
state theory 176
Stewart, John 4, 67, 68, 173, 213, 214
Stoke-on-Trent 127
  City Council 185
Stoker, Gerry 46, 122, 127, 135, 151, 170, 173, 203, 229, 230, 231, 232, 233
strong leadership model 138
Streeck, M. 228
subsidiarity 200, 236
Suffolk 77
  merging of district councils 77
Sunak, Rishi
  government 8, 90, 113, 218
Swindon Borough Council 190

Tam, Henri 68
telecommunications 244
Thatcher, Margaret 43, 149
  governments 13, 33, 42, 44, 51, 72, 83, 120, 147, 162, 177, 211
Tocqueville, Alexis de 61, 63, 234, 251
Tomaney, John 17, 83, 92, 93, 173
Tormey, S. 229
Torrens, Colonel Robert 3, 56
Tory Party 21 25, 26, 28, 40, 209, 210
town clerk 35
town councils 2, 32, 157, 158, 239, 240
towns fund 8

Index

town planning 37, 157–61, 190
townships 234
transport boards 26
Travers, Tony 41, 109, 165
Truss, Liz 8, 90, 218

ultra-vires 36, 50, 97, 152, 203
unitary authorities 7, 28, 33, 73–81,
    87, 92, 133, 154, 200, 226,
    238, 243
United Kingdom Constitution 18,
    205–6, 225
  devolution in 215–16
United States 61, 191, 198, 214,
    219
universities 5
urban areas 30, 32, 49, 51, 66, 94,
    159, 178
urban development corporations
    (UDCs) 83, 177, 181
urban district councils 2, 28, 29,
    31, 72, 208
urban entrepreneurialism 176–7
utilitarian political thought
    175–6

volunteering 10, 236

Wales 11, 26, 23, 33, 53, 101, 148,
    202, 208, 245
  COVID 169
  directly elected mayors 136
  funding 110, 162
  government 11, 32, 33, 73–4,
    81, 82
  housing 102
  Improvement Framework 148
  joint working across authorities
    104, 106
  localism 48
  policing 104
  schools system 99
  social services 101, 106, 192

South Wales 202, 245
unitary authorities 71, 81 82
Walker, Peter 32
Wargent, M. 160
Warren, M. E. 232
Warrington Metropolitan
    Borough Council 116, 119,
    189, 193
  Local Authority Mortgage
    Scheme 189
water services 1, 26, 27, 37, 41,
    66, 82, 211, 244
Webb, Sydney and Beatrice 65,
    212, 213
Welsh Office 32
West Berkshire District Council
    190
West Midlands CA 89, 137
Westminster model 11, 19, 56, 93,
    225
West Yorkshire CA 87–8, 104,
    118, 137
Wheatley, John 2
Wheatley, Lord John 32
Whigs 3, 258, 935
white papers 125
  Levelling Up the United
    Kingdom (2022) 7, 80–3,
    87, 89, 90, 92, 95, 109,
    114, 117, 137, 156, 168
  Modern Local Government
    (2000) 49
  Strong and Prosperous
    Communities (2006) 75,
    130
  Strong Local Leadership,
    Quality Local Services
    (2001) 45, 47
Wickwar, W. Hardy 67
Widdicombe Report 205–6
Wigan Deal 188
Wigan Metropolitan Borough
    Council 188

Wilson, David 38, 75, 102, 123, 151, 162
Wilson, Harold 31
Wiltshire 104
Wirral Council 111, 193
Woking Borough Council 190
Womens' rights 59

ability to stand as candidates in local elections 29–30
franchise for 27, 29, 30
Wood, Bruce 228
workhouses 25

York City 91, 138, 191

EU authorised representative for GPSR:
Easy Access System Europe, Mustamäe tee 50,
10621 Tallinn, Estonia
gpsr.requests@easproject.com